Tritium on Ice

Tritium on Ice

The Dangerous New Alliance of Nuclear Weapons
and Nuclear Power

Kenneth D. Bergeron

The MIT Press
Cambridge, Massachusetts
London, England

This book was set in Sabon by SNP Best-set Typesetter Ltd., Hong Kong.

Printed and bound in the United States of America.

Library of Congress Cataloging-in-Publication Data

Bergeron, Kenneth D.
   Tritium on ice: the dangerous new alliance of nuclear weapons and nuclear power / Kenneth D. Bergeron.
      p. cm.
   Includes bibliographical references and index.
   ISBN 0-262-02527-2 (hard: alk. paper)
   1. Nuclear engineering—Government policy—United States. 2. Tritium—Safety measures. 3. Ice condenser reacotrs—Environmental aspects—United States. 4. Nuclear nonproliferation. 5. Nuclear weapons—Materials. 6. Tennessee Valley Authority. Nuclear Power. 7. Tennessee Valley Authority. Nuclear Operations. I. Title.

TK9023 .B47 2002
363.17′99—dc21
                                                                    2002066016

Contents

Preface: Why This Book?

It's not over. We're going to see a nuclear exchange in the next 25 years, almost surely.
Daniel Patrick Moynihan, 2000

This is a book about the changing face of nuclear war in the twenty-first century and how the U.S. government is managing, or mismanaging, the new dangers. With the Soviet Union gone and the United States engaged in a deadly struggle with murderous but low-tech terrorist adversaries, the subject may strike some readers as anachronistic or even anticlimactic. Supposedly the potential for the all-out, civilization-ending nuclear paroxysm that we each came to terms with in the twentieth century has dramatically receded. Thankfully, that is true, but it is also true that these devastating weapons are still with us, still ready for war. And now the rules for their use are quietly being rewritten, year by year, country by country.

The *complexity* of the global nuclear standoff has increased dramatically, and there are now many more ways nuclear conflicts might start. We must envision now not only the bilateral superpower conflict of old, but also regional conflicts, ethnic last stands, anonymous terrorist acts, and, as always, accidental nuclear war. Though the nuclear conflicts that might occur in the future will probably be smaller than what we had to envision in the past, even a small nuclear war would be incomparably horrible.

All these are good reasons for a revived interest in the subject, but the reason we should be not just interested, but *alarmed*, is that the U.S. government, clearly the biggest nuclear player of all, is increasingly delegating the direction of nuclear weapons policy to jaded bureaucrats who are more concerned with inside-the-beltway points than with protecting the people of the world from the devastation of nuclear war.

This book provides an insider's perspective on how matters pertaining to nuclear war and weapons are increasingly controlled by political game players and their captive technical specialists. It follows a particular chronicle about how the explosive ingredients of U.S. nuclear weapons are produced and how U.S. officials have recently abandoned a long-standing policy forbidding their production in commercial nuclear power plants. The particular material on which the book focuses is tritium, a form of hydrogen needed to turn an A-bomb into an H-bomb. The commercial power plants that will produce it are of a type known as "ice condensers"—hence the title, *Tritium on Ice.*

I will argue in this book that the abandonment of the policy isolating commercial nuclear power from nuclear weapons manufacture is an unwise retreat from this country's commitment to curb the proliferation of nuclear weapons around the world. Perhaps even more important is the trend that the decision represents: a drift from vigilance about nuclear proliferation to complacency. This trend poses a distinct danger for the future, and everyone in the world is exposed to that danger.

The bureaucrats themselves may try to obscure the issues with technical fast talk and appeals to classified information, but at the core the issues are straightforward. Advanced degrees in science are not needed to understand them, nor is access to classified information. The principal agent for restoring responsibility to the U.S. decision-making process is an informed public. That is why you should read this book. The stakes are large, and they involve you and your world.

The flip side of the question "why this book?" is why did I write it? I have spent twenty-five years as a physicist in the service of one of the U.S. government's three nuclear weapons laboratories. The greater portion of my career at Sandia National Laboratories involved two subjects: the safety of commercial nuclear reactors and the production of tritium for nuclear weapons. Until recently, the two subjects were quite distinct. Now, the aforementioned reversal of policy means that they intersect directly over the safety of the two nuclear power plants that are to be modified to produce tritium. My professional experience with the safety profiles of these particular reactors and my understanding of the high-stakes politics of tritium production lead me to fear that scientific objectivity about the potential for severe accidents at these sites will be lacking.[1]

And objectivity in the face of the powerful players in this complex game will be sorely needed. There are serious grounds for worry that ice condenser plants could undergo catastrophic accidents, exposing nearby populations to fatal doses of radioactivity. The fact that the operator of the plants is the Tennessee Valley Authority, a federal agency with a long history of compromising nuclear safety, exacerbates the potential danger. Careful study of these concerns is of critical importance before the government proceeds down the path of modifying the plants, but instead the key safety issues have received little attention.

The trade-offs between our modern society's need for electricity and the need to protect the public from the methods of its production are not easy to balance, nor are the trade-offs between national security and nuclear arms reduction. But we cannot expect our government to pursue policies reflecting the interests of the public unless the public is aware of the issues and creates the incentive for officials to stay focused on their responsibilities. This book is a contribution toward that goal.

Just thirteen years ago the oil tanker *Exxon Valdez* ran aground in Alaska's Prince William Sound, causing the worst environmental disaster in U.S. history. The cause? Press accounts in the aftermath pointed to the ship's captain, Joseph Hazelwood, supposedly inebriated to incapacity when he should have been piloting the ship. But the true cause of the grounding and the subsequent botched recovery operation was deeper and more troubling. John Keeble, in *Out of the Channel*,[2] shows that years of corporate pressure to increase profits had created a working environment for Alaska tanker operations that made such a disaster inevitable. Keeble describes safety standards trimmed to bare bones with little thought of their adequacy, equipment and services critical for safe navigation downgraded to save costs, and safety procedures routinely violated or ignored. Then, one clear and cold March night in 1989, an undermanned, overtired, and underqualified crew slowly steered the massive oil tanker into a well-marked reef.

The root cause of the *Exxon Valdez* disaster lies in the collective behavior of a whole community of people, including the officers and seamen of the fleet, the people who established and managed the oil company's safety standards, the people who enforced those standards, and most of all the leaders on both the private and government sides who created the incentive environment for all the players. There was something wrong with the priorities of these people, and after the disaster much attention was paid to realigning their priorities so that similar disasters would be avoided in the future.

Today there is something wrong with the priorities of the agencies charged with managing the government's actions on nuclear weapons and war. The time to address these problems is now, not after irreversible disaster occurs.

Acknowledgements

Many people have helped me with this project, and I could not have completed *Tritium on Ice* without their kind and generous assistance. For his expert editing and for helping me learn to write in English, not technicalese, I am forever indebted to Donald Spencer. For their ideas and their reviews, I thank Reid Bandeen, David Strip, Elaine Gorham, and Dorothy Spencer. I owe David Williams a debt of gratitude for reviewing in detail the account of his conflicts with the Nuclear Regulatory Commission and Sandia National Laboratories about scientific integrity in reactor safety analysis. I am greatly indebted to Curtis Overall for helping me understand the events surrounding his discovery of safety problems at TVA's Watts Bar plant and his subsequent ill treatment at the hands of his employer. I also thank Ann Harris for her invaluable assistance with research on TVA and its whistle-blowers. I am grateful for the resources available to me both on-line and in the physical world at the University of New Mexico libraries and at the U.S. Nuclear Regulatory Commission's Public Document Room. I also want to express my appreciation for the thorough and thoughtful job that Michael Harrup did on the editing; the book is much improved for it. Finally, for her reviews of drafts, her assistance in FOIA research, and mainly for putting up with me during this long project, I will forever be in debt to my life mate, Teresa McGrew.

1

A Covenant Breached

We of this nation, desirous of helping to bring peace to the world and realizing the heavy obligations upon us arising from our possession of the means of producing the bomb and from the fact that it is part of our armament, are prepared to make our full contribution toward effective control of atomic energy.

Bernard Baruch, 1946

I have selected the Tennessee Valley Authority's Watts Bar and Sequoyah reactors as the preferred facilities for producing a future supply of tritium. . . . It is the best deal for the taxpayer.

Bill Richardson, 1998

Nuclear War in the Twenty-First Century

In the last half of the twentieth century, people worried a lot about nuclear war. For those of us who kept up with world news and lived in the potential nuclear battle zones of the Northern Hemisphere, such worries were hard to avoid. From the early 1950s through the 1980s, novels, magazines, street demonstrations, movies, and television brought these fears into focus for us. Millions of Americans watched ABC's *The Day After,* in which Jason Robards tried to run a medical clinic in Kansas in the days following an all-out nuclear war, only to join the death toll from radiation poisoning. Many of us secretly wondered in those days whether we had the courage to face a post-holocaust world.

Most of the time, though, the prospect of nuclear war in our time was not a vivid, waking fear, but more an unspoken dread. The possibility of nuclear war between the Soviet Union and the United States was seldom a topic of casual conversation, but fear of it provided a dark, unconscious background to our lives.

The strength of those fears can be measured by the relief we felt when the superpowers finally backed off from nuclear confrontation. Today, after more than a decade of disengagement between the Russians and Americans, the dread is mostly gone. Some of the twentieth-century visualizations of nuclear war now seem old fashioned, like grainy images of children ducking and covering and Nikita Khrushchev at the United Nations, pounding his shoe. These old images seem quaint, even campy.

It is human nature to celebrate escape from a life-threatening crisis. So is the tendency to dismiss the residual danger. But nuclear weapons are so destructive, and nuclear war so difficult to control once started, that it would be foolish to indulge in wishful thinking about the danger of nuclear war in the twenty-first century.

But today, for most people, the dread is simply gone. We no longer have movies or marches or TV shows to help us visualize nuclear wars of the future. If we did, though, you would see some differences from the imaginings of the past.

First and foremost there would be different candidates for the nuclear-armed combatants. For example, in one scenario you might see Pakistan and India allowing their conflict over Kashmir to escalate into a catastrophic nuclear nightmare, with tens of millions of deaths. Another plot line might start with an anonymous nuclear strike against Tel Aviv, followed by massive Israeli nuclear retaliation against Iran. Even the U.S. war against worldwide terrorism might be imagined to go nuclear. Thinking farther into the future, one would have to consider new nuclear states and new enmities. As nuclear weapons spread to more players, the combinations multiply, while the likelihood and severity of potential nuclear wars grow.

The nuclear-armed combatants in these new visualizations might be different from those in our imaginings of the past, but the nature of their conflicts will be driven by some of the same cold logic that emerged in the twentieth century nuclear standoff. Still applicable will be terms like "preemptive strike," "decapitation," and "launch on warning." Still present will be the tendency for a conflict to escalate rapidly and without control, since the ability to use whatever nuclear weapons a nation has deteriorates within hours or days of the start of a nuclear war. Still mind boggling will be the scale of death and destruction.

Eight nations are known to possess nuclear weapons today, and it is highly likely that more will acquire them in the twenty-first century. Given the tensions of the world and the unfortunate human propensity to strike out in anger against rivals, there is a good chance that at least one nuclear war will occur in the twenty-first century. If it does, there is little doubt that it would be the most destructive event in history.

If nontrivial nuclear exchanges do occur, anywhere in the world, then death and disease of civilians and armed forces due to the use of nuclear weapons will be a glaring and potent image for every human being on the planet. Cancer will continue to be a major killer, but radiation will be a suspected cause in every case. Without doubt, life will go on, but everything will be irrevocably changed.

Given this hypothesis, it is worth wondering how history will judge the people and governments that introduced nuclear technology and managed its promise and its danger. The United States will come in for the most intense scrutiny, because all paths lead from one event: the Manhattan Project. Moreover, the U.S. continued in the post–World War II period to lead in the technical development of nuclear weapons and nuclear electric power. The Soviets followed, out of fear and ambition. True, the rise of nuclear technology was probably inevitable, and in an alternate universe, its rise might have taken a different path. But in this universe, it was the United States that brought nuclear weapons into the world.

Perhaps a future of widespread nuclear conflict is inevitable, but history will judge us by what we did to avoid the worst outcomes.

This book is not about the likelihood and consequences of nuclear war in the twenty-first century, but rather about a recent, little-noted change in U.S. policy on tritium for the nuclear arsenal. In December 1998 Secretary of Energy Bill Richardson decided that the United States would produce tritium for nuclear weapons in commercial nuclear power reactors. This unheralded, seemingly innocuous decision abandoned a long-standing policy in the United States of separating civilian and military uses of nuclear energy. The new policy is bad for U.S. national security and for world security. It also turns out to be bad for the health and safety of the people who live near the power plants that are to be used for this purpose.

Tritium is an isotope* of hydrogen that is, essentially, perishable. It is the "H" in "H-bomb." The inventory of tritium in each weapon in the U.S. nuclear arsenal slowly decreases through radioactive decay, and if enough time passes, the weapon's performance will be severely degraded. Thus, a part of the job of managing the nuclear stockpile is to recharge each H-bomb periodically with fresh tritium. A steady supply of tritium is thus needed to maintain the U.S. arsenal of nuclear weapons. For the time being, this supply can come from the weapons that are being decommissioned under the terms of the nuclear arms treaties now in force between the United States and Russia. But once that temporary supply is exhausted, a new production facility for fresh tritium will be needed, since all the cold war–era facilities have, for reasons of safety, been shut down. The Department of Energy foresees such a need's occurring by 2006, though in reality no tritium will be needed for a decade or more beyond that date.

There are numerous viable options for obtaining tritium for the nuclear stockpile, but in Richardson's 1998 decision, the government chose a path that is inconsistent with the nation's interest in avoiding widespread nuclear conflict in the twenty-first century. One would assume that such a portentous policy decision would be made with agonizing attention to the costs and benefits of the change. In fact, it appears that the decision was substantially crafted at a low level in the U.S. government, that the secretary was ill prepared to address the broad issues involved, and that the White House was hardly aware of the decision or its significance.

The worrisome truth is that lapses of this sort have occurred periodically over the history of the U.S. government's management of the dangers that arise from the deployment of nuclear technology. There has been a remarkable unevenness in behavior with respect to these dangers, with periods of intense vigilance and intelligent action interspersed with mindless complacency and indirection. During the complacent periods,

---

* Atoms with the same number of protons but a different number of neutrons are called *isotopes* of the same element. Tritium has one proton and two neutrons, so it is an isotope of hydrogen, whose normal form has one proton and no neutrons. There is one other hydrogen isotope, deuterium, which has one proton and one neutron. The physical properties of tritium and deuterium are essentially identical to those of hydrogen except when nuclear reactions are involved.

policy often migrates to middle-level bureaucrats who operate far from public view and whose decisions are unlikely to reflect the best interests of the nation or of the world.

The United States and the world can ill afford this kind of inconsistency. We stand at a critical transition in the history of nuclear weapons. If the twentieth century is characterized as the age of the bilateral nuclear standoff, the twenty-first will very likely be the age of broad proliferation of nuclear weapons and the means to deliver them, an age when even small and regional conflicts can escalate into nuclear wars with profound and unpredictable effects on the world economy, the global environment, and international security.

But public attention to the threat of nuclear war and the spread of nuclear weapons has declined markedly since the end of the cold war. This is unfortunate, because an aware public is the best means of keeping the government focused and vigilant. This book presents the tritium story in the context of the larger trends in U.S. nuclear policy, showing how and why the new policy came to be and what it portends for the future that will judge us.

Wrong Two Ways, No Way Right

According to the U.S. government's new plan for obtaining the tritium required to recharge its nuclear weapons, three commercial nuclear reactors operated by the Tennessee Valley Authority (TVA) will make tritium during the normal course of their electricity production. Two of the reactors are at the Sequoyah nuclear power plant, and the third is at the Watts Bar plant. All three lie on the banks of the Tennessee River not far from Nashville.

The reactors are "commercial" in the sense that they are designed and licensed solely to produce electricity for commercial sale on the grid. To produce tritium the reactors will have to be modified substantially, but when they come back on line after the modifications (now scheduled for around 2006), they will still churn out kilowatts for the TVA's customers in seven southern states. What will be different is that the TVA will at that point have a new customer that once a year or so will drive special trucks up to the power plants and load up bundles of twelve-foot-long, pencil-thin rods that have been irradiated inside the reactor. Heavily armed troops will guard the whole operation, because these rods will contain tritium bound for the hydrogen bombs of the U.S. nuclear arsenal.

The amount of tritium in modern nuclear weapons is remarkably small, just a few grams in each bomb, but it has a significant effect on explosive yield. Figure 1 is a sketch of the kind of fission weapon used in the bomb dropped on Nagasaki, with one addition: a mixture of deuterium and tritium (D-T) is present at the center. When the explosive in the weapon is set off, the plutonium sphere implodes until the fission chain reaction starts. The D-T then undergoes fusion reactions (two atoms fuse to form a helium atom), which vastly accelerate the fission reaction. Such a weapon is said to be "boosted," since the D-T multiplies the explosive yield many times over. Some of the weapons in the U.S. nuclear arsenal are much more complicated than this diagram indicates, but all are boosted, and hence all need their tritium replaced from time to time.

As noted above, using commercial reactors for producing any of the explosive ingredients of nuclear bombs represents a dramatic departure from the policies of the past. Ever since the Manhattan Project in the 1940s, nuclear materials for defense have been produced at dedicated military reactors located in deeply remote parts of the country, surrounded by layers and layers of guarded fence.

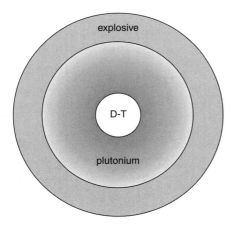

Figure 1
Conceptual drawing of a simple boosted fission weapon.

This book will show that the plan to produce materials for nuclear weapons at commercial nuclear power plants is dangerously and foolishly wrong in two important ways. It is wrong, first, because it will increase the likelihood that nuclear weapons will spread to countries or groups that now do not possess them. It is wrong, second, because the modifications necessary to produce tritium for weapons will make these three reactors, already marginal in terms of safe operation, even more likely to undergo accidents that could expose thousands of people to deadly radioactive doses.

The Impact on Nuclear Weapons Proliferation
There is a widespread belief that the peaceful side of nuclear energy has little to do with its military side, but that is false. The nuclear fuels used in power reactors are the same materials as the nuclear explosives for bombs. The specialized technology for enriching the former is the same as for the latter. The physics of the energy release is the same.[1] It is only through strict administrative controls that the use of nuclear energy for commercial electricity can be prevented from causing proliferation of nuclear weaponry.

In chapter 2 we will see that the U.S. government has, over time, come to recognize these requirements and has worked closely with other nations to establish a far-ranging system of constraints that has grown into a vast international nonproliferation regime. The system is complex and pervasive, encompassing

· barriers on international commerce in nuclear explosive materials
· export controls on critical nuclear weapons technology
· tight secrecy on weapons design information and on the technology for producing nuclear weapons materials
· intrusive in-country monitoring by the International Atomic Energy Agency (IAEA)
· a variety of other government policies and processes

Through many of these functions runs a key principle: strict isolation of civilian nuclear plants from military missions. The principle of "no dual use" for commercial reactors has its roots in the Manhattan Project of the 1940s and Eisenhower's Atoms for Peace initiative in the 1950s. It has been reflected faithfully in the policies of eight presidential administrations. Secretary Richardson's decision of December 1998 was the first significant breach of it.

But even aside from historical tradition, there is today an important practical reason for adhering to the principle of separation. It involves the attitudes and behavior of other countries, particularly signatories and potential signatories of the Nuclear Nonproliferation Treaty (NPT), which will be discussed in chapter 4. This international agreement is the binding mechanism for worldwide restraint on nuclear weapons proliferation. It is also one of the greatest American diplomatic achievements of the twentieth century. It is effectively a contract between the five nations that officially possess nuclear weapons and other countries that agree to eschew acquiring them. In exchange for that agreement, the nuclear "haves" agree not only to assist the "have nots" in their nuclear electricity industries, but also—and this is a key point—to work toward reducing and eliminating nuclear arms worldwide.

One hundred eighty non–weapons states have signed the NPT, but some nations severely criticize it as a cynical means of perpetuating the asymmetry between the weapons states and the non–weapons states. They complain that technical assistance on nuclear electricity is nothing but a way of perpetrating a kind of high-tech imperialism and that the weapons states' commitment to eliminating their nuclear arsenals is a sham. India refuses to sign the NPT for those reasons. It has now acquired a substantial arsenal of small nuclear weapons. India's bitter rival Pakistan has followed the same path.

Clearly, the continued success of the NPT in the twenty-first century depends critically on the sincerity and credibility of the United States's actions with respect to reducing nuclear arsenals and avoiding nuclear proliferation. The new tritium policy sends a wrong signal to potential nuclear-armed countries. Many in those countries have said so.

As chapter 5 will show, the Department of Energy (DOE) has rationalized the new tritium policy with white papers and public presentations that brush aside the policy issue with sophistry, deception, and artful legalese. But the policy issue is profoundly important, and the breach is substantive and irresponsible.

The Impact on Public Safety

The safety of the particular reactors chosen for the new tritium job was apparently not a factor in Secretary Richardson's 1998 decision to allow tritium production at commercial nuclear power plants. The thinking was, no doubt, that if the Nuclear Regulatory Commission (NRC) granted operating licenses to these three reactors, they must be safe. But as chapter 3 will show, nuclear safety experts know that when it comes to protecting the public from accidental radioactive releases, there are vast differences between the best of our reactors and our worst.

From a safety perspective the U.S. government could probably not have made a worse choice of a type of commercial reactor for this new military mission. All three of these TVA reactors are "ice condensers," so designated because they are equipped with gigantic arrays of wire baskets filled with chipped ice to absorb the steam and heat that would be released in a nuclear reactor accident. The containment buildings housing these great ice chests are small and weak compared to the awesomely large and strong containments that are considered the safest, a class that includes that of the Three Mile Island plant that underwent a core meltdown in 1979.

Out of the 104 commercial nuclear reactors currently operating in the United States, only 9 are ice condenser plants. All were manufactured by Westinghouse Electric Company. Numerous studies have shown that this type of plant is exceptionally vulnerable to a wide range of core melt accidents that their more robust brethren handle well. This bad situation is likely to be made worse by the modifications planned for the reactors at Watts Bar and Sequoyah, as chapter 6 will show. The reasons for fearing deterioration in safety as a result of the planned modifications lie as much in the potential impact on the TVA management's commitment to safety as in the way the engineering changes might affect the progression of events during a reactor accident.

The obvious question arises, If these changes result in unsafe plants, won't the NRC prohibit them? Indeed, the NRC must review the changes and either approve or reject the proposed amendment to the TVA's operating licenses that would allow the plants to produce tritium. That review is expected to be completed sometime in 2002. Many of the safety issues involved are subtle and technically complex. For reasons laid out in chapter 6, there is cause for concern that the NRC will not take the high ground on this license amendment review, that the technical staff will take a superficial perspective, and that the decision will be made at the highest levels of the NRC to let the TVA and DOE have their way.*

Besides elaborating on the charges listed above, this book will also try to explain why these three agencies of the federal government are collaborating to implement the new policy, despite the danger it represents to the people of Tennessee and the rest of the world. By delving into some of the hidden agendas that influence the behavior of these organizations, we can sometimes see the logic of their actions. The message about how the public's well-being is set aside in these complex bureaucratic games is disturbing, perhaps even more so than the tritium policy itself.

Dance of the Hidden Agendas

Picking on government agencies is unfair sport. Rare is the federal, state, or local agency unembarrassed by stories of wrongheaded policy, foolish decisions, and incompetent execution. Fortunately a free press ensures that most government agencies operate in the full view of stakeholders: voters and their representatives, interest groups, and so on. The bigger the issue, the more attention is paid. So the usual process is that an agency makes a mistake, some kind of uproar occurs, the agency backpedals (or not), pressure is applied from above, and things get fixed (sort of). And then on to the next cycle.

But it is a more serious matter when there is a persistent bias in an agency's behavior that reflects a set of more or less unstated assumptions about priorities within the organization. These understood priorities are quite separate from and sometimes in conflict with the organization's official charter. Such hidden agendas are less susceptible to correction by external scrutiny because their influence on organizational behavior is more likely to be carefully packaged and because reform in these areas is more likely to be resisted by those in control. Specialists in the theory of organizations have developed sophisticated methods for studying such processes, but average citizens understand the basic concepts. We know

---

* At press time, the NRC still has the TVA's license amendment requests under review.

about tax assessors' being tough on new parts of town, easy on older neighborhoods. We know about redistricting commissions' drawing strange voting boundaries to favor the powers that be. We know about water and highway projects that make little sense until you know who owns the land nearby.

When it happens at the level of the great federal agencies charged with serving the public interest in things nuclear, it is not always so obvious what is going on. The agencies' ability to obscure their motivations is aided by the technical nature of nuclear issues and by the discomfort some nonspecialists feel when confronted with scientific jargon and intentionally confusing explanations. This book will look at the hidden agendas of the key players in three federal agencies that have been brought together to implement the new tritium policy: the DOE, which needs the tritium for its nuclear weapons; the TVA, whose electricity-producing reactors will make the tritium; and the NRC, which must review the proposed changes in the reactors and pass judgment on their safe operation. There is a risk of oversimplification in such an analysis, but it is not possible to gain a true understanding of why the new tritium policy is being pursued and what it portends without exploring how these federal agencies are pressured from within to compromise the interests of the public they are supposed to serve.

The DOE lies at the center of the new policy. It is a vast, loosely co-ordinated collection of bureaucratic fiefdoms and classified nuclear weapons production facilities. Promotion of commercial nuclear power and production of nuclear weapons both lie within its charter, resulting in occasional temptations to bridge the traditional gulf separating military and civilian uses of nuclear technology. It is a notoriously intractable agency, hamstrung by conflicting internal requirements and paralyzed by deeply embedded no-win situations for its leaders. As chapter 5 discusses, selecting a technology for new tritium supplies has been a DOE mission for over twenty years, a mission that should not have been a great challenge, given the department's extraordinary budget and technical resources. But the decision process has floundered under the political pressures of selecting one technology over another or one site over another. Finally, in 1998, under intense budgetary pressure from Congress, Richardson, at that time the newly appointed Secretary of Energy, made the surprise choice of commercial reactors for the supply of tritium. The decision has all the markings of following the path of least resistance. To the secretary, it had the delightful property of shuffling most of the hard work off to the TVA and NRC. The staying power of the DOE's hidden agenda with respect to tritium production is reflected in the fact that the new tritium policy persists even after a change of administration.

The TVA is another strange federal beast. Created during the depression to bring electricity and prosperity to the impoverished mid-South, the TVA has grown to be the largest electric utility in the nation, today operating more or less independently of federal funds.[2] Its headlong plunge into nuclear electricity in the 1970s is generally regarded as the agency's biggest failure, leaving it with a $26 billion debt and just five operating reactors out of the seventeen originally ordered. As detailed in chapter 6, the TVA's nuclear division has a record of safety violations, reactor accidents, and intervention by the NRC that is by far worse than that of any other utility in the nation.

Much of the reason for the TVA's poor financial and safety record can be traced to the management structure of this strange throwback agency. A three-person board of directors appointed by the president and approved by the Senate rules the authority. The board is remarkably autonomous, reporting to no member of the cabinet and exempt from much of the oversight to which other power companies are subject.

Many in Congress find the TVA's arrogance and independence infuriating, and recently there have been vigorous attempts to dismantle the agency and sell off its electricity-producing assets to private utilities. Throughout the TVA's history, it has been able to fend off such threats, partly through the protection provided by congressional delegations from the seven states in which it operates. Nonetheless, the board fears dismantlement more than any other threat. And herein lies the secret behind the TVA's cooperation with the DOE on the new tritium policy. If the TVA takes on this new defense mission, it becomes effectively a part of the nuclear weapons establishment. The practical barriers to dismantling this great nuclear dinosaur would then suddenly become insurmountable. Check and checkmate.

Finally there is the NRC. Unlike the TVA, it is a relatively modern agency, having been created in 1974 when the old Atomic Energy Commission was split into the NRC and what is now the DOE. Unlike the

DOE, its official mission is straightforward: it is supposed to ensure that the public is safe from all nonmilitary nuclear activities. But internally the NRC is damaged goods. In 1979 the accident at the Three Mile Island (TMI) plant forced the NRC and the industry it regulates to do something about core melt accidents, events deemed incredible before TMI. As chronicled in chapter 3, the NRC responded to the challenge, but the political reaction from the financially burdened nuclear industry has made the agency extremely sensitive about core melt accidents. One can sense a kind of "see no evil, hear no evil, speak no evil" quality in its recent behavior regarding the possibility of such accidents.

Unfortunately, core melt accidents are at the heart of the very significant safety problems of the TVA's three ice condenser reactors. To properly address those problems will require a considerable degree of courage and integrity on the part of individuals at several levels within the NRC. Current regulations allow the regulators to ignore safety problems of this type, even if they dominate the risk to the public. As chapter 6 will discuss, the NRC is likely to follow this easier path in reviewing the TVA's request to modify its reactors to make tritium for nuclear weapons.

Behind the actions of any federal agency there are no doubt dozens of hidden agendas, some subtle, others simple, some broadly understood, others selfish and covert. Some are even harmless. In the case of bad policy, however, it is essential to study what seems to lie beneath the surface. In the chapters that follow, the impact of hidden agendas on the actions of agencies and of individuals will be revealed through events from recent history. In some cases these hidden agendas explain why officials took certain otherwise inexplicable actions. In other cases the agendas are revealed when individuals in the organization choose to ignore the hidden requirements and pay a high personal price.

2

War's Child: The Birth and Nurture of Civilian Nuclear Energy

It is not clear that the public will accept an energy source that produces this much radioactivity and that can be subject to diversion of materials for bombs.
Enrico Fermi, 1944

How It Began

It was 8:16 A.M. and the people of Hiroshima, Japan, were going about their business, thinking about what had to be done that day, what happened yesterday, or perhaps their families. Then, in an instant, the sky turned white, and the world was changed forever. Three days later the same thing happened in Nagasaki. Six days later the three-and-a-half-year-long war between Japan and the United States was over.[1]

It was thus in war that nuclear energy was introduced to the world.* It might have been different. In an alternative universe the science behind the atomic bombs that destroyed Hiroshima and Nagasaki in 1945 might have been explored in peacetime, and everything about the role nuclear energy plays in our world might have been different.

But it was in 1939, on the very brink of war in Europe, that two German scientists discovered that neutron bombardment could cause uranium atoms to split apart and release additional neutrons in the process. As the storm clouds of war gathered, a number of scientists in Germany, England, and the United States realized that nuclear chain reactions could be the basis for weapons of extraordinary violence. Soon, discussion in scientific journals about the new findings went ominously silent.

* The adjectives "atomic" and "nuclear" are synonyms, though the latter has gained prevalence.

Over the next five years the United States made an unprecedented investment in the secret weapon with which President Truman ended the war with Japan. At first, the war-weary American public reacted to the news with relief and rejoicing. But as time passed, news reports, photos, and films of the utter devastation in the Japanese cities brought apprehension and concern. The two bombs dropped on Hiroshima and Nagasaki killed 240,000 people.[2]

U.S. leaders feared first and foremost that this terrible new technology would spread to other nations, its awesome power driving an arms race that could threaten the very existence of Western civilization. In the Baruch Plan, an extraordinary gesture of internationalism, the United States even offered to turn control of nuclear technology over to an international agency. But Soviet leader Josef Stalin, ever suspicious and resentful of the United States, would have none of it. By the early 1950s, the dreaded nuclear arms race was on.

The first serious planning about nuclear energy for peaceful purposes took place against this anxious background. The potential for producing electricity from nuclear reactors was understood from the earliest days of the Manhattan Project. The plutonium for the Nagasaki bomb had been produced in a nuclear reactor that generated a great deal of heat as a by-product. Every engineer knows that if you have heat, you can make steam, and from that you can make electricity. But to move from hypothetical possibility to a practical system for delivering electricity to homes and industry, many enormous barriers would have to be overcome.

In the past it had been the role of entrepreneurs in the private sector to bring about the transition from the technical feasibility of an idea to a moneymaking industrial enterprise based on that idea. But the case of nuclear energy seemed to be different. There was, for one thing, the intimate connection between the technology for making nuclear electricity and that for making nuclear weapons. And some say there were also the factors of guilt and wishful thinking. If the rise of nuclear electricity could usher in a new age of prosperity and progress based on unlimited, cheap energy, then the pain from the images of dead and dying Japanese civilians and the anxiety about the nuclear arms race might be balanced by a corresponding element of hope for the future. It was in the context of these issues that President Dwight D. Eisenhower and his advisors, free-enterprise philosophy notwithstanding, saw the need for the federal government to bring commercial nuclear electricity into the light of day.

Atoms for Peace, Please

The energy needs of a world that was rapidly expanding its industrial infrastructure were a subject of much discussion even in the 1950s. For example, many analysts understood that Japan's fateful decision to attack the United States at Pearl Harbor was largely motivated by its need to maintain access to petroleum in Southeast Asia.[3] For the United States, however, fossil fuel was generally seen to be in good supply, and no constraints from limited energy resources appeared to threaten a vigorous postwar economic boom.

Nonetheless, soon after Eisenhower took office as president in 1952, he and his advisors became captive to a vision of a future in which atomic energy would power the continent and America would lead the world into a new age of peace and prosperity. With remarkably little input from scientists and engineers, Eisenhower introduced the world to his vision of "Atoms for Peace" in a dramatic speech to the United Nations in 1953.[4] By doing so, he committed the U.S. government to fostering and promoting peaceful uses of nuclear energy all over the world while somehow avoiding the spread of nuclear weapons.

The people delegated to implement Eisenhower's vision were enthusiastic, but they would have to overcome a number of hurdles, including the need to

· tightly control inventories of the fissile ingredients of atomic bombs, uranium and plutonium, to prevent diversion to foreign weapons programs
· control international proliferation of key technologies for producing uranium and plutonium
· loosen the stringent controls on technical information and fissile materials imposed by the Atomic Energy Act of 1946
· develop safe and efficient reactors in the absence of strong market incentives for private investors
· overcome private-sector exposure to the unknown liability of reactor accidents

• deal with nuclear waste, for which neither technology nor legislation existed

This was a tall order, indeed. With the benefit of hindsight, the Atoms for Peace initiative has been widely judged to have been highly optimistic. As early as 1963 David Lilienthal, the first chairman of the Atomic Energy Commission and one of the principal architects of early U.S. nuclear policy, confessed, "We were grimly determined to prove that this discovery was not just a weapon. This led perhaps to wishful thinking, a wishful elevation of the 'sunny side' of the Atom."[5] The centerpiece of the Atoms for Peace program, and its most remarkable element, was the way that weapons-grade uranium and plutonium would be controlled. The Manhattan Project had demonstrated that powerful atomic bombs could be made either with uranium, which was used in the Hiroshima bomb, or plutonium, the key ingredient of the Nagasaki bomb. Atoms for Peace would be a failure if other countries could acquire these bomb materials because of the development of civilian nuclear energy.

For uranium, the key was preventing the spread of enrichment technology. Natural uranium is unsuitable as a nuclear weapons material or as fuel for the kind of reactor being pushed in the Atoms for Peace program. The fraction of the fissile U-235 isotope, about 0.7 percent, in natural uranium is too low for either purpose. The rest of natural uranium is the nonfissile U-238 isotope.* The Manhattan Project had created huge, secret industrial facilities to produce uranium with a higher fissile content, a process known as "enrichment." Nuclear weapons required enrichment to 80 percent or 90 percent, but nuclear fuel for American reactors needed a U-235 fraction of only 3–4 percent.

The problem for the people implementing Eisenhower's Atoms for Peace program was that the technology for enrichment was the same for fuel as for bomb material. Eisenhower's people needed to open up commercial atomic energy to the world and at the same time remove the incentive for other countries to develop enrichment technology on their own.

The U.S. solution to the dilemma was this: power companies would bring natural uranium to the great enrichment facilities in the United

---

* U-238 has three more neutrons than U-235, but those neutrons make it more stable and less apt to disintegrate when struck by a neutron from outside the nucleus. Thus the terms "fissile" for U-235 and "nonfissile" for U-238.

States, and they would receive in return the slightly enriched uranium fuel their reactors needed. The customers, whether foreign or domestic, would pay only the actual costs of the enrichment services. In this way any country could pursue peaceful nuclear energy without the need to develop expensive enrichment facilities that might also be able to produce bomb material.

Controlling plutonium required different measures. The steady neutron bombardment of U-238 in the fuel of a reactor creates small quantities of plutonium as time goes by. It was essential to prevent the users of U.S. reactor fuel from chemically processing the spent fuel to extract its plutonium for weapons. To accomplish this, Eisenhower called for the establishment, within the framework of the United Nations, of a new international body whose inspectors would track reactor fuel from the time it left the U.S. enrichment facility to the time it was returned to the United States as spent fuel. Thus, to get the benefit of U.S.-supplied fuel, each participating country had to agree to intrusive monitoring of the fuel and inspections of the reactors using it. As an additional precaution, the United States would maintain a high degree of secrecy about the technology for chemically separating plutonium from spent fuel, a technology known as "reprocessing."

It was an amazing plan, really. Here was a relatively conservative, free-market-loving Republican president proposing that the United States get into a new business, providing profit-free industrial services from classified military facilities to all qualified customers, foreign or domestic. And he was furthermore calling for the creation of an international agency with unprecedented authority to carry out intrusive inspections in any country agreeing to the deal. That this remarkable proposal was being made at a time when there was no energy crisis looming attests to the emotional power of that image of the "sunny side" of atomic power, counterbalancing the terror of nuclear weapons.

With enthusiastic support from Congress, the Atoms for Peace program developed over the remainder of the 1950s and into the 1960s, with each of the hurdles outlined above addressed one by one. A key step was the formation of the Atomic Energy Commission (AEC), a decidedly civilian agency that would continue the country's nuclear weapons work but also guide and promote civilian applications at home and abroad. The plan was to incubate and facilitate a domestic nuclear power industry until it was a self-sufficient economic concern. Similar accommodations were also to be extended to international partners, so that the nuclear industry could develop globally, with the United States, naturally, well in the lead. Consistent with Eisenhower's vision, the IAEA was established in 1957 to coordinate the Atoms for Peace program at the international level.

The Atomic Energy Act of 1954 relieved the restrictions of the 1946 act with respect to private-sector and international involvement in nuclear power and laid out the overall framework for a dual-track implementation of nuclear technology. Military applications would continue as before, but peaceful applications would proceed along a path that was insulated from the exigencies of national security. Instead, the federal government would create policies and institutions that would deal with those exigencies. Prohibition of using commercial reactors to produce weapons material was one such policy.

A cooperative research and development program between the federal government and private companies addressed the need to design and test the large and expensive prototype reactors required to establish confidence in the new technology. The government even subsidized some of the first large-scale commercial reactors for electricity production.

The private-sector liability problem was eventually solved with the Price-Anderson Act, which limited the liability of utilities and other private entities for nuclear reactor accidents. The utilities were required to purchase liability insurance for each reactor that would cover up to $60 million dollars in damages; if any accident cost more than that, the government would foot the bill.[6] Similarly, the nuclear industry was not required to solve the waste disposal issue (an impossibility in the early years, since the overall national approach to the nuclear fuel cycle was highly uncertain).

For every problem that arose, Atoms for Peace had a solution. The bigger the obstacle, the more creative the approach applied to overcoming it. Behind the program was a "can-do" attitude that had served Eisenhower well on the European front in World War II. But time would reveal deep flaws in the assumptions underlying this program, flaws that have a direct bearing on the issues now facing the United States regarding the new tritium production program.

Nuclear Energy Dreaming

The unconsidered enthusiasm that leaders in the U.S. government brought to the promotion of civilian applications in the early days of nuclear energy is today a thing of wonder. There was actually a vigorous program (more than $4 billion in year-2000 dollars)[7] to develop a nuclear-powered airplane. Think about that for a moment. The congressmen and administrators who promoted the program knew that planes crash and would always crash. The crash of an atomic plane would certainly release large quantities of highly radioactive materials into the atmosphere. Perhaps the proponents of nuclear planes had a poor appreciation of the health hazards of radioactive fission products, yet the scientific knowledge was available at the time.

At any rate, the use of nuclear power for electricity was a much more sensible concept, and soon corporate partners found the government's enthusiasm infectious. Large companies like General Electric and Westinghouse recognized the technical and financial risks associated with developing nuclear technology, but the government's willingness to share (or fully absorb) those risks overcame any early hesitation they may have had.

The first reactors to put electricity on the grid (starting in 1957) were either partially or fully subsidized by the AEC's Power Reactor Demonstration Program. Six years after the first of these was completed, an electric utility for the first time placed an order for a nuclear power plant without the benefit of a government subsidy. To overcome the utility's anxieties about uncertain capital costs, General Electric (GE) had offered a "turnkey" deal: a fixed-price contract, payable upon operation. Soon Westinghouse followed suit with turnkey power plant proposals, and each nuclear vendor took several additional orders for plants from utilities around the country. These early contracts were priced to beat the competition from fossil fuel. Clearly, the companies offering the contracts had a vision of a nuclear electricity future that would justify significant early financial losses (GE lost about $3.5 billion in year-2000 dollars in its first seven turnkey plants).[8]

Following that aggressive pump priming, U.S. utilities started lining up to order power plants. In 1965–67 a total of fifty-six orders were placed for nuclear reactors. (This is more than half the number in operation today.) The size of the reactors was also increasing dramatically: the average capacity ordered in 1967 was about 900 megawatts, compared to about 550 megawatts four years earlier.

This level of investment was possible largely because the federal government sheltered the nuclear reactor vendors and the utilities from the unique risks associated with this new and potent technology. The government carried out the research, funded the demonstration plants, limited the vendor and utility financial liability, and allowed the looming issue of radioactive waste disposal to be deferred. Then, as the engineering and construction challenges of these enormous and complex facilities became clearer, the nuclear industry also began to seek relief from burdensome requirements related to public safety. The government would find it considerably more difficult to provide relief of that sort, and from that tension emerged a dominant theme for nuclear energy in the twentieth century: the balancing of public benefit from the new power source against the health risk from hypothetical reactor accidents.

The AEC had been established to manage both the development of the new energy industry and protection of the public from its hazards. These conflicting roles created concerns early in the government's nuclear power program, but the shortage of technical experts was cited as adequate justification for merging these two functions in one organization. To some extent, the Advisory Committee on Reactor Safeguards (ACRS), autonomous by statute, filled the need for independence in the two functions, as its area of concern was exclusively the safety issue. But the ACRS could only study and advise; it could not carry out research or impose requirements.

The AEC's commitment to reactor safety assessment was clearly secondary to its interests in advancing nuclear technology and assisting the fledgling industry. Whatever safety budget existed was modest, and even that was not even fully spent, with an average 8.5 percent of the commission's safety budget left unspent during 1965–68.[9] As the plants on the drafting tables became increasingly large, the ACRS repeatedly raised alarms about the need for more research on critical safety issues. But the AEC's research arm was not persuaded, choosing instead to emphasize work on the breeder reactor, which would usher in the age of the plutonium fuel cycle.

In 1974 Congress finally did something about the clear conflict of interest inherent in one organization's having the responsibility for both industry promotion and public protection. The AEC was split into the NRC and the Energy Research and Development Administration (ERDA), with lines of responsibility clearly separated. Not long afterward, ERDA was merged with many other agencies to become the bureaucratic behemoth known as the DOE.

The staff and management of the NRC were by and large drawn from its predecessor organization, so dramatic changes in attitudes and activities were not initially apparent. Then in March 1979, a commercial power reactor in Pennsylvania experienced a type of accident that, by the assumptions of the nuclear industry and the federal regulators, could not happen: the reactor core melted down. At that moment, the transformation of the NRC into an independent regulatory agency truly began.

How the NRC responded to the challenge of the TMI accident and how its regulation of nuclear reactor safety has evolved in the ensuing twenty years will be discussed in chapter 3. But first, I will briefly review how the underlying links between nuclear weapons and civilian nuclear power were managed by two presidents in the 1970s.

A Tale of Two Presidents

With the Atoms for Peace initiative, President Eisenhower staked the security of his country on the premise that a healthy civilian nuclear industry could develop in parallel to and in isolation from its military counterpart. Reflecting the optimism of the 1950s, he gambled that the benefits of an unlimited supply of power from nuclear energy could be gained without the corresponding cost of spreading nuclear arms around the world. Part of the gamble concerned whether future administrations would recognize and honor the commitments implicit in the two-track nuclear strategy Eisenhower initiated.

Unfortunately, there has over the years been an ebb and flow regarding U.S. attention to the dangers inherent in nuclear technology. Intense vigilance is followed by a slow slide into complacency, which is then often punctuated by a crisis caused by external events. Such a crisis may then trigger a flurry of activity, heightened awareness, and strengthened controls. And then, slowly, attention drifts again. In the intervals of complacency, decision making can descend into middle levels of the federal government (and virtually all nuclear matters have become federal matters), where hidden agendas can lead to policies and decisions quite contrary to the interests of the public.

For an understanding of today's challenges, such as the new tritium policy, it is illuminating to review the records of two presidents: Richard Nixon and Jimmy Carter. The presidencies of these two men were more or less contiguous, separated only by Gerald Ford's partial term after Nixon resigned in disgrace in 1974. The contrast between how nuclear proliferation was handled in the successive administrations is striking and helps us understand how burdensome a covenant presidents since Eisenhower have inherited and how unevenly it has been respected.

The Nixon Administration Reneges on Enrichment Services

Eisenhower believed that one of the keys to a successful dual-track strategy was managing the supply of enriched uranium and controlling enrichment technology. The centerpiece of his offer to the world was a commitment on the part of the U.S. government to providing enrichment services to all companies and countries that agreed with the basic rules of international inspection and oversight.

In retrospect, Eisenhower had other options, and his failure to consider them is a discouraging aspect of the history of nuclear energy. For example, commercial nuclear power is eminently feasible with "heavy" water* for the coolant and natural uranium for fuel, as the Canadian nuclear program has admirably demonstrated. But the United States, strongly influenced by Admiral Hyman Rickover's vigorous nuclear submarine program, took the path of using slightly enriched uranium for fuel and ordinary water (or "light" water) for cooling. On this path, uranium enrichment was a necessary part of the civilian fuel cycle, and thus prevention of nuclear weapons proliferation depended heavily on administrative controls separating military and civilian uses of enrichment.

---

* "Heavy" water (D_2O) is identical to ordinary (or "light") water (H_2O), except that its hydrogen is deuterium, a hydrogen isotope with one neutron added to the single-proton nucleus of common hydrogen.

Richard Nixon came to the White House in 1969 with a zealous mission to scale back government, eliminate interference in the free marketplace, and transfer to private enterprise all functions that did not absolutely belong in the sphere of government. In *Nuclear Power and Nuclear Proliferation*, the definitive book on nuclear policy shifts in this era, Michael Brenner wrote, "It is easy to underestimate the heavy political and ideological weight borne by the privatization plan. For the Nixon people in the early 1970s, the nuclear energy issue did not mean reactor safety, or the environmental nuclear dangers of poorly planned waste disposal, or the threat of terrorist seizure, or the proliferation of weapons states. It meant getting the enrichment business off the back of the federal government."[10]

Then, as now, the federal nuclear establishment had powerful friends in Congress and knew how to defend its turf. The Production Division of the AEC employed thousands of workers at three enormous diffusion plants at Paducah, Kentucky; Portsmouth, Ohio; and Oak Ridge, Tennessee. These plants could provide all the enriched uranium needed by both the military and civilian sectors in the early 1970s, but the AEC saw greatly expanded capacity in its future. The only question was how many plants and when they would be needed.

The broad-based government push to commercialize nuclear power had by this time stimulated aggressive nuclear electricity programs in the United States, Europe, and Japan. Planning adequate enrichment facilities to supply the future fuel needs of the resulting global fleet of power reactors was an exercise in educated guesswork, but it was as clear to Nixon's people as it was to the AEC that more production capacity would be needed soon. Being true believers in free enterprise, however, Nixon's people insisted that the expansion occur via privatization, not expansion of AEC's dominion. They worked with leaders in the private sector to form two industrial consortia that would take over the enrichment job from the government. Then they demanded that the AEC transfer the classified enrichment technology to the consortia so that planning for new, private facilities could begin. To keep the squeeze on, Nixon paralyzed productivity improvements at the AEC's existing facilities by impounding congressionally appropriated funding.[11] The AEC's allies in Congress retaliated by threatening to forbid the transfer of the secret enrichment technology to the private sector. Nixon backed down, but the battle over privatization of enrichment services raged on.

The AEC's leaders were chastened by the effectiveness of this thrust into their empire and backed away from some concepts they cherished, such as reactor fuel prices that were subsidized to stimulate the growth of nuclear energy. But they felt that time was on their side; their analyses suggested that new capacity would not really be needed until 1982, well beyond even a second Nixon term. They could win the confrontation by the age-old tactic of government bureaucracies: just go slow.

Nixon's people would have none of this and crafted a plan that would sabotage the AEC's ability to maneuver in the political arena. A key administration official, James Connor, was inserted into the agency, where he took charge of planning, evaluation, and analysis. A lawyer by training, Connor worked with other White House loyalists to craft new procedures and policies on enrichment contract terms and agency book-keeping. These changes seemed on the surface to be routine upgrades of government operations, arguably bringing them closer to private-sector norms. But they were a time bomb that would eventually cause an international crisis tarnishing the reputation of the United States and profoundly compromising its world leadership in nuclear affairs. Brenner argues that the catastrophe was well planned and consciously executed by free-market zealots operating from mid-level management positions in the federal government.[12]

The change in contract terms seemed simple enough; it was a switch from "requirements contracts" to the more businesslike "fixed-commitment contracts." The older format reflected the paternalistic, nuclear-promoting attitude of Atoms for Peace. It committed the U.S. government to providing whatever fuel a client needed throughout the life of a reactor, as long as the government was informed at least six months in advance of any changes in fuel needs. This amazingly generous arrangement was replaced by the much tougher fixed-commitment contract, which dramatically moved the burden of uncertainty from the supplier to the customer. It required the buyer to commit to a specific schedule of enriched fuel purchases, and it secured the commitment with large cash deposits and severe penalties for changes in schedule or quantities. Astonishingly, the customers had to forecast ten years of fuel deliveries and commit to the contracts eight years before first delivery of fuel, thus requiring up to eighteen years of prescience. Only an unregulated monopoly could dictate such arrogant terms to its customers. But of course, the idea was to break the monopoly by creating irresistible pressure to privatize the uranium fuel supply business.

It gets worse. In the same dry bureaucratic prose with which these dramatic changes were announced to the world, the AEC reminded its customers that U.S. law would not allow the agency to enter into any fuel supply contracts that would cause the enrichment facilities to be oversubscribed. The administration's interpretation of this restriction was admirably frugal: only existing AEC enrichment capacity would be factored into the calculation of oversubscription, even though the initial fuel contracts would span eighteen years. No one believed that there would be no enrichment capacity added during that time frame, but the AEC accountants, watched carefully by Connor, stood by the policy.

To reactor owners in the United States and foreign countries, the message between the lines was as clear as day: "first come, first serve." Governments of fuel-importing nations howled at the reversal of policy, but the hard reality was that the United States was their only possible supplier of nuclear fuel, other than the unreliable Soviet Union. And so, as Brenner tells it, "[t]he great enrichment rush began. Utilities at home and abroad did rough calculations and then sought a place near the front of the line forming at the doors of AEC headquarters in Washington. A prudent utility could do only one thing: make the most generous estimate of prospective needs and get a lien on a share of the finite AEC enrichment capacity."[13] The new policy was made official in January 1973. By June 1974 the U.S. government's enrichment capacity was fully booked for the next nine years, and in July of that year the United States announced it was suspending acceptance of additional enrichment contracts.[14] In just eighteen months, Eisenhower's promise to fuel the world's nuclear reactors had been undone.

The international reaction to these events was, at first, disbelief. Then the protests mounted, increasing in potency and stridency until the State Department desperately importuned the AEC to back off. But Nixon's appointees turned a deaf ear to these complaints. Brenner points out that career bureaucrats in the AEC could have worked to redirect the calamitous policy but gambled that the uproar would help them get the funding they needed for new enrichment plants. Meanwhile Connor and his White House allies believed the crisis was worth the pain because it would lead eventually to privatization. Strange bedfellows.

Over the next year, a war raged within the Nixon administration over the reversal in nuclear policy, but it would not be settled by the president. In the spring of 1973, his life was changed by John Dean's testimony before a Senate committee chaired by Senator Sam Ervin. Dean convincingly described the president as an active conspirator in a cover-up of his administration's involvement in a burglary of Democratic Party national headquarters in Washington's Watergate Hotel. In October of that year, Nixon fired Archibald Cox, the special prosecutor appointed to investigate these charges. Over the winter, calls for impeachment of the president echoed across the country. Nixon was impeached by Congress in July 1974 and resigned the following month.

Meanwhile the State Department, low on the totem pole of the Nixon administration, struggled to contain the international crisis involving nuclear fuels that was erupting around it. It found a magic bullet in an obscure executive order signed by Eisenhower as part of the Atoms for Peace program in 1955. The order asserted State's supremacy over the AEC in matters affecting foreign policy and national security. Confronting the AEC with this trump card at precisely the time when Nixon was about to be impeached by the House of Representatives, the State Department won a number of begrudged concessions. The AEC had another reason to back off from its hard line. The industrial consortia it had cobbled together for a private enrichment venture were disintegrating as some of the big players failed to see how they were to make money from the deal.[15] A more flexible policy on AEC enrichment contracts was pounded out, leaving many issues unresolved but allowing the diplomats at State to show the world that sanity about nuclear fuel was slowly returning to the U.S. government. Ironically, Nixon issued a statement approving the revised fuels policy on the day he departed the White House.[16]

The damage done by the engineered enrichment crisis was profound and lasting. Says Brenner: "From a non-proliferation standpoint, the effects were uniformly bad and quickly observable. . . . The outcome was to weaken U.S. leverage on the nuclear programs of other states while offering those states a rationale for acquiring technology that would substantially lower the barriers to weapons manufacture."[17] There could not have been a worse time for this turn of events, as there were two European consortia looking for capital and customers for their competitive enrichment services. With the shattering of the world's confidence in the United States as a reliable fuel supplier, these ventures were strongly boosted. For decades, the United States would expend enormous diplomatic effort trying to rein in the burgeoning international market in enriched uranium fuel. And what is discouraging is that the architects of the crisis knew what they were doing. They just valued the privatization objective more highly than the nonproliferation objective that was supposed to be at the heart of the nuclear policy of the United States.

The parallels with recent events concerning tritium production, to be discussed in chapter 5, are quite remarkable. In both cases, the nation's commitment to nonproliferation was compromised by a perceived higher objective; in Nixon's time it was privatization, whereas in today's case it is cost savings. In both cases, a pattern of impasses with Congress motivated the administration to manipulate internal policies to work around obstacles to the chosen strategy; in Nixon's time the solution was the artificial saturation of enrichment capacity, whereas today it is the reinterpretation of U.S. policy on dual-use nuclear facilities. In both cases, a key player in the policy changes was a lawyer imported into the middle of the federal nuclear bureaucracy. In both cases, the critical events occurred while the president was distracted by impeachment proceedings. And in both cases, the credibility of the United States as a champion of nuclear nonproliferation was deeply compromised.

Nixon's resignation was not the only event of historic proportions to intrude on the uranium enrichment crisis of 1973–74. In May 1974, India surprised the world by exploding a nuclear fission device, thereby becoming the sixth nation in the world to possess nuclear weapons. Following a pattern to be repeated often in the history of federal agency attitudes about nuclear dangers, the drift in vigilance that had allowed India to develop a nuclear capacity with apparently no knowledge on the part of the U.S. government was instantly replaced by alarm, and the government frantically searched for ways to mitigate the dangers India's action revealed.

Jimmy Carter Defers the Plutonium Economy

The Indian bomb came as a complete surprise to the architects of the U.S. nuclear energy program. Conventional wisdom held that international safeguards such as the IAEA's inspections of reactors fueled with U.S.-enriched fuel would prevent would-be nuclear proliferators from obtaining plutonium. Canada, however, had sold India a reactor that, since it used natural uranium as fuel, was not subject to the requirements the U.S. imposed for its enrichment services. Nonetheless India had committed itself, in bilateral agreements with Canada, not to use the fuel supplied by Canada as the material for a bomb and to submit to safeguards similar to those demanded by the United States. But the Indian scientists had gotten around that promise by refining their own locally obtained uranium and exposing it to neutron bombardment in the Canadian reactor. They extracted plutonium from this legally unfettered uranium by running it through a reprocessing facility that they had built at a cost of $35 million (year-2000 dollars). To add insult to injury, it was later learned that the facility's design was based on training in reprocessing technology the Indian scientists had received in the United States, courtesy of the AEC.[18]

The Indian achievement revealed important loopholes in the international system for preventing proliferation of nuclear weapons and a serious drift in the AEC's vigilance about critical nuclear weapons technology. Soon officials and knowledgeable academics in the United States and abroad were looking for other weaknesses and fallacies in the nonproliferation system. They soon found that the path the United States was following toward its civilian nuclear future was based on wishful thinking and unfounded assumptions. At the heart of the problem was the plan to use plutonium as reactor fuel.

The early architects of U.S. policy on commercial nuclear energy believed that the world supply of natural uranium was quite limited, so that unless another nuclear fuel was found, the envisioned halcyon nuclear age would be brief. Their solution was plutonium, which could be produced simply by exposing the otherwise useless U-238 to the storm of neutrons in a specialized nuclear reactor called a "breeder." Until 1974, the almost universal view in the nuclear community was that the finite store of U-235 was simply nature's way of getting humankind started on a nuclear economy based on plutonium, which would be in plentiful supply for over a thousand years.

After the Indian bomb, people started to ask the question that should have been asked long before. What about plutonium bombs from diverted reactor fuel? Actually, there was a ready answer from the true believers in nuclear energy, and it came in two parts. First, safeguards would prevent proliferators from diverting plutonium from the civilian economy, and second, plutonium extracted from spent reactor fuel was unsuitable for bomb making. The Indian explosion cast doubt on the first argument. The second argument, as it turned out, was also in error.

The plutonium that is extracted from spent commercial fuel is slightly different from that used in nuclear weapons, and the difference has to do with isotopic composition, just as the difference between reactor-grade and weapons-grade uranium does. The key isotope for plutonium's chain reaction in a bomb is Pu-239, but all reactor-produced plutonium has heavier isotopes—Pu-240, Pu-241, etc.—mixed in. Of these, Pu-240 causes the greatest problems for bomb design. It is considered a "contaminant" because it produces a steady stream of neutrons that tend to cause a "fizzle" instead of an explosion.

The more time a batch of U-238 is exposed to neutron irradiation in a reactor, the greater the percentage of contaminant isotopes in the plutonium that is created. Thus the military reactors that produced plutonium for weapons used relatively short uranium exposure times before the irradiated material was removed for reprocessing. This approach resulted in weapons-grade plutonium, defined as plutonium having less than 7 percent Pu-240. In contrast, commercial power reactors have very long exposure times, and the Pu-240 fraction can be 19 percent or higher. This fact led to the belief that commercial spent fuel would not be useful for would-be proliferators.

It is now known that fission weapons can be made with plutonium extracted from commercial spent fuel. It was also known in 1974, since the United States had tested such a weapon in 1962, but this fact was kept classified until 1994.[19] As it turns out, the distinction between weapons-grade and non-weapons-grade plutonium is more about economics than physics, since bombs made with higher contaminant fractions are feasible, just heavier and more difficult to make. Besides, it would not be hard for any proliferator to obtain weapons-grade plutonium clandestinely by exposing U-238 for a shorter period of time than the bulk of the fuel in a commercial reactor, just as India had.

President Carter is generally remembered for turning the great ship of the U.S. government away from the plutonium economy, but it was actually Ford's administration that moved first. During the 1976 presidential election campaign, Carter scored points against the Republican administration over the issues of plutonium and the India bomb. In the week before Election Day, Ford attempted to defuse the issue by releasing a major statement laying out a new vision of U.S. nuclear policy. In it, the president called for enhanced international commitments to controlling the spread of nuclear weapons and declared open to question what had heretofore been unquestioned assumptions in the country's nuclear policies. The connection between civilian nuclear power and weapons proliferation was identified as a critical concern, and according to the president's statement, the "United States should no longer regard reprocessing of used nuclear fuel to produce plutonium as a necessary and inevitable step in the nuclear fuel cycle."[20]

It would be up to Jimmy Carter, who won the election handily, to take on the challenge of refashioning the government's nuclear policies and processes in light of the issues raised by Ford's announcement. Carter, who had some training in nuclear engineering, waded into the complex issues of nuclear power and proliferation soon after taking office in 1977. He was greatly impressed by a report commissioned by the Ford Foundation and carried out by the technical think tank, Mitre.[21] The Ford/Mitre report exposed to the light of day the risks inherent in the plutonium economy and took exception to the prevailing belief that the world's supply of uranium would soon be exhausted unless a plutonium fuel cycle was used to stretch the available resources.

Carter addressed domestic aspects of the plutonium policy by calling for the cancellation of two plutonium-related demonstration facilities, one a reprocessing plant and the other a breeder reactor. This immediately drew withering criticism from the entrenched nuclear bureaucracy in his own government, the large nuclear corporations expecting lucrative design and construction contracts, and the congressional delegations in the regions that would benefit in jobs from the plants.

At the same time Carter took on these domestic opponents, he turned his attention to the knotty international aspects of plutonium commerce. He viewed with great concern the imminent deal under the terms of which Germany was to build a large reprocessing facility in Brazil. The vision of thousands of pounds per year of weapons-usable plutonium moving in and out of a reprocessing plant in Brazil by way of river or rail transport would surely cause any U.S. president some anxiety. Carter saw this as a giant step down the slippery slope of nuclear weapons proliferation and stridently argued against the deal to the principals. Clumsiness tended to characterize the Carter administration's activities, and the attempt to turn the Germany/Brazil deal around was received coldly by both governments.

Sobered by this demonstration of the weakened U.S. influence on nuclear policies of other nations, Carter grimly set out on a mission of international education and dialog. One of the highlights of this campaign was the International Fuel Cycle Evaluation (INFCE), a series of meetings and joint projects that began in October 1977 and continued for over two years. Its participants were technical and political specialists from all over the world, broken up into subgroups to study a wide variety of complex issues related to international nuclear power. INFCE was a framework not for negotiations, but for analysis, and its voluminous output established a solid technical basis for international dialog on nuclear issues. In the period during which INFCE was in session, several myths were punctured, such as the picture of worldwide scarcity of uranium deposits. And at long last, the study of the connections between military and civilian uses of nuclear technology became a professional discipline, with a transnational network of specialists sharing common terminology and a basic understanding of the issues.

The final reports of the INFCE published in 1980 adopted a more sanguine perspective on the plutonium fuel cycle than Carter had hoped for, reflecting a compromise between the American perspective and its fierce opponents in Europe.[22] In the four years of Carter's administration, his people failed to achieve the strong international control and oversight that they saw as essential for a proliferation-resistant nuclear fuel cycle. The needed controls were too intrusive and expensive, and it was simply too late to turn back the clock. Too many governments had made irrevocable commitments to the pursuit of plutonium as a reactor fuel, and for many of them energy security was seen as being on a par with national security.

Nevertheless, Carter's international crusade against plutonium was not without effect. The policies of key nuclear players, such as France, Great

Britain, and Japan, were substantially moderated as a result of the work of INFCE and the persistent diplomacy of the United States. The momentum of the transition to mixed plutonium/uranium fuel in light-water reactors was essentially stopped cold.[23] The Brazilian reprocessing plant was never built. The sophistication of safeguards and technical controls on fuel transfers was much improved. And the world's awareness of civilian nuclear power as a pathway for weapons proliferation was dramatically deepened. It is fair to say that without Carter's efforts, the quest by nations like North Korea, Libya, and Iraq for nuclear weapons would probably by now have succeeded.

These two vignettes of different presidents dealing (or not) with nuclear proliferation shed light on the fifty-year history of the interplay between the civilian and military uses of nuclear energy. We have, on one hand, President Nixon, whose people blithely abandoned the commitment from the Eisenhower era to ensure a reliable world supply of enriched uranium fuel and thereby opened the door to increased nuclear proliferation. And on the other hand, we have President Carter, who was forced by the Indian bomb to look deeper into the implications of that covenant, deeper even than Eisenhower's advisors saw, and turned the country and much of the world away from the plutonium economy.

There are lessons from these contrasting stories that are relevant to the new tritium policy. We can clearly see the operation of hidden agendas in the Nixon administration's manipulation of enrichment services contracts, leading to policies contrary to the best interests of the public. The same kind of bureaucratic game playing on tritium production will be revealed in chapter 5. We also see how plutonium policy prior to Carter's intervention was founded on the false premise that a shortage of uranium would appear in the near future. Today the technocrats in the DOE justify the new tritium policy by claiming that the existing tritium supply will be exhausted by 2006, which chapter 7 will show is a self-serving underestimate by twenty years or more. But perhaps the most important connection is a positive one. Carter's thorough airing of the proliferation issues related to plutonium led to a reversal of an unwise government policy despite vigorous opposition by vested interests. Perhaps the same type of reversal may be possible for the new tritium policy.

3

Nuclear Reactor Safety: Confidence versus Vigilance

To prevent accidents as serious as Three Mile Island, fundamental changes will be necessary in the organization, procedures and practices—and above all—in the attitudes of the Nuclear Regulatory Commission, and, to the extent that the institutions we investigated are typical, of the nuclear industry.
John Kemeny, 1979

The Fallacy of the "Design Basis Accident"

One of the central themes of this book is that the interests of the public are being poorly served by some of the institutions set up within our society to deal with nuclear technology. A recurring issue is nuclear reactor safety. To understand fully the implications of the U.S. government's decision to make tritium in three commercial reactors owned by the TVA, it is important to understand nuclear reactor safety as an institution, that is, as a set of regulations and procedures, a collection of organizations each with its unique roles and traditions, and a community of individuals with their own expectations and interests. This chapter explores that institution, how it works, and how it came to be what it is.

To a remarkable degree the character of nuclear reactor safety in the United States was shaped in the hectic 1960s, when nuclear power burst upon the commercial electricity scene. With the avalanche of orders for nuclear power plants came a corresponding surge in applications for licenses to build the plants. The federal regulators were poorly prepared for the onslaught, but they knew they could not go about reviewing each application on a case-by-case basis as they had for the earlier demonstration reactors. Given the huge amount of capital involved, industry felt compelled to pressure the government to streamline the review process, shorten the review period, approve plants early, and especially, avoid second thoughts after construction had begun. Above all, the industry needed clear guidance on what the government regulators would approve and what they would not.

Fortunately, all of the players in the nuclear game at the start of the 1960s believed ardently in the promise of nuclear energy. They looked back with admiration on what the previous generation of engineers and scientists had accomplished in the Manhattan Project and felt they were carrying on the same tradition. They were bright, committed, and confident.

A major challenge for regulators in the early 1960s was to craft a set of safety requirements that would protect the public without taking the job of designing nuclear reactors away from the private sector. Given the unique nature of nuclear reactors and the accidents they might undergo, this undertaking would require a remarkable degree of technical insight, not to say clairvoyance, since the rules had to be developed before any large commercial plants were constructed.

A crude analogy might help convey this difficulty. Imagine that right after the automobile was invented the government decided to back a rapid expansion of the auto industry, promising financial and technical support as needed. Suppose then that government engineers were told to write a rule book for the various safety features in these cars (brakes, tires, lights, and so on). To do so, they would have to imagine all the emergencies that might occur: stuck accelerator pedals, brakes that fail, gasoline leaks, whatever. Then they would have to write the rule book for the auto designers to follow, being careful not to actually design the vehicles themselves. Now suppose that industry and the government then proceeded to build fifty million or so of these cars along with a few hundred thousand miles of highway. The rhetorical question is this: how appropriate do you suppose the safety standards would be?

The analogy to the nuclear industry is crude indeed, if only for the fact that nuclear power plants were being built to last forty years, not the ten or so of the typical automobile. But this much of the analogy holds true: the underlying philosophy of the safety rule book guiding the design of all U.S. commercial power reactors was established before any significant experience with such reactors was obtained.[1] When experience later was acquired, sometimes painfully, the regulations for operating the reactors could be modified somewhat to account for unexpected vulnerabilities, and some minor changes in the plants could be made, but many of the vulnerabilities lay deep in the design of the plants and could not easily be remedied. This is particularly true of the ice condenser plants that are to be used to produce tritium for U.S. nuclear weapons. To show how this strange situation came about, a short history of reactor safety is needed, with a particular focus on that last line of defense, the final barrier protecting the public from radioactive fission products: the containment building.

Reactor Safety Basics

When viewed as machines for producing electricity, nuclear power plants are fairly simple, simpler than an internal combustion engine, for example. Figure 2 shows the basic pieces of a typical commercial reactor. The heart of the system is the water-filled steel pressure vessel. Inside it is the reactor core, consisting of hundreds of fuel rods suspended vertically in the cooling water. When a U-235 atom in the fuel is struck by a neutron, it splits apart, or fissions, into a number of smaller pieces. These pieces include smaller atoms, called "fission products," and a few neutrons, which may then strike other uranium atoms elsewhere in the fuel, keeping the whole process going.

The overall rate of fissioning throughout the core is controlled by the positions of a set of control rods interspersed among the fuel rods. The

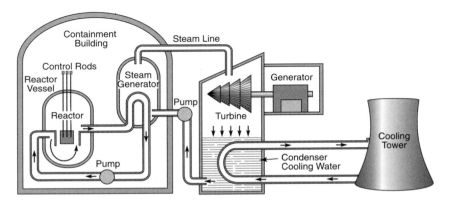

Figure 2
Schematic diagram of pressurized-water reactor.

control rods are made of materials that absorb neutrons. Thus, the overall rate at which uranium atoms in the core are bombarded by neutrons can be increased by moving the control rods out of the core or decreased by pushing them deeper into the core. Correspondingly, the rate of fissioning, and therefore the heat produced, increases or decreases. To shut the reactor off, the control rods are pushed all the way in.

The rest of the system is just high-quality plumbing. The nuclear core generates a prodigious amount of heat, which is carried away by pressurized water flowing continuously through the core, out into large pipes, and then into gigantic heat exchangers called steam generators. The resulting steam drives turbines to produce electricity. Fossil-fueled plants work essentially the same way, except that instead of a reactor core there is a (much larger) combustion chamber that burns coal, oil, or natural gas.

Nuclear engineers saw many advantages to nuclear electricity in comparison to its fossil fuel competitors. But to realize these benefits, they had to address the unique safety challenges of this new technology. These challenges arise from the fact that the fission products left after a uranium atom splits apart are highly radioactive—much more radioactive than the uranium itself. From the moment a fuel rod begins producing power, it becomes laden with fission products that can never be allowed to come into contact with human beings. The complexity of nuclear reactors emerges not from the requirement to produce electricity, but from the requirement to prevent the escape of fission products.

What makes this challenge even more daunting is that the fission products continually generate heat within the fuel rod. This heat is called "decay heat" and is only a small fraction of what the reactor produces while operating at full power. The problem is that the decay heat doesn't shut off when the reactor is shut off.

It is decay heat that makes the engineering of nuclear power plants as difficult as it is. The system must be designed to ensure that high-pressure water continues to flow through the core even after shutdown. Many modern automobiles run electric-powered fans to cool the engine after the ignition is shut off, but only for a minute or two. In contrast, a nuclear core's decay heat must be cooled for weeks and months after a shutdown. Safety systems must ensure that this flow continues under any plausible set of circumstances, including massive earthquakes, electric grid failures, operator errors, tornadoes—essentially anything that is reasonably possible over the life of a power plant. If water were to stop flowing in the core, it would only be only a matter of hours before the core and all the steel structures holding it in place melted into a red-hot liquid that would proceed to melt through the foot-thick-steel pressure vessel in which it is enclosed.

The early U.S. experimental and demonstration reactors relied chiefly on two features for protecting the public from release of radiation:

1. highly reliable safety systems that ensured the flow of cooling water for all conceivable conditions
2. remote siting—the public was entirely excluded from a zone in the vicinity of the plants, and the population density was required to be very low over a much larger area around them.

As experience was gained with these early reactors, the nuclear industry added more levels of redundancy to the safety systems, recognizing that as the scale of the reactors was increased to the size needed for commercial power production, the consequences of potential accidents also increased. The first conceptual designs for commercial power reactors captured all the experience gained from the smaller demonstration reactors and went farther, incorporating unprecedented levels of reliability into the design and fabrication of the reactor and its safety systems. Consequently, the leaders of the nuclear industry had high confidence that any reactor accident that could release radioactivity outside the plant would be so unlikely as to be not worth worrying about. They felt it was time to be relieved of the remote-siting requirement, since the cost of transmitting electric power from remote sites to population centers hundreds of miles away would put an undue burden on the economics of the new energy source.[2]

Nevertheless, when utilities pressed the government for permission to build plants close to populated areas, the AEC insisted on an additional level of protection: they called for a *containment*.[3] This is a large, hermetically sealed, freestanding building housing the reactor. The idea was that in the extremely improbable event that the internal safety systems of the reactor failed, the containment would capture the steam, gases, and fission products that escaped and thus prevent their release into the environment. The philosophy of adding redundant layers of safety systems, each backing up the next, came to be known as "defense in depth," and requiring a large containment building for commercial nuclear power plants was its ultimate expression.

Some experience in the design of containment buildings had already been gained in the government's early experimental reactor program. Since the reactors in this program were small, building a leak-tight spherical shell around them required no more than a straightforward implementation of existing industrial practice at the time. But scaling those buildings up by the factor of fifty or more required for commercial-scale reactors[4] would call for great innovation or great expense and probably both.

The compromise of requiring a robust containment in exchange for allowing plants to be located near population centers was one of the defining events in the history of U.S. commercial nuclear reactor regulation, but there was no quantitative analysis behind the compromise. As can be seen in the authoritative history of nuclear regulation by George Masuzin and Samuel Walker, the commissioners at the AEC felt that this was a reasonable trade-off, but no one made any attempt to prove that a containment was either necessary or adequate.[5] Regardless, robust containments became a regulatory requirement for all nuclear power stations.

It was characteristic of the early development of reactor safety policy that the federal regulators (i.e., the AEC and the ACRS) were open to intuitive trade-offs between the benefits of additional engineered safety features (like the containment) and closer proximity to population centers. No systematic process for making such trade-offs existed.[6] In many cases, the utilities learned what would pass muster by submitting license applications and waiting for acceptance or rejection by the federal regulators.

Such a casual approach to specifying safety requirements was clearly incompatible with the high capital cost of the new plants and with the surge in plant orders that occurred in the early 1960s. The industry insisted on clear guidance from the government but at the same time cautioned the regulators to leave the actual job of designing to their engineers.

Fortunately, the leaders of the AEC were as optimistic about nuclear energy as their private-sector counterparts and pursued a solution to the safety requirements dilemma with enthusiasm. The Holy Grail in the early days of nuclear energy regulation was something called the "maximum credible accident." The top regulator in the AEC set this as his principal focus,[7] and by about 1962 a consensus developed that the government could achieve the twin goals of ensuring safety and leaving the design to industry by specifying one or more of these "maximum credible accidents" in its safety requirements. It would then be up to the designers to come up with various redundant safety features that would guarantee that such an accident, should it occur, would be kept under control.

The key accident chosen to set standards for safety systems was a "pipe break" accident. In the scenario for such an accident, the designer was to assume that one of the large pipes connected to the reactor broke in two while the reactor was operating, causing the entire inventory of water in the system to be ejected as a steam-water mix in a matter of seconds. It was understood that worse accidents, like a runaway nuclear reaction, were entirely possible, so the term "maximum credible accident," was clearly a misnomer. Eventually the terminology was changed to "design basis accident," and the regulators outlined several of these stylized events, each challenging a different aspect of the power plant. And the government asserted that any plant that could withstand the design basis accidents was adequately safe.

But to ensure a predictable regulatory environment (i.e., no surprises from the regulators after construction began), a set of rules was also needed for performing the calculations proving that the safety systems coped adequately with the design basis accidents. Therefore the AEC formulated, over a period of several years, a highly detailed and prescriptive process that each reactor owner would follow to obtain a license to build and operate a commercial nuclear reactor. The basic structure and philosophy of these licensing requirements were established in the late 1960s and have changed little since.[8] Many of the safety concerns that exist today about the fleet of U.S. reactors stem from serious shortcomings in the licensing process, shortcomings that have been present from the beginning.

The critical flaw in this regulatory approach is that the design basis accidents are limited to conditions in which there is always enough water in the reactor core to submerge the fuel completely. In other words, the combination of equipment failures that would be required for any portion of the fuel rods to lose contact with cooling water was considered to be so unlikely that it need not be considered. This central assumption was justified on the basis of engineering judgment, and it simplified the reactor design process significantly.[9] Unfortunately, the assumption is not valid, as the 1979 TMI accident showed.

Nuclear reactor accidents in which fuel is uncovered long enough to start melting are called "core melt accidents" or "severe accidents." It is certainly true that they are extremely unlikely and that safety systems should, for the most part, focus on the types of accidents considered in the license applications, that is, the design basis accidents. But by allowing severe accidents to be disregarded entirely, the government invited design choices that were unwise.

In the early 1960s containment building design took two paths. The first was a straight scale-up of the early containment shells. Containments developed using this design principle came to be called "large dry" containments and were remarkable achievements of civil engineering. Typically the size of a large high school gymnasium, they could withstand pressures of sixty pounds per square inch (about that of a bicycle tire) or more without leaking.

The second path for containment design sought reduced cost and construction time by striving for a smaller containment building. This could be achieved by rapidly cooling the steam from a pipe break before it could expand into the containment volume. If the large dry containments are considered a "brute force" method of containing an accident, these alternative methods might be deemed "ingenious" designs, because they require the plant to be divided into three zones: the reactor, an intermediate zone where the hot steam would be captured and quenched, and the outer zone that was the actual containment building.

Westinghouse's ice condenser containment was one of these ingenious designs. It was cheaper than the large dry concepts, and Westinghouse demonstrated that it accommodated design basis accidents beautifully. But in later years the ice condenser containment has been shown to be ineffective for many severe accidents. To understand this dichotomy, it is necessary to look more closely at the design basis accidents.

Ingenious Containments

The most important design basis accident for the containment has a colorful name: double-ended guillotine break. The license applicant is to assume that a section of the reactor piping is sliced open (as by a guillotine) at two nearby locations and the intervening pipe simply disappears. The pressurized water in the reactor would then surge out in a steam-water jet at the maximum possible flow rate. It is a stylized and unrealistic scenario, but that is intentional. The idea is that in this idealized accident, steam would flow out more rapidly and the containment would be more highly pressurized than in any realistic pipe break. Moreover, the scenario has the added benefit of requiring calculations that are easy to do: experts don't need to waste a lot of time arguing about how a real pipe might break, as long as they agree that this imaginary case is worse than anything that could happen to a real pipe.

A nuclear reactor contains a great deal of water that is very hot and highly pressurized. If a double-ended guillotine break were to occur in one of the large pipes connected directly to the reactor vessel, most of that water would escape (flashing to steam, mostly) into the containment building in a matter of seconds. Any ordinary building, even if it were very well sealed, would pop doors and windows (and some walls, no doubt) immediately, releasing steam and radioactivity to the outside atmosphere. But containment buildings are extremely strong and well sealed. The nuclear industry pushed the state of the art for steel welds, reinforced concrete, and seals around penetrations (like pipes) to build containments that could withstand such extraordinary pressure.

Large dry containment designs solve the engineering problems of the design basis accident with brute force: the typical containment building is made very large, very strong, and more or less in the shape of a partial sphere (the shape that maximizes ability to contain pressure). Additional safety is provided by large arrays of sprinklers that can flood the atmosphere in the building during an accident, thus reducing the pressure and washing out the dangerous fission products before they can leak out of the building. In some cases, huge industrial chillers supplement the containment sprays. Today, most commercial plants use large dry containments. They are typically designed by the architecture/engineering firm contracted to the utility, rather than by the reactor vendor.

Because such large structures are expensive and time-consuming to build, two of the big reactor vendors, GE and Westinghouse, explored alternative concepts that would allow a smaller, less expensive, and more standardized containment building to be constructed that would nonetheless meet the AEC's requirements. Standardization was attractive from a cost standpoint. Large dry containments are typically one-of-a-kind structures, partly because they are so large they have to be engineered to fit the site, and partly because of the practice of placing a separate contract with an architecture/engineering firm to design and construct the building. These firms were masters in the art of advanced civil engineering, and they continually advanced new concepts in concrete and steel construction. All this meant that each containment building was a unique solution to the problem of coping with the design basis accidents.

GE and Westinghouse understood the high cost of one-of-a-kind facilities, and each saw a competitive advantage if they could amortize the cost of a new containment design over many nearly identical plants and at the same time save money by making the buildings smaller and less robust. A smaller, weaker building would need less concrete, less steel, less labor, and less time to build. From a corporate perspective, there was surely another attraction to the standardized containment concept: any utility that signed up for one would give a larger piece of the power plant construction budget to the reactor vendor and less to the architect/engineer.

Each of the two companies saw that the key to getting a smaller containment approved was to satisfy the design basis accident requirement by quenching the steam rapidly as it escaped from the reactor. The GE design forced all the hot steam to bubble through a large pool of cold water before it could get into the containment building. Actually, "bubble" doesn't convey the violence of the process, but GE's extensive testing showed that the "pressure suppression pool" concept worked: the pool captured so much of the steam that there was a much smaller pressure rise in the containment building than in traditional large dry containments, even though its volume was only a fraction of that of such containments.

Westinghouse took the quenching concept a step further. With its ice condenser containment design, steam from any pipe break had to pass through a tall chamber filled with ice flakes suspended in wire baskets. As with the pressure suppression pool, the steam from the pipe break would condense rapidly on the surface of the ice, and only a small fraction would pass all the way through the ice chest and into the main containment volume. Again, this ingenious arrangement allowed the containment to be smaller and weaker yet still satisfy the licensing requirements for the design basis accident.

Many utilities were impressed with the new containment concepts. Over the following decades GE sold dozens of the suppression pool plants, using experience gained with the early versions (called "Mark I") to guide the design of two subsequent generations (designated "Mark II" and "Mark III"). The Westinghouse design did not evolve as much, and eventually only nine ice condensers were completed in the United States. Three of them are operated by the TVA—two at the Sequoyah plant and one at Watts Bar, as noted in chapter 1. These are the reactors that the Department of Energy wants converted to the production of tritium.

Unfortunately, ice condenser containments have serious design flaws. As with GE's suppression pool containments, they deal well with design basis accidents but are much less effective than large dry containments in coping with severe accidents. According to the licensing rules set up in the 1960s, they did not have to be. It took an actual nuclear accident in the 1970s to reveal the fallacy inherent in those rules: the fallacy of the design basis accident.

The Incredible Occurs

On March 28, 1979, a routine problem at unit 2 of the TMI nuclear station escalated into the most serious commercial reactor accident in U.S. history. The accident began when a faulty electronic signal caused two feedwater pumps (which create the flow in the circuit shown in the center of figure 2) to shut down. Since it is essential for water to flow in this circuit, there is an emergency feedwater pump just for such a situation. Two valves on the piping from this pump had been inadvertantly left closed, however, after some maintenance work—a grievous error. The result: no cooling water flowed in the steam generator, so there was no way to remove heat from the primary system (left side of figure 2). This caused pressure and temperature in the reactor to rise, so another safety device went into action: a relief valve opened and steam from the pressure vessel was vented into containment. That worked. Pressure and temperature began to drop.

By this time the control rods had been automatically inserted to shut the reactor down, and the heat produced by the core immediately dropped to the decay heat level of around 10 percent of the operating power. Two separate anomalous events had occurred, the faulty signal to the feedwater pumps and the blocked flow path for the emergency feedwater pump, but there are so many redundant safety features, like the relief valve, that the plant was not really in very much trouble.

The real trouble began when the pressure relief valve failed to close after the pressure returned to normal. This possibility had been considered in the design of the safety systems, but what happened next had not. The instrumentation on the control panel incorrectly indicated that the relief valve was closed and also gave a false reading of water level in the vessel. Operators were trained to follow procedures, not to doubt their instruments. What they didn't know was that the relief valve was venting a good portion of the water in the reactor vessel into the containment. It did so for over two hours, but the control room was a chaos of flashing indicators and audible alarms, and the operators continued to misdiagnose the crisis. The water level dropped almost to the bottom of the vessel. The incredible had happened: the core was dry.

Hydrogen is one of the hazards that is characteristic of severe accidents but absent in design basis accidents. When the core is uncovered, steam in contact with overheated fuel rods reacts chemically to produce hydrogen gas. In the TMI accident, more and more hydrogen was generated as the water level dropped. This hydrogen leaked out the same stuck-open relief valve that was draining the core of water. The hydrogen concentration in the containment increased until it exceeded the flammability level, and then it ignited. A muffled bang was heard in the control room, but few if any of the people there understood what they were hearing.[10] Such was the limited understanding of severe accidents at the time.

The pressure spike caused by the hydrogen burn showed up clearly in the data records analyzed by specialists after the accident. It was a pulse of pressure equal to about half the design rating of the containment building. Any normal industrial building would have been blown wide open, but the TMI containment building was a large dry design that was one of the sturdiest in the country. Consequently, there was relatively little radioactivity released to the outside environment.

A greater potential challenge to the containment was the melting fuel itself. Temperatures in the core reached 5,000° F and higher,[11] well above the melting point of steel and of the reactor fuel. About half the core melted and flowed downward, much like lava flowing down the side of a volcano. A substantial amount (about twenty tons) reached the bottom, where it formed a hot, molten puddle.[12] There was a real possibility that it could melt its way through the vessel and into the containment, with unpredictable consequences.

Eventually, someone in the crowded control room realized the relief valve was stuck open and ordered another valve closed. This shut off the leak. Over the next hours and days plant engineers carried out steps that stopped the melting of fuel and brought the reactor under control. But before TMI was stabilized, hundreds of thousands of people had been evacuated or had voluntarily fled their homes, some for several weeks.

In the following weeks and months many committees and panels studied the TMI accident exhaustively and from many angles. Most concluded that it was caused by operator error: the reactor operators, though not nuclear engineers, should have correctly diagnosed the situation despite contradictory readings from their indicators. If they had, core damage would not have occurred and the event would never even have made the news.

But in his provocative 1984 book *Normal Accidents*, Charles Perrow disagreed. He pointed instead at the very nature of nuclear power plants, complex, tightly coupled systems that are prone to failure modes quite different from mishaps in more forgiving systems like factories. He argued that in such systems minor faults can interact with each other in unpredictable ways, and unplanned couplings among different parts of the system can rapidly escalate the severity of abnormal conditions. He observed that thirteen seconds into the TMI accident, several independent faults had conspired to make the plant's status a complete mystery to the operators. He coined the term "normal accident" for such events, since he believed that they emerged "normally" from the complexity and tight coupling of the system. Redundancy, in his view, might fend off some accidents, but by making system failures more difficult to diagnose and control, redundancy can also increase the likelihood of normal accidents.[13]

Perrow's scholarly assessment may not have found many adherents among the engineering types at the NRC and in the nuclear industry, but everyone knew that things would never be the same after TMI. The accident was a watershed in the history of U.S. nuclear power. The NRC had been formed only four years earlier to take over the job of regulating commercial nuclear power from the AEC. Up until the TMI accident, the NRC was staffed mostly by former AEC personnel and was pretty much going through the same motions as its predecessor. The accident, however, galvanized the new agency. The event brutally revealed that key assumptions underlying the industry's approach to safety and the government's approach to regulation were deeply flawed. Over the next few years both industry and government played an intense game of catch up as they tried to adjust to the new reality.

Since then, scientific understanding of the TMI accident and other potential severe accidents has advanced substantially as a result of the work done by the NRC and industry. One of the most important insights is that, although all containment designs are robust to the steam loads of the design basis accident, some are much less effective than others in coping with the added challenges of hydrogen and molten fuel that characterize severe accidents.

In a way, there was a bright side to the message that the TMI accident brought. Subsequent "what if" studies showed that, although the reactor vessel came perilously close to failing (which would have caused molten fuel to be ejected at high pressure into the containment), the TMI containment was a strong remaining layer of defense. The studies showed that even if wiser heads had not terminated the accident when they did, the resultant challenge to the containment when the vessel failed would almost certainly have been insufficient to cause the containment to fail (i.e., to leak large amounts of radioactivity into the atmosphere). The intuitive compromise insisted on by the regulators, requiring robust containment for plants near population centers, was vindicated, as was the brute force approach of the large dry containment.

In contrast, the ingenious containment designs that achieved cost savings by including a quenching system (either water or ice) do not have the same resistance to severe accidents. The rest of this chapter will show

how scientific studies in the post-TMI era revealed that pressure suppression and ice condenser containments provide far less defense in depth than their robust counterparts. For these plants, one of the founding principles of commercial reactor safety—that nuclear plants sited near population centers must have a strong and effective containment—was compromised.

Seven years after the TMI accident, something much worse happened in the Ukraine: the violent explosion of a reactor at the Chernobyl nuclear site. Because it was partly driven by a nuclear chain reaction, the accident was unbelievably violent, spewing dangerous radioactivity into the atmosphere, where it spread all over the world. The released radioactivity was several hundred times the combined quantity from the Hiroshima and Nagasaki bombs.[14]

Fortuitously, the extremely energetic nature of the accident actually diminished its impact on human health. Thirty people exposed to intense radiation at the reactor site died within weeks of the accident, but because so much of the radioactivity was lofted to high altitudes, the surrounding communities experienced remarkably low ground level doses. Nevertheless, radioactive contamination occurred over a vast area, and eventually 336,000 people had to be evacuated from Belarus, the Russian Federation, and the Ukraine.[15]

Subsequent analysis showed that this horrible event was a result of irresponsible behavior by operators, who had purposely defeated many safety features to perform a dangerous experiment with the reactor. A deeply flawed reactor design was another factor, prompting the U.S. nuclear establishment to emphasize loudly and often that its commercial reactors could never undergo such a violent accident.

True as that might be, subsequent study of the underlying causes of the Chernobyl accident yielded lessons that were fully applicable in the United States. Chernobyl brought about a new appreciation for the institutional context of reactor safety. The concept of a "safety culture" emerged as an intangible but critical factor in all aspects of safe nuclear power: design, fabrication, maintenance, and operation. From this perspective, it is pointless to focus on errors or misconduct by reactor operators without also looking at their incentive environment. As a major study of Chernobyl for the IAEA concluded, "[t]he accident can be said to have flowed from deficient safety culture, not only at the Chernobyl plant, but throughout the Soviet design, operating, and regulatory organizations that existed at the time." More important, at least in regard to the safety of the TVA reactors that are to be used for tritium production, is that study's emphasis on management's role in shaping the motivational environment: "Safety culture . . . requires total dedication, which at nuclear power plants is primarily generated by the attitudes of managers of organizations involved in their development and operation."[16]

In the U.S. nuclear establishment, such abstract concepts were at first no better received than Perrow's systems theories. The initial emphasis for the NRC and the nuclear industry after the TMI and Chernobyl accidents was to find practical ways to accommodate, without having to shut down any power plants, the new reality that severe accidents could really happen and were really dangerous.

The New Science of Severe Accidents

In hindsight, the fundamental flaw in the government's approach to reactor safety was the artificial distinction it made between "credible" and "incredible" accidents, particularly since it used a rather soft connotation of the word "credible." The formulators of the original licensing approach knew core melt accidents were possible: an accident at one of the experimental reactors had shown that.[17] But they felt that reactors could be made adequately safe by protecting against all the accident scenarios that were likely enough to be worth thinking about. Intuitively, they judged that core melt accidents didn't fall into that category. They looked at safety from a black-and-white perspective: some accidents one worries about, some are so unlikely that one doesn't. What they learned from TMI and its aftermath was that the measure of importance of a particular type of accident is not just its probability but the *product* of its probability times its consequences. On that basis, core melt accidents, unlikely as they are, dominate nuclear power's threat to public health.

A simple example may help. If a hang glider manufacturer hired a safety engineer to evaluate a new design for its safety characteristics, a fairly straightforward approach would suffice. The engineer would study the kinds of accidents that had happened with other hang gliders, analyze what went wrong in most cases, and modify the design so those things wouldn't go wrong with the new design. What is straightforward about this task is that the event to be avoided is a crash—any crash. In a sense, all crashes are equal, because they result in the same consequence: the injury or death of one person.

In contrast, a nuclear power plant accident has the potential to cause fatalities ranging in number from none or a few to tens of thousands. This wide range of outcomes changes how designers must think about safety. For example, if a particular type of event that occurs only once in 10,000 years causes 10,000 fatalities, its contribution to public risk is one fatality per year. This would be far more important than a different type of event that occurs every ten years, but on average causes a fatality only 1 percent of the time (its contribution to public risk is 0.1×0.01, or 0.001 fatalities per year).

Reactor safety analysts now know that nuclear power plants are a special type of complex system whose risk to the public is dominated by "low-probability, high-consequence events." For such systems, safety engineers are not focusing on the right issues if they arbitrarily ignore all low-probability events. Because of the huge range of accident consequences, it is necessary instead to think about the *risk profile* over a wide range of event probabilities.

Early in the history of the nuclear industry there were hints of this reality. A study done for the AEC in 1957 estimated that a severe accident could cause 3,400 deaths and cost $7 billion in property damages.[18] Eight years later the study was revised to account for the larger plant sizes being considered at that time. The new numbers were so shocking that the AEC suppressed publication of the report. The chairman at the time later said, "we didn't want to publish it because we thought it would be misunderstood by the public."[19] The truth appears to be that the AEC misunderstood it.

Nuclear reactors have some of the most reliable and redundant safety systems of any man-made facilities. But as TMI showed, systems can fail, people can err, and sometimes more than one thing can go wrong at a time. Despite clever design, careful manufacture, and dutiful maintenance, multiple failures of safety systems can and will occur.

Severe reactor accidents—those involving melting of the core—are expected to be quite rare, occurring in the United States less than once in a generation, perhaps. But if the health consequences are large enough, they are a more important threat to the public than more likely but more benign accidents. Ignoring core melt accidents in designing reactors was therefore a huge mistake.

Before TMI, there was recognition by some that core melt accidents dominate public risk. For example, in 1974, the AEC commissioned Norman Rasmussen of the Massachusetts Institute of Technology to lead a major study[20] that systematically evaluated public health impacts of nuclear reactors, focusing necessarily on the improbable but highly consequential "beyond–design basis" accidents. It was a seminal study that after TMI became the starting point for greatly expanded efforts. But the AEC's goal for the Rasmussen study was primarily to deal with growing public opposition to nuclear energy by comparing its risks quantitatively with other risks that society routinely accepts.[21] It was never intended to modify the government's approach to reactor design or regulation.

After TMI, everything changed. Now the question was, how could these risk-dominant events be factored into regulation? The new challenge to the NRC was to sort out what types of potential accidents were "risk-significant," having the property that their probability times their consequences was large, and to decide what should be done about them.

In the early 1980s the NRC embraced this new perspective with grim diligence. Great sums for new research were requested from Congress and granted. To establish a higher degree of credibility for the new research, the NRC engaged the services of the DOE's great nuclear weapons laboratories, such as Sandia and Oak Ridge. In parallel, the nuclear industry formed the Industry Degraded Core Rulemaking (IDCOR) consortium to supplement the government program and to ensure that if "rulemaking" (that is to say, new regulatory approaches) were to take place, the industry's interests would be well defended. Eventually severe-accident research became an international enterprise, as Japan and Europe established their own programs (primarily after the great scare they got from the horrendous Chernobyl accident).

The NRC's severe-accident research program had to find new ways of thinking about reactor safety and to develop entirely new fields of science and engineering. The probabilisitic methods pioneered in the Rasmussen study were expanded and computerized, leading to a new field of statistics called "probabilistic risk assessment." Specialists in the new field developed sophisticated computer programs that categorized various types of abnormal events and followed the causal connections from one event to another, using probabilistic treatments when it was not known which of several outcomes might occur. The new science of severe accidents spawned a new mathematics of probabilistic calculation that today is being applied to all sorts of other enterprises besides nuclear power, such as evaluating the safety of nuclear weapons.

In addition to the new probabilistic techniques, effective safety assessment required information about what can happen, physically, when the core begins to melt and relocate and when core debris breaks through the reactor vessel boundary and enters the containment. Since it is not possible to carry out experiments on severe accidents with real reactors, a variety of test facilities were needed that could simulate the extreme conditions of a severe accident. The NRC (and its counterparts all around the world) made large investments in such facilities, and the experiments performed in them yielded many new insights about what might occur in severe accidents.

A third element of the NRC's new research program was the development of computational simulation software. When low-probability events are considered, the possible combinations of conditions and configurations are overwhelming. It would be impossible to conduct experiments for all possibilities. For that reason, the NRC sponsored the development of sophisticated computer programs that could calculate how conditions in a hypothetical accident would evolve. These "codes" used theoretical models for the physical processes involved but were grounded in reality by checking how well they could predict the results of experiments in the severe accident test facilities. As time went on, hundreds of person-years were invested in these codes, and in a way they took on a life of their own, embodying hundreds of thousands of lines of computer code and becoming more complex than any one individual could comprehend. They had names like MELCOR, for modeling core melt progression, and CONTAIN, for studying events in the containment.

Within a few years, the NRC's research program had yielded abundant insights about the nature of severe accidents and nuclear power plant risk. If this knowledge had been obtained before all the U.S. plants had been designed and built, the plants could have been designed to be intrinsically resistant to core melt accidents. Instead, the agency in 1983 or so was left with few winning strategies. Certainly, shutting down all nuclear power plants would have been foolish: all risk studies showed (and still show) that nuclear energy is on a par with other energy sources as far as risk to public health is concerned. The agency's challenge was instead to steer an objective course, working with the industry to minimize wasted regulatory effort, while at the same time maintaining a high degree of vigilance and integrity in dealing with the issues that truly affect public health and safety.

It became apparent in the mid-1980s that studying severe accidents was something that could be funded, delegated, and executed readily enough, but doing something concrete with the results of such studies posed many dilemmas for a federal regulatory agency. Prioritizing actions was particularly challenging. Early regulatory responses to TMI were often ad hoc and inconsistent and met with hostility from the industry. It seemed that the only rational basis for decision making would be systematic, quantitative assessments of public risk based on the knowledge and tools developed in the research program.

The new probabilistic tools measured public risk in quantities such as the average number of fatalities per year of reactor operation. Balancing risk reduction against the cost of changes was an appealing decision strategy, but adequate studies of the risk posed by reactors were not available. The NRC's research organization therefore embarked on the extraordinary NUREG-1150 project, so named from the document number of its major report, *Severe Accident Risks: An Assessment for Five U.S. Nuclear Power Plants.*[22] This massive, coordinated assessment of quantitative risk and its uncertainty took many years and hundreds of specialists to complete, but it established a firm foundation for factoring severe-accident issues into regulatory practice.

The NUREG-1150 study analyzed five different plants, each representing a different containment concept and together spanning the entire fleet of U.S. nuclear power plants. The five types and the plants chosen to represent them were as follows:

· large dry containment (the Zion plant)
· large dry subatmospheric containment (the Surry plant, whose containment is held at negative pressure compared to the outside environment)

- Mark I suppression pool containment (the Peach Bottom plant)
- Mark III suppression pool containment (the Grand Gulf plant)
- ice condenser containment (the Sequoyah plant)

Although the study took far longer and cost far more than originally planned, the picture that emerged from the project had, by 1987 or so, established the battle lines for the emerging conflict with the nuclear industry over severe accidents.

Resistance Builds

The history of commercial nuclear power is notable for the contrast between the rosy picture motivating the early headlong plunge into a nuclear future and the bitter experience of the people who signed up for it. One after another, the assumptions that lay behind that rosy picture were found to be invalid or were made invalid by government action. The federal government did not, for example, find a solution to the spent-fuel disposal problem, and its decision to abandon the plutonium fuel cycle (see chapter 2) accelerated the nuclear waste crisis. Extraordinary levels of inflation in the 1970s and 1980s were punishing to the capital-intensive economics of nuclear power. In many cases local opposition to power plants near population centers forced more time, attention, and money to be spent on public safety than had been envisioned. Then, of course, TMI and Chernobyl occurred, with devastating impacts on public acceptance. In contrast to the land rush atmosphere that began around 1965 (199 plants ordered in ten years), new plant orders dried up completely by 1977, and construction of many previously ordered plants was canceled.

In the years following TMI, the industry gamely prepared for changes in regulations and even in the plants themselves, since the accident had revealed deep flaws in the safety philosophy of commercial nuclear power. But the early regulatory actions by the NRC were often poorly motivated and implemented with a heavy hand. The industry felt unnecessarily burdened with new regulations that appeared to add nothing to safety or reliability. By the time the NRC established, in the form of the NUREG-1150 reports, a solid scientific basis on which to ask for safety improvements, the atmosphere between industry and the regulators had become adversarial and bitter.

This is not to say that common ground was not found for some changes. Through their own research and that of the government, many utilities saw ways to modify their plants to reduce the likelihood of a severe accident in the first place. These insights came from the so-called front end of the probabilistic risk analyses: the analysis of how various failures of control systems and safety features interact to create a core melting situation. Even if no serious harm were done to the public (as was the case with TMI), a core melt accident would almost certainly end the life of the reactor as a producer of electricity. Hence utilities had a double incentive—public safety and capital preservation—to improve the front-end safety picture of their nuclear power plants. Consequently, a broad range of plant changes were made, often at the initiative of the plant owners, to reduce the likelihood of a severe accident.

When it came to the "back end," that is, those events that might occur after core melting, the industry's motivation to make changes was not as strong. The costs reactor owners would incur to modify the containment buildings to better protect the public would do nothing to restore the lost revenue stream from the ruined plant. Recognizing this reality, the government chose to organize its NUREG-1150 study around the five major containment types, assessing in detail both the front end and the back end of a representative plant for each type. In 1987 the stage was set for a series of bitter conflicts over containment improvements between the NRC and the industry it regulated.

Of the five containment types studied in NUREG-1150, two were notable for their poor performance in severe accidents. Those two were the "ingenious containments" first developed as integrated features of the power plant to save costs and shorten construction time: the Mark I pressure suppression containment and the ice condenser.

To translate research results into positive action, the NRC initiated the Containment Performance Improvement (CPI) program in the late 1980s. The idea of the program was to review from a generic (i.e., not plant-specific) standpoint what changes in each of the five containment types might be justified in the interest of public safety. Rather than taking on all five types at once, the program was to address one at a time, from the most problematic to the least.

The performance numbers for the Mark I plants and the ice condenser plants were fairly similar,[23] but the CPI program decided to take on the

Mark I plants first. There was a good reason for giving these plants priority: twenty-four reactors in the United States used General Electric's Mark I design, whereas only eight used Westinghouse's ice condenser concept.[24]

The Mark I severe-accident problems arose from a variety of event scenarios, mostly due to the small size of the containment. One of the most troublesome scenarios involved the molten core, which analysts had come to call "corium," penetrating the bottom of the reactor vessel and pouring onto the containment floor. The corium would be so hot in such an event that it would flow essentially like water, and if enough flowed out of the vessel, it would form a large, shallow pool that would come into direct contact with the steel liner of the containment building. No steel can stand up to such temperatures, and numerous calculations indicated that the core material would soon melt through, creating a pathway from the highly radioactive containment atmosphere to the external environment.

Such hypothetical scenarios and the theoretical calculations surrounding them were the grounds for fierce arguments between the safety analysts of the NRC and those of the nuclear power industry. Years of bitter controversy passed, but in 1989 the NRC issued guidelines that recommended specific (and expensive) changes to the Mark I containment buildings. Legally, the NRC couldn't mandate the changes, but the language they used carried a sufficiently threatening tone[25] that most of the Mark I owners made at least some of the specified modifications.[26] But the battle had repercussions that went far beyond the technical arena.

For years, Congress had heard the nuclear industry's complaints that it was being regulated to death. The dire economic state of nuclear power certainly supported the claim of imminent demise, and the charge of overregulation resonated with the political atmosphere in Washington during the administration of President Ronald Reagan. The NRC's response to pressure from the industry, Congress, and the administration to address these complaints was to move out managers who seemed too enthusiastic about dictating industry's actions and move in people who agreed it was time to end the obsession with the TMI accident, at that point some ten years in the past.

In 1988, NRC management published new guidance for its research program, entitled *Integration Plan for Severe Accident Closure*

(SECY-88-174).[27] This plan introduced the novel concept that the goal of research on severe accidents should be to show that they were not a problem and that further research was unneeded. This "closure" philosophy conflicted sharply with the principles of scientific objectivity, but it nonetheless became the organizing principle for the NRC's approach to severe accidents from that point onward.

The CPI program collided head on with this new management philosophy. The CPI program's recommended Mark I improvements were duly endorsed by the new management, though in a form somewhat diluted from earlier conceptions. But the rest of the CPI program was summarily terminated within a year of the release of SECY-88-174. The CPI program's final report devoted two sentences to the ice condenser plants, suggesting that any problems that existed should be assessed and dealt with by the plant owners.[28]

At this point in the story of the NRC's response to TMI's rude awakening, a familiar pattern is emerging. The initial, vigorous program of research and reassessment, set against a background of resistance from vested interests, was running out of steam. A new attitude was emerging that reflected a new agenda for the agency, the need to soften the impact severe-accident research was having on the operations and image of the nuclear industry. Ten years had passed since the TMI accident. What the public knew was that there had been a lot of work on reactor safety, and electric utilities were cancelling, not ordering, nuclear power plants. A strident but small sector of the population remained energized about reactor safety, but the proponents of vigilance in the NRC did not have the kind of broad-based citizen support that other regulatory agencies, like the Environmental Protection Agency, enjoyed.

The growing obscurity of reactor safety allowed key people in the NRC to move forward with a plan to implement the new agenda regarding severe accidents. To them, the epitaphs were written, and it was time to put the corpses in the caskets. They were aided in this enterprise by the complexity and subtlety of severe-accident issues. But hidden agendas can be clearly revealed when specialists within the system choose not to cooperate. Then, if the energy behind the agenda is strong enough and an individual is stubborn enough, the conflict between the system and the individual generates enough heat and light to reveal what is really going on.

Just such illumination was provided when a prominent, respected scientist working under contract to the NRC refused to go along with a rush to judgment about a thorny severe-accident issue called "direct containment heating" (DCH), an accident scenario believed to be a potential problem for all containment types. It became one of the most visible and contentious severe-accident issues the NRC ever dealt with and persisted as a source of rancor well into the 1990s. The next section explores this debate and focuses on the story of how one conscientious researcher tried to maintain scientific integrity, even in the face of potent political pressure, and lost.

Shoot the Messenger

DCH eventually provoked one of the most intense and sustained conflicts between the NRC and the nuclear industry about containment vulnerabilities, but awareness of the scenario emerged slowly after the TMI event. One of the aspects of the TMI accident that caught engineers by surprise was that so much of the core melted even though the pressure in the reactor remained very high. This occurred because the steam leak into the containment was not due to a large pipe break, as envisioned in the design basis accident, but rather to a stuck-open valve, an accident in the "small pipe break" category, which, by design basis philosophy, should be less threatening to the containment than a large-break accident. But in reality it proved to be a greater threat.

Analysts studying the TMI event began to indulge in "what if?" exercises about this high-pressure situation. What if the corium at the bottom of the vessel had melted through? Wouldn't the melt then be sprayed with great force into the containment? Was that a good thing or a bad thing compared with what was expected for a low-pressure accident?

The irony that the movie *The China Syndrome* had been released just before the TMI accident was a source of great consternation on the part of nuclear power advocates. The title derived from a hypothetical type of accident in which a large quantity of molten fuel penetrates the steel reactor vessel and pours onto the concrete floor of the containment building. The relentless decay heat in the fuel would keep it so hot that the concrete would be slowly consumed as gravity drew the mass of molten corium toward the center of the earth.

The terminology "China syndrome" was a bit of gallows humor that caught on, but no one really envisioned the corium's penetrating deeply into the earth. The real danger in this scenario comes from the cauldron-like interactions between the corium and the concrete, producing prodigious quantities of gas and heat. The resulting high pressure has the potential to rupture the containment building, releasing massive quantities of radioactivity into the outside atmosphere.

Early speculation about TMI-like accidents suggested that there might be a silver lining for this kind of event, compared with the classic China syndrome variety. Instead of having a self-heating, red-hot pool of corium melting its way through concrete, you might have wide dispersal of the melt, driven hard by the pressurized steam coming out of the reactor vessel. The result might be that the corium would be more widely distributed throughout the building, and hence it might cool down more and be unable to melt concrete.

To explore these and other issues, the NRC sponsored a series of experiments at Sandia National Laboratories in Albuquerque, New Mexico. It was of course not possible to use real nuclear fuel (which is extremely dangerous stuff), but the Sandia scientists developed methods to melt mixtures of materials with similar properties. They also learned how to use pressurized gas to drive the molten mixture out of a hole in a simulated reactor vessel to see how thoroughly the fuel simulant would be dispersed. Initial tests, performed outdoors in the desert south of Albuquerque, demonstrated that the melt would indeed be efficiently swept out of the reactor cavity. Some of these tests were conducted at night, and the molten fuel simulant was ejected in a brilliant arc hundreds of feet into the air, like a giant Roman candle.

When the researchers went on to perform the same experiment inside a closed building, a surprise awaited them. The steel building was violently lifted off its concrete pad, shearing the stout bolts fastening it down. Thus was born the concern about DCH as a means of overpressurizing the containment building. Over the next fifteen years, DCH would become one of the most contentious issues in reactor safety.

What had happened in the indoor test was that the driving gas had broken up the melt into small droplets, not unlike the spray of droplets from a garden sprayer. These droplets were so small and so hot that they burned in the presence of the air in the building. The result was a rapid heating and pressurization, similar to accidents in grain elevators when finely dispersed dust ignites. A more vivid picture might be that of setting off a Roman candle inside the trunk of a car.

These first experiments were performed in the early 1980s, and as additional tests and theoretical analyses were performed, DCH became increasingly important in assessments of severe accidents in U.S. reactors. The NUREG-1150 study found that DCH was one of the largest contributors to public risk for several of the containment types, because if DCH were to cause a breach in the containment, the release of radioisotopes to the environment would be very large, since so much of the radioactive material would be suspended in the containment atmosphere at that time. As for most things, timing is everything for severe accidents, and the DCH scenario has poor timing: virtually simultaneous reactor vessel failure and containment failure. Many other accident scenarios involve a long delay between the two events, so the airborne radioactive material can slowly settle out onto containment surfaces; consequently, much less radioactivity would be released if the containment were finally to fail.

Throughout the 1980s the NRC invested heavily in research on DCH, and the nuclear industry responded with its own research and analysis (generally attempting to minimize the threat). But the issue was exceptionally resistant to a confident resolution.

The NUREG-1150 risk study was based on what was essentially a snapshot of scientific understanding of severe accidents as of about 1985. The study showed that some containment types were much more resistant to severe accidents than others and that, in particular, the large dry containments held up very well to most challenges. Only DCH appeared to be a potent threat to such containments. Since containments of this type represented 57 percent of the entire U.S. reactor fleet,[29] there was a strong incentive to determine how significant the threat from DCH was. So the NRC continued to invest research funds in more experiments, more modeling, and more probabilistic analysis.

This unprecedented, sustained investment in a single severe-accident scenario began to pay off in the late 1980s. The experiments and codes were showing that a number of mitigative effects would occur in a DCH event at the same time as the melt ejection, chemical reaction, and atmosphere heat up. The trend of the results was to reduce the peak pressure calculated in accident simulations, compared to earlier studies. But the analysts still found important scenarios that resulted in pressures above what large dry containment buildings could handle.

The slow pace of scientific progress on this issue was a source of frustration to NRC management, who were taking a no-nonsense approach to severe accident research, exemplified by the 1988 *Integration Plan for Severe Accident Closure* mentioned earlier. But even more potent was the message from Congress expressed in the form of reduced budgets for the NRC.

The nuclear industry was facing dire times in the late 1980s, and many of its leaders believed that the current difficulties were due in large part to image problems: if the public understood nuclear energy better, there would be more support for it. Then, they believed, the other economic problems the industry was facing would be more amenable to solution. For these nuclear cheerleaders, spending time discussing severe accidents was highly counterproductive to improving nuclear's public image and had no corresponding benefit. Many members of Congress were sympathetic to these arguments and saw the NRC as the quintessential self-focused government bureaucracy, standing in the way of the country's economic prosperity and greatness. Such attitudes even began to show up in the commission itself, whose members, unlike the NRC staff, were presidentially appointed and Senate-approved officials, attuned to the political atmosphere favoring deregulation.

The NRC's predicament worsened with the transition of its funding base from taxpayer funds to industry fees in 1991. Now, when nuclear industry lobbyists complained to Congress about overregulation, they were heard even more sympathetically as the ones paying the bills. Congress responded with steady decreases in NRC funding (which, despite being off-budget, was controlled by Congress) and in many cases provided guidance on how the budget was to be allocated among the NRC's functions. Reflecting these forces, the overall research budget for the NRC declined sharply after its peak shortly after the TMI accident, as figure 3 shows.

The NRC's continued frustration with slow progress on severe accident "closure" led to more assertive measures to control the outcome of research. In the 1990s, the NRC's research came more and more to consist of developing information that would justify the foregone con-

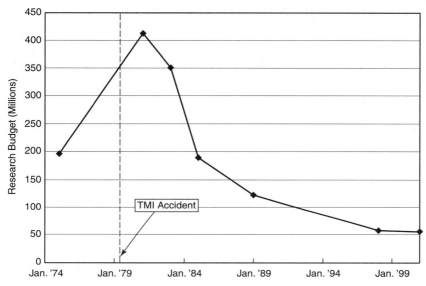

Figure 3
NRC reactor safety research funding before and after TMI (in year-2000 dollars). *Source:* Data for years prior to 1985 from letter from Carlyle Michelson, Chairman of ACRS to Kenneth Carr, chairman of NRC dated June 13, 1991 (available at NRC's Public Document Room). Data for later years from U.S. Nuclear Regulatory Commission, *Budget Estimates Fiscal Year* ••, NUREG-1100, volumes 1–17, published annually (•• = year) since 1985.

clusion that the top reactor "issues" were not a problem for any plant. This concept of closure for severe-accident issues was articulated in a 1992 report, the *Revised Severe Accident Research Plan*.[30] The following statement from a briefing to the commission by the NRC's director of research illuminates the new perspective: "[The *Revised Severe Accident Research Plan*] describes the progress and our understanding of important severe accident phenomena. It defines the research that would lead to closure of core melt progression, direct containment heating, which as I said before was an early containment failure mode, and fuel coolant interactions."[31] The commissioners warmly received the report's message that the continued research program was effectively a mopping-up campaign.

In the ensuing years, the conflict between the philosophy that the goal of severe-accident research was to justify its own termination, on one hand, and the actual state of knowledge in the various subject areas, on the other, became a source of great frustration to the participants in the research program. The NRC's duty to maintain vigilance concerning reactor safety had come into direct conflict with the interests of the flagging U.S. nuclear industry.

To accelerate progress on closing the DCH issue, the *Revised Severe Accident Research Plan* laid out a more aggressive and more coordinated effort on DCH research. The NRC chose Sandia National Laboratories to lead a team of national laboratories and other contractors in this project, which was named the DCH Issue Resolution project.

Sandia's management was gratified by the confidence that the NRC displayed in choosing it as the lead laboratory for this program. It was a logical choice. Sandia's experimental facilities and expertise in the area were unparalleled; they were the developers of the CONTAIN computer code, which was the NRC's leading analysis tool for DCH; and finally, Sandia had been the NRC's principal contractor for its NUREG-1150 project.

Sandia is primarily a nuclear weapons laboratory for the Department of Energy, and as the cold war was drawing to an end, budgets for such laboratories were tight and uncertain. Sandia's director of nuclear energy technology, Nestor Ortiz, had been trying to get his managers and their staffs to apply customer-focused management concepts such as total quality management. Being awarded the contract to lead this important new NRC program was a vindication of his efforts. At the same time, he recognized that leading the DCH Issue Resolution Project would be a challenging assignment, since the project would be conducted in a fishbowl environment. The customer was already frustrated at the slow pace of progress and would no doubt pay close attention to see whether the new funding and streamlined organization involved in the project was paying off.

The DCH Issue Resolution Project was to proceed in phases. The initial phase would focus on only one reactor, the Zion nuclear power plant, located near Chicago. Later phases would systematically apply the same methods to the remaining plants. The Zion plant had a large dry containment that was quite strong. It was considered a good representative of the most robust class of containments in the country and had been thoroughly studied in the NUREG-1150 project.

Mathematical methods for accident analysis had reached a point by this time that the NRC could establish a quantitative criterion for resolving the DCH issue at Zion. It wanted Sandia to show that if the reactor vessel failed at high pressure, there would be only a 10 percent or less chance that the containment would leak. It was a way of expressing the philosophy of defense in depth in quantitative terms.

Most experts thought that Zion would have a containment failure probability much less than 10 percent, but the challenge for the project was to develop a method for doing the calculation that was applicable to all reactors and that found favor with a panel of external experts selected by the NRC. Once the method was developed and accepted, the project could proceed with the remaining U.S. plants until all had been studied. It was hoped that all plants could be covered by 1994.

The project ran into trouble in early 1993, when the first draft of the Zion report was submitted for internal peer review at Sandia. Many reviewers took exception to what they considered a lack of rigor in the analysis. Numerous assumptions were challenged as unjustified, and the analysis was criticized for ignoring important phenomena or treating them incorrectly. The treatment of uncertainty was a particular source of criticism: some felt that uncertainties were being grossly underrepresented.

In scientific work, it is normal for peer reviews to generate questions that technical authors resolve with either revisions to the initial report or explanations that satisfy the reviewers. In this case, however, the report authors had a good sense of what the NRC contract managers expected, and they found it difficult to find compromises that satisfied their peers at Sandia. Tensions within the program grew.

The internal arguments over Sandia's peer review soon spilled over to the authors. One of the report authors was from Sandia, and two were subcontractors to Sandia from the University of California at Santa Barbara (UCSB). In the course of trying to resolve the reviewer comments, bitter disagreements between the two organizations developed. This rift stymied progress. Although the UCSB authors technically reported to Sandia, the lead professor maintained separate lines of communication with the NRC's research director, the man who had already gone on record to the commission about the expected outcome of the DCH program.

Internal review comments were still not resolved in June 1993 when the NRC directed that the external committee of experts it had selected review the report.[32] When the comments of those reviewers came in, many of the criticisms they expressed paralleled those of the Sandia reviewers. They questioned such things as how the authors decided what the conditions were in the reactor vessel at the time it failed, that is, the quantity of melt at the bottom of the vessel, its temperature, and its metallic content. Some, like the Sandia reviewers, questioned the use of simplistic models for pressurization of the containment, when more detailed treatments were available. And some of them felt that the treatment of uncertainties was just too superficial, again consistent with the earlier internal review.

As this crisis worsened, Ortiz got personally involved and attempted to apply total quality management methods to this contentious situation. He appointed a total quality committee of his managers to facilitate technical resolution of the disagreements between the authors and the reviewers. The committee's work served to clarify many of the concerns and to organize the disagreements into clear categories but also concluded that the impasse had not been overcome.[33] Ortiz reported this unfortunate state of affairs officially to the NRC in January 1994, a full year after the Zion report was first submitted to reviewers.

The NRC was not sympathetic: this was not the kind of progress it had expected when it entrusted the DCH Issue Resolution Project to Sandia. Brian Sheron, the director of NRC's severe accident work, wrote back to Ortiz, "[T]here are instances where it appears that the authors and the SNL [Sandia National Laboratories] internal review committee are no longer supporting the conclusion in the report, i.e., DCH issue is resolved for the Zion NPP [nuclear power plant]."[34] Later in the same letter, Sheron sharpened the point: "Therefore, when responses to the peer reviewers' comments appear to be unenthusiastic and do not stand behind the conclusion in the report that DCH is essentially resolved for the Zion NPP, it is very unlikely that we can resolve DCH for other PWRs [pressurized water reactors]." Sheron called on Sandia to reevaluate its responses to the peer review comments. Thus the Sandia total quality committee concluded that the authors had yielded too little to reviewers' criticisms, but the NRC customer felt they had yielded too much.

One of the most persistent critics of the Zion report was David C. Williams, the top DCH calculational analyst at Sandia. While the report authors struggled with both internal and external peer review comments, Williams had been looking carefully at some of the experimental test results and found convincing new evidence that the DCH methodology used for the study on Zion was seriously flawed. To his great surprise, though, no one in the program was interested in his findings.

Williams was an internationally respected expert in computer modeling of accident conditions in containment buildings. He had spent much of the previous ten years studying DCH and was generally recognized as the most knowledgeable analyst in the world on the subject. Over the years, he had guided the development of DCH models in the NRC's massive CONTAIN computer code. He followed the experiments on DCH closely and used insights gained from the tests to improve CONTAIN's treatment of physical reality.

In the spring of 1994, Williams was frustrated by the fact that no one was paying attention to the important new results he had obtained. Worse, he found he was excluded from the meetings Sandia had set up with the external review committee to work out the Zion report problems. Unable to convince his management that he belonged in these meetings, he offered to prepare material for others to present, but this offer was rejected. He complained about this in a memorandum that summarized the new information and cautioned, "An outside observer could conceivably interpret my exclusion from the Peer Review Meetings as implying that there is a desire by Sandia management to conceal the findings summarized above from the Peer Review group."[35] The meetings proceeded without Williams's involvement. He acquiesced and turned to other assignments, little knowing that the impediments to his continued professional work would become greater.

The grueling business of resolving the myriad technical disagreements over the Zion report continued over the summer, and Sandia finally found a path to bring the vexing Zion work to an end. In December 1994, two reports were published simultaneously. The first was the original report with only minor changes, authored by the UCSB and Sandia authors. The second did not include the UCSB authors; it was called a "supplement" to the first and contained commentary and (unresolved) criticism about the main report, without contradicting the conclusion that the DCH issue was resolved for Zion. This was an odd compromise, but it got Sandia past the roadblock. It was hardly a satisfactory outcome, since most of the substantive criticisms that Williams and other internal reviewers had raised were ignored.

To his great disappointment, Williams was not allowed to be involved in the follow-on work extending the analysis to other nuclear plants. He was a very capable scientist, however, and there was plenty of other work in Sandia's Nuclear Energy Technology Center to keep him busy.

He at least had the satisfaction in 1994 of completing a large report culminating years of improvement to the CONTAIN DCH models, showing in exhaustive detail how well (or not so well) these models agreed with the dozens and dozens of DCH experiments that had been performed over the previous ten years. This extremely technical treatise was for Williams a magnum opus, highlighting many years of his professional career. Normally, such technical reports are routinely submitted to the NRC for approval before they are published and distributed to technical organizations and libraries throughout the world. This approval step was not for ensuring the technical quality of the work—that was Sandia's job. Rather, the approval step was intended to prevent such things as premature release of safety policy information. In the case of Williams's CONTAIN assessment report, there should have been no problems of that nature: it was strictly a discussion of the science of accident modeling. This "hands off" policy regarding the technical content of contractor reports was conveyed in the formal procedures of the NRC's Office of Research (RES): "While the RES has responsibility for setting the scope, conduct or methodology, and objectives of research, there should be no interference with the contractor presenting his judgement as to the nature and interpretation of the research results."[36] By this time, however, the entire DCH issue had become so politicized that the NRC refused to give Sandia permission to publish the report,[37] even after Ortiz had offered to publish it as a Sandia report, with no NRC affiliation and at no cost to the government. Thus, years of Williams's work came to nothing from the all-important perspective of scientific publication. The NRC's action was clearly inconsistent with its own "hands-off" policy, but at that point Sandia management essentially gave up on Williams's cause. It had done what it could do.

Williams's sense of justice was badly frayed by this time, and he tried to find relief through Sandia's ethics organization. He was concerned with the damage to his career, of course, but he also had broader concerns. He wrote:

For over 12 years, DCH has been recognized as a major nuclear safety issue. The DCH issue resolution project has offered sweeping conclusions that DCH presents little or no threat in all plants studied to date, which include the most common type of plant in the U.S. It would be surprising if general acceptance of this claim did not result in reduction of efforts to understand DCH better and/or reduction in precautions taken to minimize DCH threats. If, as I believe, there is substantially greater uncertainty concerning the conclusions of the DCH resolution work than is being acknowledged, general acceptance of those conclusions would result in overconfidence concerning DCH that could eventually degrade safety.[38]

Since Sandia's Ethics Office was established to deal with issues of a legal nature and had no real mechanisms to assist in scientific controversies such as this, it directed Williams back to his line organization. Ortiz again tried to implement additional total quality management processes to ameliorate the situation, but Williams was to get no satisfaction from them. In reality, a federal contractor like Sandia has few means other than persuasion to bring pressure on a customer in such a situation. In 1996, Williams had an opportunity to retire early from Sandia with an incentive package (part of a downsizing), and he decided to leave.

David Williams was not an antinuclear troublemaker. He was a brilliant scientist, holding a Ph.D. in nuclear chemistry from the Massachusetts Institute of Technology. He had started his career in nuclear energy as an enthusiastic promoter of nuclear power. Early on, he spent a great deal of his private time in promotional activities, such as speaking in favor of nuclear power at public meetings. He was a scientist who had achieved the highest level of technical achievement at Sandia, the prestigious rank of Distinguished Member of the Technical Staff. He had an international reputation as one of the most capable reactor safety analysts in the world. Yet he left Sandia feeling angry and defeated.

This has been the story of one severe-accident issue. It is not, unfortunately, an isolated case. There is no doubt that the NRC conveyed to Sandia and its other contractors the conclusions they expected from the contracted research. Facing the kind of pressure created by the NRC on the DCH Issue Resolution project, it is not easy for a contractor such as a national laboratory to maintain an open mind. The long tradition of technical integrity in the laboratories' research is certainly a bulwark against blatant distortion of research results. But management must also consider its commitment to the customer paying the bill. Ortiz had to think not only about Williams's concerns, but also about the livelihoods of the hundreds of other scientists and engineers in his center. Total quality management processes are not well suited for resolving such conflicts. (Williams, for his part, believes Sandia was at least as responsible for the shortcomings of the DCH Issue Resolution project as the NRC was.)[39]

The contrast is sharp between the forthright research atmosphere surrounding the NUREG-1150 project and the way things were handled with the DCH Issue Resolution Project ten years later. The earlier project recognized the importance of factoring in the opinions of many different experts, who might not see every issue the same way; at that time Williams was an important and respected player on the expert panels the NRC convened to wrestle with the uncertainties of hypothetical severe accidents. Ten years later, his expertise was of no value to the NRC, because he refused to conform his technical opinions to the positions adopted by NRC management.

Ice Condensers, the Little Containments that Don't

As noted above, the pattern of intense vigilance triggered by an external event, followed by a slide into complacency, seems to be characteristic of the federal government's attention to the hazards of nuclear technology. It appeared in the history of U.S. nonproliferation policy presented in chapter 2, and it can be seen in the context of the NRC's attitudes toward severe reactor accidents in the decades following TMI, as just described in the story of David Williams and the DCH Issue Resolution project. It may very well be true that the benefits of nuclear technology are worth the risks, but the risks are persistent and long-term and cannot be properly managed with such uneven attention by the agencies charged with protecting the public's interests.

Similarly, today's public indifference about nuclear war and proliferation allows the federal government's new tritium policy to move forward despite its grave shortcomings. But there is also a more direct connection between the DCH Issue Resolution work and the new tritium policy.

It concerns the safety of the ice condenser plants that TVA will modify to be able to produce tritium.

After the Zion report was finally published, NRC and Sandia proceeded to evaluate the DCH threat for one group of reactors after another, eventually declaring the issue "resolved" for all large dry containment plants without a significant hitch. Then, around 1996, they decided to take on one of the problem containments, the ice condenser.

The last time ice condensers had been in the NRC's spotlight was in the late 1980s, when the CPI program had been poised to assess systematically the performance of ice condensers in severe accidents. Then the program was abruptly terminated, as discussed earlier in this chapter. It seemed then that ice condenser containments had dodged a bullet, avoiding the intense scrutiny that led NRC to call for containment changes at the more numerous Mark I plants. The DCH Issue Resolution program put the ice condenser containments, with their remarkable weaknesses, right back in the spotlight.

For the ice condenser work, Sandia was the only contractor involved, since NRC's research budgets had been squeezed dramatically in the years following the infamous Zion DCH report. But the starting point for Sandia's specialists was not auspicious. Given the NUREG-1150 results, it was not apparent to them how ice condensers could be found resistant to DCH.

In 1997 Sandia submitted to the NRC its draft report on DCH Issue Resolution for ice condensers. It concluded that, unlike all the containment types studied previously, ice condensers could not meet the "success criterion"—containment failure probability less than 10 percent—for resolution of DCH. The report also pointed out that DCH was not the only problem ice condensers had. In many sequences, if DCH were hypothesized by fiat not to cause the containment to fail, some other challenge would.

Characteristically, the NRC project managers did not publish this report and instead contemplated ways to salvage the commitment the NRC's management had made to the commission to close the DCH issue. The broad vulnerability of ice condensers to a variety of severe accident challenges, not just DCH, led the NRC to commission Sandia to do a systematic evaluation of ice condenser response to the entire threat spectrum. This is exactly what the CPI program was going to do nine years earlier, but there was a difference. In those days, the goal was to decide if changes in the containments were called for. Now, the purpose of the work was to demonstrate there was no longer a need for research on DCH.

Sandia carried out the integrated study of ice condenser vulnerabilities in 1998 and 1999. The report it submitted to the NRC showed quantitatively what most analysts expected: that these containments provide far less defense in depth than conventional containments.

The problem with these reactors is that the volume of the containment building is small compared to large dry containments, but the reactor core is about the same size. The ice suspended in the massive banks of wire baskets (see figure 4) would certainly be effective in absorbing the steam from a pipe break accident, but severe accidents tend to overwhelm the ice. Buildup of hydrogen is a particular problem, since removing steam from a steam-hydrogen-air mixture increases the concentration of hydrogen, making the gas more combustible, even detonable.

Figure 4
View of ice baskets from top deck of ice chest. Each wire basket is a forty-eight-foot-high cylinder. The entire ice condenser containment holds more than 1,000 tons of ice.

One of the safety features in these containments is an array of strategically located hydrogen igniters, essentially spark plugs, that would burn the hydrogen off before the concentration got too high. But there are some conditions in which the igniters do not work, such as in the "station blackout" scenario, in which all electrical power is lost.

Some of the difficulties of the Mark I containments also derived from their small volume, but the hydrogen combustion danger had been eliminated by the use of an inerted (that is to say, nitrogen-filled) containment building. Without oxygen in the atmosphere, the hydrogen cannot burn. In contrast, the atmosphere in the ice condenser containments is ordinary air, and hydrogen combustion is a major severe-accident problem in such containments even without DCH. The Sandia analysts found that DCH and hydrogen combustion could occur simultaneously and cause containment failure in ice condenser containments for accidents that large dry containments could easily survive.

The revised Sandia report concluded, as had its original report, that the ice condensers could not meet the 10-percent containment failure criterion for DCH. But because an integrated analysis had been done, the NRC had another way to declare victory. Since there were so many other ways for the containment to be compromised, it turned out that DCH was a minor contributor, on a probabilistic basis, to the overall probability of containment failure. This was partly because most severe accidents were found not to result in high-pressure ejection of corium into the containment. For those accidents, the containment's resistance to DCH was a moot point. In other cases, the containment failed because of hydrogen combustion before melt ejection occurred, again making the containment's resistance to DCH irrelevant.

Since the focus of the project was DCH, not overall protection provided by the containment, the NRC chose to view the Sandia results in a positive light, and in June 2000 Ashok Thadani, the NRC's director of research, announced that the DCH issue had been resolved for ice condensers.[40] His logic? Since it was not possible to declare victory on the basis of the original success criterion, the NRC used a new criterion, that despite being vulnerable to DCH, these containments were equally vulnerable to a wide variety of more likely events. The logic was equivalent to saying, "why worry about automobile gas tanks exploding due to collisions from the rear if most collisions are from the side or the front?"

From the narrow perspective of the DCH Issue Resolution project, the NRC decision may have been logical. But from the perspective of how well the public is protected from reactor accidents, the message of the Sandia study was bleak. The calculations showed that ice condensers are very susceptible to failure under a wide variety of severe accident conditions, not just DCH. If, for example, electric power to the igniter system were lost, hydrogen could build up to the point that either random sparks or restoration of power to the igniters would trigger an overwhelming hydrogen burn that would cause the containment to fail. The containment could fail if melt ejected from the reactor vessel built up on the containment shell and melted through. The containment could fail if there were a large "spike" of steam created by rapid mixing of molten debris with a pool of water beneath the vessel.

Station blackouts posed a particular problem. Because many of the containment's safety features require AC power (rather than battery, or DC, power that other plants use), ice condenser containments are more or less "sitting ducks" in such an accident. Unless power is restored, failure of the reactor vessel, release of corium into the containment, and containment failure are all virtually inevitable. The Sandia study found, for example, that in the event of a station blackout, the Sequoyah's probability of containment failure was about 97 percent.[41]

Thadani's memorandum announcing the success of the DCH Issue Resolution effort recognized this darker picture:

The recent ice condenser study . . . concluded that the ice condenser plants are more vulnerable to early containment failure than large dry containments, but that this vulnerability is not due to DCH. In fact, early containment failure in ice condensers was dominated by non-DCH hydrogen combustion events rather than by DCH, and was seen largely to depend on plant specific probabilities for station blackout (ice condenser igniter systems are not operable during station blackout events).

Despite this recognition the NRC, still gun-shy about the politics of severe accidents, has not vigorously pursued the issue of ice condenser vulnerability.[42] As described at the beginning of this chapter, in the early days of nuclear power the AEC required effective containment systems as a trade-off to balance the increase in public risk due to locating nuclear power plants near population centers. But for many of the most important accidents, ice condenser plants pose essentially the same risk to the public as the same plants would with no containment at all.

What has all this to do with the DOE's selection of the Sequoyah and Watts Bar plants to be the first commercial power plants to produce nuclear weapons materials? As far as DOE has been concerned, nothing. The safety of the plants was irrelevant to the DOE selection. What mattered was the fact that, of all the utilities operating nuclear power plants in the United States, only the TVA could be persuaded to cooperate with the nuclear weapons program by producing tritium in its reactors.

Chapter 5 will explain how this occurred. But before that discussion, it is time to switch attention from the danger of nuclear reactor accidents to the other downside of the government's decision to produce tritium in commercial reactors: the danger that it will encourage proliferation of nuclear weapons throughout the world.

4

Nuclear Nonproliferation: The Devil Is in the Details

In a world boiling with local (and not so local) hatreds, the retrogression of arms control raises the question of whether the Cold War, instead of being the high point of danger in a waning nuclear age, will prove to have been a mere bipolar rehearsal for a multipolar second nuclear age.

Jonathan Schell, 2000

Nonproliferation 101

Thinking about nuclear war is a pretty depressing thing to do, but it used to be worse. It used to be called "thinking about the unthinkable," back when the two superpowers bristled with nuclear weapons on hair-trigger alert, and President John F. Kennedy predicted there would be fifteen to twenty-five nuclear-armed states by the 1970s.[1]

Today there is some good news about this depressing subject. Not only have the United States and Russia taken a few steps back from the brink, but Kennedy's predicted growth in the nuclear "club" never happened. Even better, recent years have seen countries turn away from nuclear weapons after having once possessed or vigorously pursued them. For example, South Africa possessed six bombs but destroyed them in 1991 before revealing their existence to the world and announcing a new policy of abstention. Also encouraging, fewer nuke "wannabes" are active now. The 1998 issue of the Carnegie Endowment's *Tracking Nuclear Proliferation* compares the current situation to the 1980s: "The seven states that are of greatest concern today were already then considered proliferation threats. Moreover, it is now known that Argentina, Brazil, Romania, and Taiwan all then took steps of one type or another to pursue nuclear arms but backed away or renounced their acquisition."[2] Table 1 shows the Carnegie report's tally of countries that

Table 1
Countries with current or past weapons programs

Nuclear Weapons States	Renunciations	Non-NPT Nuclear Weapons States	High-Risk States
United States	South Africa	Israel	Iran
Great Britain	Brazil	Pakistan	Libya
China	Ukraine	India	Iraq
Russia	Algeria		North Korea
France	Argentina		
	Belarus		
	Romania		
	Kazakhstan		

Source: Rodney W. Jones and Mark G. McDonough, *Tracking Nuclear Proliferation* (Washington, DC: Carnegie Endowment for International Peace, 1998).

possess or have pursued nuclear weapons at one time or another. The first category, "Nuclear Weapons States," involves a legal distinction established by the NPT, to be discussed in more detail later in the chapter. The good news in the table is the "Renunciations" category, which includes not only South Africa, but also seven other countries that had at one time made substantial progress in weapons building but have since abandoned such ambitions. Countries in the third category, "Non-NPT Nuclear Weapons States," possess nuclear weapons but are not among the original five weapons states. They refuse to sign the NPT, since that would require that they relinquish their weapons. Of these, India and Pakistan have proudly proclaimed their possession of nuclear weapons and have demonstrated them with recent underground tests. Israel, the third member of the category, acknowledges nothing but is believed to have more than 100 deployable weapons. Finally, there are four countries considered to be in the "High Risk" category; it is believed that they do not yet possess nuclear weapons but have shown strong inclinations to obtain them, despite having signed the NPT. They are all considered "rogue" states and have been highly resistant to diplomatic and economic pressure to abandon their pursuit of the nuclear bomb. Despite the last two categories, the overall picture is a positive one, because it shows that the complex international nuclear nonproliferation regime is working.

This relative success to date is, however, no guarantee that the situation will not unravel in the future. The effectiveness of the nonproliferation system depends on a delicate interplay among positive incentives for each non–weapons state to forgo its quest for nuclear weapons and a series of barriers that makes acquiring them expensive and difficult. In today's rapidly evolving world, either side of the equation could change, leading to a dangerous expansion of nuclear weapons capabilities in the world. It is essential for the continued success of the nonproliferation system to adapt it to changing conditions and to maintain a high degree of vigilance in implementing it.

The starting point for nonproliferation is convincing non–weapons states that acquiring nuclear weapons will not add to their national security. Perhaps the most visible mechanism of accomplishing this goal is the network of bilateral and multilateral security arrangements that reduce international tensions and promote peaceful relations among states. During the cold war each superpower extended a nuclear umbrella over many nonnuclear allies, in part to discourage them from pursuing nuclear weapons on their own. With the cold war over and international terrorism overturning traditional assumptions about national security all over the world, it would be prudent to assume that some nations may reevaluate their posture vis-à-vis nuclear weapons in the coming years.

Supplementing the network of mutual-security alliances is the NPT itself. It is effectively a contract between two groups of states. The nuclear arsenals of the five weapons states (the first category in table 1) are acknowledged and more or less accepted for the time being. All other signatories must forswear pursuing nuclear weapons and allow IAEA inspections and monitoring (generically termed "safeguards") of the nuclear reactors in their countries.

The original five incur a different set of obligations. For one thing, they agree to provide enriched nuclear fuel and technical assistance on civilian nuclear energy to the non–weapons state signatories. They are also committed to working sincerely toward nuclear arms reduction and eventual abolition of nuclear weapons, a provision known as Article VI that is principally directed at the United States and Russia.

Since the NPT was established in 1970, the United States has worked very hard to convince non–weapons nations to join the NPT framework.

The type of persuasion applied has depended on the circumstances. Undeveloped countries did not attract a great deal of attention, but industrialized countries that did not sign the NPT were subjected to intense diplomatic and economic pressure to reconsider. This pressure has generally been in the form of incentives, such as foreign aid, technical cooperation on civilian nuclear power, and enriched nuclear fuel. The United States most often provides these benefits, but other nations have also contributed.

A major problem during this campaign to persuade industrialized nonsignatories to sign the NPT has been the need to overcome the perception that the treaty is asymmetric and unfair. India has been highly vocal in this regard, claiming that the treaty is simply an institutionalization of the military dominance of five nations over the rest of the world. It criticizes the elements of the treaty that impose restrictions on the nuclear activities in the non–weapons states but place no similar constraints on the weapons states. It believes that Article VI is a cynical sham, that the weapons states will never give up the nuclear bombs and intercontinental ballistic missiles that give them such a great military advantage.

The United States has taken concrete steps to blunt such criticism, following a number of policies that voluntarily impose the same burdens on its nuclear program that the treaty imposes on the weapons states. One of those policies is to prohibit production of nuclear weapons materials in commercial nuclear reactors. Another is called the voluntary offer, whereby the United States agrees to allow IAEA inspections at its commercial nuclear plants to verify that this commitment is being honored.

It has taken a lot of time and effort for such inducements to bear fruit, but today 180 non–weapons states have signed the NPT. Only four countries, Cuba and the three members of table 1's third category, have not signed.[3] Thus, the NPT, established and fostered from the start by the United States, must be considered one of the great diplomatic achievements of the twentieth century.

The United States's new tritium policy is a departure from the previous policy prohibiting production of nuclear weapons ingredients in commercial reactors, but it is not a departure from U.S. law or the NPT. As part of the campaign to encourage international participation in the

NPT, Congress did pass a law prohibiting production of fissile materials for weapons in commercial power plants, but that provision, known as the Hart-Simpson amendment to the Atomic Energy Act, did not cover tritium. Thus, prior to 1998 every presidential administration adhered to the policy prohibiting the use of commercial reactors for tritium production, but such adherence was not established by legislation. Part of the reason tritium was left out of the Hart-Simpson amendment is that there are commercial uses of tritium, such as for runway lighting and exit signs, that might be inconvenienced by such a provision. But the main reason for its exclusion from the amendment was probably the perception that barriers to producing fissile materials were sufficient of themselves to prevent acquisition of nuclear weapons. The potential availability of weapons-grade fissile material on the black market (discussed later in the chapter) is changing that perception, however, and now is the time to be focusing more attention on tritium in the context of nonproliferation, not less.

The NPT and its system of safeguards, administered by the IAEA, is one of two key international mechanisms for controlling nuclear proliferation. The second system is independent of the NPT, but consistent with it; it is the export control system agreed upon by a collection of nations referred to as the Nuclear Suppliers Group (NSG).[4] In 2000 this group had thirty-four members, including essentially all countries capable of manufacturing nuclear technology, with the unfortunate exception of China.[5] They agree on a list of materials, devices, and information that will be subject to export control, and they agree to export such items only upon receiving certain concessions from the importing nation. Such concessions include the agreement not to reexport, to submit to IAEA-like inspections of how the items are used, and to abide by the NPT.

The list of items subject to export control includes not only things that are primarily nuclear in nature, but also a variety of dual-use items that have legitimate civilian uses besides their potential nuclear weapons application. Examples from the current list are "detonators and multipoint ignition systems" and "electromagnetic isotope separators."[6] Enforcement of export controls is up to each supplier nation, but there is active exchange of information among them about standards and interpretations, so a reasonably uniform system operates worldwide.

The NSG scrutinizes the list constantly and updates it annually, as technology advances and new information on the activities of proliferators is revealed.[7]

These two systems, IAEA safeguards and export controls, have been reasonably effective in controlling proliferation, but not perfectly so, as the examples of Israel, India, and Pakistan attest. Even more alarming, after the 1991 Persian Gulf War, UN inspectors in Iraq discovered evidence of a surprisingly advanced nuclear weapons program that had been carried out clandestinely in spite of full implementation of IAEA safeguards in that country. It was only because Saddam Hussein invaded neighboring Kuwait and brought about a devastating international military response that the Iraqi nuclear weapons program was halted before Iraq had functioning bombs.[8] This close call prompted a searching review of IAEA safeguard mechanisms, and the lessons learned have prompted a number of improvements to the IAEA's inspections system.

Largely in response to alarm about Iraq's clandestine nuclear weapons program, many advanced industrial nations pushed after the Gulf War for renewed commitment to strict export controls on dual-use technology and materials. In 1991 the NSG met for the first time in fourteen years in the Hague. There the United States proposed a broad expansion of export controls to cover a variety of items that were not until that time strictly controlled. Prominent among the U.S. suggestions, and significant for the subject of this book, was tritium and the means for its production.[9] As chapter 5 will discuss, the new tritium policy may require the United States to find ways to circumvent the intent of the export control system if it persists in its plans to modify commercial reactors for tritium production. This is an ironic but discouraging twist for the nation that has called most strongly for high-technology export control to prevent nuclear proliferation.

The example of Iraqi progress in clandestine nuclear weapons programs is not anomalous; throughout the history of the nonproliferation regime, flaws in the systems have allowed countries with nuclear ambitions to work around its provisions. Of particular recent concern are the shortcomings revealed in the dangerous nuclear arms race now taking place between India and Pakistan.

How India got around international agreements and developed a plutonium bomb in 1974 was described in chapter 2. Pakistan followed a much easier path. According to the *New York Times*, "China, a staunch ally of Pakistan's, provided blueprints for the bomb, as well as highly enriched uranium, tritium, scientists and key components for a nuclear weapons production complex, among other crucial tools."[10] With help like this from its northern neighbor, Pakistan conducted a series of underground nuclear tests over a three-day period in May 1998. Pakistan's decision to test was an angry response to India's surprising resumption of nuclear tests earlier that month. Significantly, both countries' tests involved bombs boosted with tritium.[11]

The nuclear armaments of Pakistan and India have been a complicating factor in the ongoing war now being waged by the United States and its allies against international terrorism. The possibility of terrorists' gaining access to nuclear weapons adds a chilling new dimension to the dangers of proliferation. The calculus of terrorist use of nuclear explosives is quite different from that of use by a national government. A government may be able to build and stockpile nuclear weapons, but fear of nuclear retaliation will usually be a potent deterrent to using them. Proliferation experts generally discount the possibility of nonstate terrorists' building their own nuclear weapons, but the danger that they might obtain one from a national arsenal by theft or collusion is very real.[12] If that were to happen, the deterrent effect of "mutually assured destruction" would inhibit widely dispersed clandestine organizations like Al Qaeda less than state governments.

From these examples it is clear that the nonproliferation regime can be effective only if international commitment to it remains vigorous and if it evolves with the times. Today, the international environment is changing rapidly in the aftershocks of the end of the cold war and the disruption caused by state-supported terrorism. It is essential to assess the implications of those changes for nonproliferation policies and processes. The remainder of this chapter will focus on those implications in two areas: the control of nuclear materials (in the next section) and the control of weapons information (in the following one).

Nuclear Materials Control: Everything Has Changed

As it was in the 1940s, the first step today for an aspirant to nuclear weapons status is obtaining a sufficient quantity of fissile material, either highly enriched uranium (typically 90-percent U-235) or plutonium (which can be variable in the mix of its isotopes). Both materials are extremely difficult to produce at the quality needed for efficient nuclear weapons. Hence, the international nonproliferation regime has set great store on controlling access to these materials and to the technology for producing them. Notable by its absence for most of this period has been intense concern about tritium. The logic for the relative neglect of tritium as an area for concern was probably something like this: one cannot build a boosted nuclear weapon, much less a two-stage thermonuclear device,[13] if one cannot build an efficient fission weapon. Thus, the focus of nonproliferation efforts has been on prevention at the entry level of nuclear weapons.

Recent changes in the worlds of technology and international politics invite reexamination of the philosophy implicit in the nuclear nonproliferation efforts to date. The most important political change is the disintegration of the Soviet Union and the continuing deterioration of governmental control in the countries that made up the Eastern bloc. Thousands of nuclear weapons and hundreds of tons of weapons-grade fissile materials, once controlled closely by the authoritarian Soviet government, have become vulnerable to diversion or loss as Moscow's economic and political strength has waned. Certainly, the United States and other Western nations have worked energetically with the nations of the former Soviet Union to prevent disaster, and those efforts have borne fruit. For example, all strategic nuclear weapons have now been removed from the three non-Russian states—Ukraine, Kazakhstan, and Belarus—that at one time possessed them.[14] Also, technical assistance from the West has improved Russian technology for tracking and protecting the nuclear materials it inherited from the Soviet Union. But it is nonetheless a source of great concern that these weapons and materials still exist and are owned by a government that has lost its grip on many aspects of the society it once firmly controlled.

The quantities of these weapons and materials are staggering. Unclassified estimates put the amount of weapons-usable uranium and separated plutonium now stored in Russia at about 1,400 tons.[15] This is in theory enough to make 120,000 nuclear weapons,[16] far more than the total number of warheads currently in existence in the world. This astonishing number is likely to increase because Russia's aggressive weapon disassembly program, driven by the two Strategic Arms Reduction Treaties (START-I and START-II), will continually add to the stores of surplus fissile material.

Experts on the subject are generally pessimistic about the prospects for protecting these materials from diversion into the black market or clandestine sale by Russian officials. The weapons-usable nuclear materials are believed to be stored in nearly 400 buildings at sixty sites throughout the country.[17] Matthew Bunn, a specialist in this subject at Harvard University, recently wrote:

Much of the fissile material in Russia is in facilities with no effective portal monitor at the door to set off an alarm if someone walks out with plutonium or HEU [highly enriched uranium]; poorly trained, conscript guard forces go unpaid for months at a time; no major facilities have carried out a measured physical inventory in this decade; electricity that provides the lifeblood of alarm and sensor systems is sometimes cut off for non-payment of bills; and all this takes place in a society where corruption is endemic and violent organized crime groups with extraordinary resources control large sections of the economy.[18]

This is not just a short-term problem. The quantities of fissile material in Russian stockpiles are so large that there is simply no feasible way to bring their protection up to Western standards any time soon. In an encouraging step, the United States has agreed to purchase 550 tons of weapons-grade Russian uranium, blended in Russia with natural uranium to create fuel for civilian reactors. The price works out to be about $21 million per ton.[19] But the purchase will be spread out over a period of ten years, and a lot can happen in ten years. What if another buyer offers $50 million for a ton, unblended? That would be enough to make over sixty bombs.

If significant diversion of, say, more than a ton of weapons-grade fissile material does happen, that changes everything. The barriers to entry into the nuclear club would be dramatically lowered for the nations or organizations that could obtain uranium or plutonium in such quantities. It is not a happy thought, and the governments involved are exerting intense efforts to prevent such a diversion from happening. But for the purposes of assessing U.S. tritium policies, a good working assumption is that it is possible, if not likely, that superpower-quality fissile material will be available, at a price, within the next ten years.

If the hypothetical material that escapes Russian control were highly enriched uranium, the remaining technical barriers to producing an effective weapon would be negligible. Almost thirty years ago, U.S. nuclear weapon designer Ted Taylor described a variety of ways to produce potent uranium weapons using "home-brewed" technology.[20]

Plutonium bombs, on the other hand, require a precise spherical implosion, which in Taylor's day was vastly more difficult to accomplish than what was needed for uranium bombs. But today the digital revolution and worldwide commerce in high technology have brought to market astonishing capabilities in precision manufacturing, sophisticated explosives, and advanced digital control systems. True, the export control strategies of the NSG are supposed to monitor the sale and use of many of the relevant technologies, but these controls can only slow the acquisition process down; they cannot prevent it. The tension between the demands of an export control regime and the drive to expand foreign sales of high technology is unavoidable. When, like today, there is no great sense of emergency, it is difficult for caution to win out.

For much the same reason, there has been a huge increase in the availability of information about engineering techniques, high-tech materials, calculational methods, and electronics design, much of it on the Internet, where it is impossible to control who accesses the information. To put an even sharper point on it, the level of detail on designing nuclear weapons that is now available on the World Wide Web is breathtaking.[21]

All this means that the difficulty of making an effective implosion bomb has been dramatically reduced.[22] The unavoidable conclusion is that the acquisition of large quantities of Russian uranium or plutonium by one or more nuclear aspirants will almost certainly create new members of the nuclear club. Bunn puts it grimly: "If plutonium and HEU become widely available on a nuclear black market, nothing else we do to prevent the proliferation of nuclear weapons will succeed."[23] To this dark picture must be added another consequence of the Soviet Union's fall: thousands of Russian engineers and scientists who have spent their careers designing and building nuclear weapons and who are now living desperate lives in the ruins of what was once the greatest scientific establishment in the world,[24] or who have abandoned science entirely and get by from week to week in menial jobs for subsistence wages. Expertise provided by any one of the top Soviet weapons designers would have a dramatic effect on a country's nascent nuclear weapons program. The United States and other countries have invested heavily in programs that try to keep these people gainfully employed, but the problem is so large that it may be unsolvable in the long run. A prominent German specialist in nonproliferation noted, "Given the incentives that wealthy proliferators can offer, it would be a miracle if no one accepted."[25]

Now let us take the logic a little further. Given high-quality fissile material and high-quality implosion, boosting with tritium can make the new club member's bomb many times more powerful than it otherwise would be. Boosting can also stretch a limited supply of fissile material to make a larger and more powerful arsenal. If the tritium were available, why would this hypothetical nation or group not take that additional step? Think about this: all current U.S. nuclear weapons, whether simple boosted weapons or two-stage thermonuclear devices, are boosted. Not one is a pure fission weapon.[26] From the unclassified literature, it does not appear that adding fusion boost to a workable implosion fission weapon is particularly difficult. It is mostly a matter of ensuring that deuterium and tritium are present at the center of the implosion.[27]

How much the barrier to creating boosted nuclear weapons has been lowered over the years is revealed by a comparison of how long a delay ensued for different countries between the creation of their first fission weapon and that of their first hydrogen bomb. For the United States, it took seven years. For the Soviet Union, aided by spies in the Manhattan Project, it took four years. With Chinese help, Pakistan made the transition much faster: the time between its first test of a fission device on May 28, 1998, and its first test of a boosted weapon was just three days.[28]

On the positive side, there is more to proliferation than just the "how" and "what" part of the equation. There is also the "why," and the news is good in this regard. For example, there are many countries that could easily have developed a nuclear weapons capability within a few years (they are sometimes called "virtual weapons states")[29] but have not done so because they see no reason to. In the relative stability of today's international climate, most nations will not see an advantage to going nuclear. But it is unrealistic to think that doing so will never be perceived to be in the interests of any country. To believe that is to ignore Israel's nuclear history. Similarly, the Pakistanis and Indians feel fully justified in pursuing nuclear weapons. And as the decades pass, who can say which countries that now show no interest may discover the need for nuclear weapons in changed circumstances?

It is impossible to say whether the probability of further nuclear weapons proliferation will be higher or lower in the future than it was during the cold war.[30] What can be said is that the reduced physical security of Russia's fissile-material stockpile, the spread of advanced technology throughout the world, the increased availability of information on weapons design, and the possibility of Russian weapons scientists' defecting to aid another country's fledgling nuclear weapons program all point to a dramatic lowering of the technical barriers to weapons production. These trends also suggest that the transition by a new weapons state from pure fission weapons to boosted designs using tritium and deuterium should no longer be seen as subject to major technical barriers, once the proliferator has the tritium.

The implication of these changes for U.S. nuclear policy should be an enhanced sensitivity about tritium and the means of producing it.* Yet what we are seeing in recent actions by the DOE is the opposite, a relaxation of concern about the connection between tritium and weapons proliferation. How this has come about will be described in chapter 5.

But first, a parallel issue will be evaluated in the light of the changing times. If controlling who acquires nuclear materials is the export control side of nonproliferation, then the corresponding control of who gains access to information is secrecy.

The Illusion of Secrecy

Institutionalized secrecy is one of the tools that the U.S. government uses to curb the spread of nuclear weapons technology to other countries. There have always been some aspects of tritium production that have been protected by the DOE information classification system. That will continue to be so as the new tritium facilities are designed, built, and operated. How that system works, how successful it will be in protecting critical information, and what secondary effects it might have are

---

* Since deuterium is easier to make than tritium and does not decay over time, these arguments are less applicable to it than to tritium.

thus important questions for evaluating current U.S. policies on tritium production.

In part, the answers to these questions depend on the details of DOE procedures and mechanisms for protecting secret information, and in part they depend on how people behave in the environment those rules create. That is, they depend on the subtle and complex interactions between human nature and the classification bureaucracy. An effective system of information protection must strike a balance among the need to prevent damaging loss of information to potential adversaries, the need to carry out work in an effective and timely way, and the need for an informed public in a democratic society.

The current DOE apparatus for imposing secrecy on nuclear weapons information is a compromise among these requirements.[31] It is generally known as the Q-clearance system, and it had its origins at Los Alamos during the Manhattan Project. General Leslie Groves, who was in overall charge there, at first expected military-style secrecy rules to apply, with compartmentalized groups working on separate parts of the atomic bomb problem but knowing little of what was going on in other compartments. The scientists at Los Alamos rebelled, arguing that the cross-connections among different parts of the project were vital for all to understand. Otherwise progress toward the goal would be exceedingly slow. Out of this conflict emerged a compromise arrangement, based on the idea that any scientist cleared for secrets would have access to the whole range of subjects associated with work at Los Alamos.[32] Although Groves was not comfortable with this loose approach to secrecy, the isolation of Los Alamos and the multiple guarded fences surrounding the complex added a compensating degree of security.

Today's Q-clearance system of information protection at the DOE national laboratories bears a strong family resemblance to the truce painfully worked out some sixty years ago between Groves and the atomic scientists. Work on nuclear weapons is, in general, not compartmentalized. In other words, there is no official list of people authorized to know about each aspect of the project. With the Q-clearance system, one's badge shows what level one is cleared for without regard for the particulars of the project. This is not to say that the "need-to-know" requirement is abandoned entirely, only that its enforcement is delegated to the individuals doing the work. No permission is needed to reveal classified aspects of one scientist's work to another, as long as both have the required clearance level marked on their badges.

The underlying philosophy of the Q-clearance system is based on the understanding that keeping scientific information secret is much more difficult than protecting traditional national security information, such as troop locations or keys to cyphers. One reason for this difference is that the most important secret about a technical achievement like the atom bomb is often simply the fact that it can be done. The United States could hardly keep its success secret after Hiroshima and Nagasaki. It is therefore more accurate to view the role of scientific secrecy as slowing down the rate of acquisition of knowledge by adversaries, rather than preventing it entirely.[33] Imposition of secrecy also forces an adversary to expend resources doing the research and testing required to independently obtain the same data. Thus, the effectiveness of a secrecy system should be evaluated not in terms of success and failure, but rather in terms of how good a balance it strikes between the need to make technical advances and the need to slow down the acquisition of key information by adversaries. Consistent with its origins, the DOE system has emphasized technical progress over strict security, because staying ahead technologically was always seen as the way to win the arms race (whatever that meant).

Poor subjective judgments colored by wishful thinking lie at the root of many of the historical failures of DOE's secrecy system. The most famous example is the loss of detailed information about the U.S. atomic bombs to the Russians via several Manhattan Project scientists who were sympathetic to Stalin's communist regime. One of them was Theodore Hall, a brilliant young physicist who never tried to hide his Marxist beliefs or his membership in the John Reed society, an American group dedicated to the furtherance of Russian communism. At the time, Robert Oppenheimer, the head of the project, was engaged in what he called a "policy of absolutely unscrupulous recruiting of anyone we can lay hands on."[34] In this progress-oriented atmosphere, Hall was granted a security clearance despite his political affiliations and consequently had access to vast amounts of classified information, which he dispatched to Russia at his earliest opportunity.[35]

The fallibility of the DOE's secrecy system has also been highlighted by more recent revelations about losses of secret information from the national laboratories. Around 1995, it became apparent to some U.S. intelligence personnel that, over a twenty-year period, the People's Republic of China had obtained detailed design information on the most advanced thermonuclear weapons in the U.S. arsenal and had used that information to leapfrog its own nuclear weapons program by many years.[36] After this devastating revelation, other experts downplayed the damage to national security,[37] but the level of rhetoric on the failure of the DOE to protect nuclear secrets nonetheless escalated to a fever pitch, ultimately causing in 1999 a complete reorganization of the nuclear weapons program and its handling of classified information.[38]

The perceived loss of weapons information to the Chinese was reminiscent of the losses to the Soviets during the Manhattan Project, but there were many differences between the two situations that reflect how the challenge of protecting secret information has changed since then. Intensive studies of the Chinese program to acquire sensitive information showed that a large part of China's approach was simply to sift through the vast amount of publicly available information and synthesize classified information by inference. The Internet was an important tool for this process, as was information gained from thousands of contacts between Chinese scientists and their counterparts at the DOE national laboratories.

The evidence also suggests that China effectively exploited the natural human tendency of U.S. researchers to reveal what they knew, even if it edged close to classified information. The review panel convened to examine the leaks stated, "the Chinese services have become very proficient in the art of seemingly innocuous elicitations of information."[39] The low priority assigned to security issues by lab personnel also came under fire in the same report: "The predominant attitude toward security and counterintelligence among many DOE and lab managers has ranged from half-hearted, grudging accommodation to smug disregard."[40]

In 1999, the United States indicted Wen Ho Lee, a weapons scientist at Los Alamos National Laboratory, on fifty-nine counts of mishandling classified computer codes and databases with the intent "to secure an advantage to a foreign nation."[41] Investigators had discovered that Lee moved massive quantities of highly secret information from the secure computer systems at Los Alamos to an unsecure desktop computer that was connected to the Internet. But the government was unable to find evidence that any unauthorized access to this information occurred and was forced to plea-bargain the charges it had brought to a single charge of mishandling classified information.

More important than Lee's guilt or innocence regarding the other charges is what has been revealed about the gap between prescription and practice in the way weapons scientists deal with classified information. Knowledgeable scientists have defended him in the press, claiming he is just a scapegoat for the Chinese espionage debacle. The publisher of the highly respected *Bulletin of the Atomic Scientists* said that "many other scientists at Los Alamos and elsewhere have routinely violated those regulations." Others have taken great exception to the idea that lapses like Lee's are common or acceptable. Apparently, there is a wide range of attitudes toward such sloppiness across the different national laboratories and even within the same lab.[42]

The controversy about protecting classified information reveals an important aspect of how scientific secrecy works in an open society. Over time, a cultural consensus can develop in which some types of security breach are accepted by the rank and file whereas others are dealt with seriously. There are analogs in everyday life. Who really comes to a full stop at a stop sign? Who really drives 55 mph? What is culturally acceptable in breaching these rules is not the same as what is acceptable under the law, as strictly construed. The Lee case and the revelations that have emerged from it suggest that in the absence of a clear sense of emergency and a credible antagonist, it is difficult to maintain the discipline and intrusive oversight required to achieve a high degree of secrecy in technical matters.

These arguments invite a perspective that the purpose of secrecy should be seen as *delaying* the eventual diffusion of classified information, rather than *preventing* it. A natural tension between the demands of secrecy and the need to get work done is unavoidable. In some classified environments there will be a higher emphasis on secrecy. In others, there might be more emphasis on productivity.

This dichotomy has direct implications for the new U.S. tritium policy. Nuclear power plants like the ones the TVA intends to use for tritium production are protected by physical security systems that are far less elaborate than those of the U.S. nuclear weapons complex. There are virtually no controls on classified information; the emphasis is on preventing unauthorized access and sabotage. The addition of a new, secret technology for producing tritium at the plants will create two new concerns. First, there is the question of how well the secrets about the new technology will be kept. Second, there is the question of how the imposition of protections on classified information will affect the safety of the plant's operation.

It is highly likely that the answers to both will be unhappy. Backfitting an effective system for controlling classified information on an existing industrial operation is not easy and seldom successful. The implication of this observation is that soon after the TVA reactors are modified, the new technology for producing tritium, that is to say the design of the tritium-producing burnable absorber rods, will be in the hands of other countries, such as Pakistan, which is believed to be in the market for tritium production technology.[43]

But it is also likely that the new secrecy requirements, ineffectiveness notwithstanding, will have a deleterious effect on the safety of these nuclear plants. One mechanism through which safety may be compromised would be the additional security procedures required at the plants themselves to protect the classified information, complicating day-to-day operations. But more important by far is the potential impact of secrecy on oversight by regulators. Safety and secrecy are not independent. The historical record is clear that they tend to be in opposition. For example, immediately following the Chernobyl disaster, an angry *New York Times* editorial said, "Secrecy is a disease and Chernobyl is its symptom, a threat both to the Soviet Union and its neighbors."[44]

The opposition of safety and secrecy can also be seen in the United States. The next chapter begins with the discouraging story of how secrecy and isolation allowed concerns about safety and the environment to be shoved into the background during the first forty years of the operations of the nuclear weapons complex.

5

Tritium, the Lifeblood of the Nuclear Arsenal

The production of nuclear material for defense purposes by commercial power reactors licensed by the U.S. Nuclear Regulatory Commission would be contrary to the long-standing national policy to separate commercial nuclear power generation from the nuclear weapons program.

Draft Environmental Impact Statement for the New Production Reactor, 1991

Early Tritium Production

In the 1950s, early tests of the hydrogen bomb demonstrated to U.S. military planners that fission-fusion devices were far superior to pure fission weapons, since much more powerful bombs could be made with this new technology. In fact, the Russians eventually tested a bomb with a record yield of sixty megatons, the equivalent of sixty million tons of TNT. Such a gargantuan weapon was of little practical importance, however, because a few bombs with yields under ten megatons would cause far more damage. For these, the advantage of the fission-fusion hybrid design was that they were much smaller, lighter, and less susceptible to accidental detonation, leading to nuclear artillery shells and nuclear-tipped missiles, as well as lightweight bombs for delivery from aircraft. In contrast, pure fission weapons were large and heavy. The largest such bomb fielded by the United States was rated at 500 kilotons, or 0.5 megaton, but it remained in the stockpile for only a few years. By 1956 all weapons in the U.S. arsenal were fission-fusion hybrids.[1]

The tritium required for these fission-fusion weapons was most easily produced in nuclear reactors via neutron bombardment of lithium, a common element on the Earth's surface. Hence, the same reactors that produced the plutonium for the fission portion of a bomb could also produce tritium for its fusion boost. All that was needed was to modify the reactor cores to allow lithium "targets" to be inserted into the reactor core. After a sustained period of reactor operation, the neutron irradiation would cause tritium to build up in the targets, just as plutonium built up in the uranium fuel. Then the tritium for hydrogen bombs would be extracted from the target material via chemical processing.

In the early years of the arms race, the United States built one nuclear reactor after another for producing plutonium and/or tritium. Between 1944 and 1955 eight reactors were built at a remote location near Hanford, Washington, and five were built at the Savannah River site in rural South Carolina. Each of these was named simply by a letter of the alphabet, such as B, C, K, and L. When the N reactor was built at Hanford in 1964, the total number of production reactors built in the United States came to fourteen. All of them produced plutonium, but only a few also made tritium.

Tritium is unique among the nuclear ingredients of a bomb in that it has a rather short half-life, which is to say that any quantity of tritium will decrease over a relatively short time because of radioactive decay. The half-life of tritium is about twelve years, so that if one were to start with a gram of tritium gas today, then in twelve years there would be only half a gram, and in twenty-four years there would be only a quarter of a gram. Another way of saying this is that 5.5 percent of any tritium inventory decays away annually. In contrast, plutonium has a half life of 24,000 years, and uranium is even more stable, so the weapons complex doesn't need to worry about replacing the losses in these fissile materials due to radioactive decay. Of all the explosive ingredients in nuclear weapons, only tritium presents this problem. But on the other hand, no other material can substitute for tritium in its role of multiplying the power of the nuclear explosion by a large factor.

Thus, during the cold war the United States needed facilities to produce not only what tritium was needed for new weapons, but also additional tritium to replenish what was lost in existing weapons through radioactive decay. Above and beyond that, a substantial quantity of tritium was produced as a reserve against any possible interruption of supply. The Savannah River site produced all of the required tritium and shared with Hanford the much larger task of plutonium production.

Savannah River and Hanford were sprawling industrial complexes employing thousands of workers sworn to secrecy. Each site spanned hundreds of square miles of unpopulated land, isolated from scrutiny by security fences and patrolled continuously by armed guards. The prevailing cold war mentality ensured that the sites would carry out their business with minimal oversight from government agencies. Pervading the entire enterprise was a sense of urgency that often led to expedient measures for dealing with the hazards of the operations. Under intense pressure to maximize production, the site contractors often ignored growing problems of toxic and radioactive wastes and treated the issue of worker safety with far less concern than their counterparts in the private sector.

On the other side of the security fence, Americans were becoming more and more concerned about safety and the environment. In 1962, Rachel Carson's *Silent Spring*[2] sounded an eloquent early warning about chemical hazards in the nation's air and water. In 1965 Ralph Nader published *Unsafe at Any Speed*,[3] a best-selling indictment of the automobile industry's safety standards. Throughout the 1970s and 1980s, new laws and new agencies imposed increasingly stringent controls on private industry and public utilities. But the nuclear weapons complex was effectively insulated from these changes, protected by its cocoon of secrecy and made insensitive by its inbred cold warrior culture.

Starting at the end of the 1980s, the DOE would encounter its greatest crisis as the cold war wound down and the light of day revealed the sharp contrast between practices at the weapons complex and the rising expectations of the public concerning safety and the environment.

The Painful Encounter with the Safety Culture

The TMI accident in 1979 shook the commercial side of nuclear energy out of its complacency, but it had little impact on the reactor operations of the nuclear weapons complex. Such was the protection afforded by geographical remoteness and official secrecy in the name of national security. But when the Chernobyl reactor blew its top off in 1986, these protections proved inadequate, in part because cold war tensions were lessening at the time, but more because of the disturbing similarities between the Russian RBMK-1000 reactor that exploded and the N Reactor at Hanford. Both were graphite-moderated and heavy-water cooled.[4] Both used highly enriched uranium, rather than the slightly enriched fuel in commercial power plants. Neither plant had a robust containment building. And both operated behind a veil of secrecy.[5]

Defenders of the U.S. weapons complex were quick to take exception to these parallels, but the pressure for an independent review of the safety of the N reactor was immense. Soon after the Chernobyl accident, the General Accounting Office carried out a study that compared Chernobyl to Hanford's N reactor, drawing alarming conclusions. For a more in-depth assessment, the DOE called upon the National Academy of Sciences and the National Academy of Engineering to conduct a thorough and unbiased assessment of the safety of all the production reactors in the complex. Of these, only five were still operational at the time: C, K, L, and P at Savannah River and N at Hanford. The review committee was authorized to obtain whatever information was needed, classified or not. Its report, published in early 1987, was scathing in its criticism of the DOE and the safety of its reactors, most of which were based on designs from the 1950s.[6] In response to this and other studies, the DOE shut down the N and C reactors in 1987 and the remaining three in the following year.[7]

Over the course of the next four years the DOE would strive mightily, spending billions, to upgrade the safety features of some of these reactors. But their safety problems were rooted deeply in their outdated designs. To make matters worse, the harsh new light of external scrutiny was exposing major problems not only at the production reactors, but also at all of the operations in the weapons complex.

The vast U.S. nuclear weapons complex is scattered over about a hundred separate sites all over the country.[8] Figure 5 shows the locations of the complex's major facilities. In the late 1980s, highly unfavorable reports emerged about negligent environmental and safety practices at all sites, but particularly at the large operations marked with diamonds in the figure. They are Hanford (numbered 6 in the map), Idaho (7), Rocky Flats (26), Oak Ridge (20), and Savannah River (30)—all places where nuclear materials for bombs were produced, isotopically enriched, or processed into final form.

These materials and their waste products are among the most hazardous substances known to man. Without meticulous attention to industrial safety, the health of workers at these sites would be at great risk. Without painstaking care in handling and disposing of the waste,

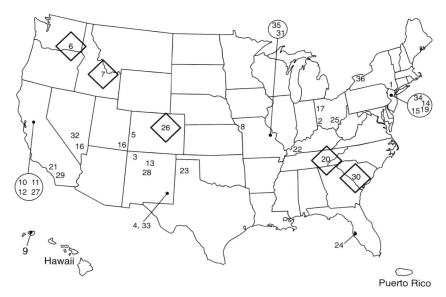

Figure 5
DOE weapons complex sites currently under environmental management. Numbers inside diamonds mark the sites where environmental problems are worst. *Source:* This map is adapted from <http://www.em.doe.gov/cercla/fig21.html>, provided by the DOE's Office of Environmental Management. It includes all facilities that are currently under the DOE/EM's remediation or management program. *Key:* **1** Colonie Site, NY; **2** Fernald Environmental Management Project, OH; **3** Gasbuggy, NM; **4** Gnome-Coach, NM; **5** Grand Junction Projects Office Remedial Action Project, CO; **6** Hanford Site, WA (excluding Pacific Northwest National Laboratory); **7** Idaho National Engineering Laboratory, ID; **8** Kansas City Plant, MO; **9** Kauai Test Facility, HI; **10** Laboratory for Energy-Related Health Research, CA; **11** Lawrence Livermore National Laboratory—Livermore Site, CA; **12** Lawrence Livermore National Laboratory—Site 300, CA; **13** Los Alamos National Laboratory, NM; **14** Maywood Site, NJ; **15** Middlesex Sampling Plant, NJ; **16** Monticello Mill Site and Monticello Vicinity Properties, UT; **17** Mound Plant, OH; **18** Nevada Test Site, NV; **19** New Brunswick Laboratory, NJ; **20** Oak Ridge Reservation, TN (excluding Oak Ridge National Laboratory); **21** Oxnard Facility, CA; **22** Paducah Gaseous Diffusion Plant, KY; **23** Pantex Plant, TX; **24** Pinellas Plant, FL; **25** Portsmouth Uranium Enrichment Complex, OH; **26** Rocky Flats Environmental Technology Site, CO; **27** Sandia National Laboratories/California, CA; **28** Sandia National Laboratories/New Mexico, NM; **29** Santa Susana Field Laboratories, CA; **30** Savannah River Site, SC; **31** St. Louis Site, MO; **32** Tonopah Test Range, NV (Sandia National Laboratories/Tonopah); **33** Waste Isolation Pilot Plant, NM (Carlsbad, NM); **34** Wayne Site, NJ; **35** Weldon Spring Site Remedial Action Project, MO; **36** West Valley Demonstration Project, NY.

there would be great danger as well to the environment and to the health of the public in the regions surrounding the sites. As legitimate revelations of abuses at the facilities spawned rumors and exaggeration, the issue of environmental and safety practices in the nuclear weapons complex soon became a scandal.

In 1989, George Bush was sworn in as president and moved quickly to deal with the crisis of confidence in the nuclear weapons complex by appointing Admiral James T. Watkins as his Secretary of Energy. Watkins had been chief of naval operations, the top job in the U.S. Navy, and brought to the new assignment a reputation for decisive and skillful management of complex organizations. He viewed the DOE's neglect of health and safety standards in its nuclear operations as inexcusable and vowed to bring the weapons complex into compliance with the law, regardless of the impact on operations. For the employees and contractors of the DOE, Watkins's four-year tenure was without doubt the most traumatic and stressful period in the department's history.[9]

Watkins soon learned what others who wanted to reform the DOE had found: the management structure of the department was so decentralized and convoluted that the secretary had precious few means of exerting real control over it. Management of operations was largely delegated to field offices that were geographically located in the hinterlands, near the major facilities. Powerful private contractors operated the facilities, employing armies of scientists, engineers, and industrial workers in the vast U.S. nuclear weapons machine. Predictably, the field offices and site contractors formed strong and lasting alliances, often working closely with their respective congressional delegations for the economic benefit of the regions where large sites were located. To be sure, the headquarters offices of the DOE were amply manned with civil servants, but central control was nonetheless weak. The overall arrangement was often characterized as feudal.

Watkins soon found that his influence on the weapons site environmental crisis was further diminished by the presence of other government players. Even before he took over the DOE, the Department of Justice and the Federal Bureau of Investigation (FBI) had developed substantial evidence of environmental misdeeds at the Rocky Flats Nuclear Weapons plant outside Denver. "Rocky" was operated by aerospace giant Rockwell International and employed about 6,000 people in various aspects of warhead manufacture. The government believed that improper storage and disposal of the deadly by-products of bomb manufacture at the site represented willful violations of environmental law. Moreover, it believed the public was at risk from these violations, since Denver's rapid expansion after the site was established in 1951 had brought civilian neighborhoods right up to the plant's fence.

Just one month after Watkins took office, the FBI and the DOE's inspector general jointly broke the bad news: they suspected that DOE field office personnel were colluding with company officials to hide widespread illegal mishandling of radioactive and hazardous materials at the Rocky Flats plant. The situation was grave, and the Justice Department had no intention of looking the other way in the interests of national security. It had decided to raid the site.

Steven Blush, who was later to become Watkins's director of nuclear safety, described the admiral's painful predicament: "For four months, while the FBI prepared to conduct a 'raid' of the plant, Watkins could take no action in order to avoid either the appearance or the reality of obstructing justice. Instead he helped the Justice Department lay the logistical groundwork for the raid, not least to avoid the possibility of a confrontation between the Rocky Flats security forces and armed agents of the FBI."[10] The FBI raid (designated Operation Desert Glow, strangely foreshadowing the upcoming military actions in the Persian Gulf) commenced one June morning in 1989. To ensure an effective operation, the FBI called upon Rockwell to assemble an emergency meeting of all senior managers for a briefing about imminent terrorist attacks by environmental militants. Under this cover story, nearly 100 heavily armed federal agents, mostly FBI, descended upon the 400-acre site and secured important locations throughout its 100 buildings. The agents remained in place for eighteen days and eventually left with over 100 cartons of evidence. Eight senior officials were indicted on criminal violations of environmental law. They were eventually spared when Rockwell pled the case, agreeing to a fine of $18.5 million.[11]

The bizarre Rocky Flats incident, coupled with penetrating and highly negative investigative journalism by the *New York Times*,[12] brought about a radical change in public attitude toward the weapons complex. At one time it had been viewed as a heroic scientific bastion in the war against an evil empire. It soon came to be seen as an arrogant radioactive polluter, hiding behind outdated notions of national emergency and mindless of the health and safety of workers and citizens. Feelings of alarm and concern spread through the weapons complex, no doubt helping Watkins capture the attention of his far-flung bureaucracy. But there was also a sense of betrayal and frustration, triggering the countervailing response of self-preservation and evasion.

Watkins soon found that his management hierarchy was unable to provide him with consistent and accurate quantitative information about safety and environmental problems at the various sites, so he embarked on a course of action typical of the nuclear Navy from which he hailed. He created an independent system of oversight reporting directly to him, the infamous DOE Tiger Teams. For three years, these squads of technical specialists, drafted mostly from the ranks of the weapons complex itself, visited the sites one at a time. They reviewed in excruciating detail all aspects of facility operations for compliance with applicable health and safety regulations. Blush recounts, "The Tiger Teams had an enormous impact, and it was not altogether a pleasant experience either for the teams or for the sites. The Tiger Teams were deeply resented, particularly by the laboratories who were being compelled to forego scientific and engineering research in order to permit in-house support groups of lesser status in the laboratories to pick over their operations."[13] Eventually, Watkins's shock treatment of the nuclear weapons complex permanently changed attitudes and behavior in the department's industrial operations. But forty years of environmental negligence left a legacy of nuclear waste that presented a colossal problem. For example, the amount of radioactively contaminated soil is 75 million cubic meters, enough to cover the island of Manhattan to a depth of 5 feet. There is enough contaminated groundwater to cover the island to a depth of 135 feet.[14] For much of this contamination, no technologies exist that can restore the environment to a safe condition.

In 1989 a new Environmental Management (EM) Office in the DOE was created to deal with remediation, or at least responsible management, of the environmental catastrophe at the weapons sites. The EM office soon commanded the largest budget of any DOE office (the 2002 budget appropriation was over $7 billion). Between 1989 and 1999, it spent over $50 billion on the cleanup job but has nevertheless made only limited progress. An additional $150 to $200 billion will be needed to finish the job, which will take an estimated seventy years.[15] More than 75 percent of those costs will be incurred at the five sites highlighted in figure 5. These estimates would be even higher if they included the costs of maintaining in perpetuity the various facilities for storing the nuclear waste that is the deadly legacy of the cold war.

Faced with this emerging picture, Watkins had the unpleasant duty of shaking up his vast, recalcitrant command and forever changing "business as usual." He had to do this despite an impatient Congress, a terrible image with the media, a hostile relationship with the Environmental Protection Agency, a growing alliance between environmental and antinuclear activists, and, at the sites, a collection of very smart facility managers who saw the cleanup as simply a way to replace jobs that were lost when the arms race ended.

Despite these troubles, concerns about the dwindling tritium reserves in the weapons complex were ever present. To deal with them, Watkins pursued a two-part strategy. First, one or more of the complex's shutdown production reactors would be refurbished and upgraded with modern safety features. Second, a top-priority New Production Reactor (NPR) program would be pushed full-speed ahead to build a major new tritium production facility that could satisfy the nation's tritium needs into the middle of the twenty-first century. The next section will show that, despite Watkins's best efforts and billions in expenditures, he was to leave office having achieved neither of these goals.

Beauty Contests

As early as the 1970s there was a broad consensus among defense planners that the aging production reactors had a limited life and that modern replacement facilities were needed. On the other hand, there was little need for continued plutonium production, since adequate supplies were available for any foreseeable size of the nuclear arsenal. The problem was tritium, because of its short half-life. Regardless of whether the arsenal was large or small, a steady supply of tritium would eventually be needed to replenish the 5.5 percent of the inventory that decayed away each year.

In the last quarter century, three phases can be recognized in the DOE's efforts to establish new lines of supply for tritium (see table 2).

Table 2
Phases of DOE efforts to replace tritium supply

	Period	Presidents	Secretaries of Energy
Phase 1	1976–1988	Carter, Reagan	numerous
Phase 2	1988–1992	Bush (G. H. W.)	Watkins
Phase 3	1992–2002	Clinton, Bush (G. W.)	O'Leary, Peña, Richardson, Abraham

The first phase was the period from the late 1970s to 1988, characterized by many false starts and stalled initiatives, plenty of controversy but no real progress. The second phase was more purposeful, driven by the shutdown of all production reactors after the Chernobyl accident. This phase coincided with the tenure of Watkins as Secretary of Energy, ending in 1992 when President G. H. W. Bush terminated the NPR program because of progress in arms reduction. The third phase lasted from then to the present and produced the DOE decision to choose irradiation of lithium targets in commercial power reactors as the favored path for producing the nation's supply of tritium. By analyzing parallel trends in each of these three phases, we can learn a great deal about the underlying forces that make decision making so difficult for the DOE.

Phase 1: The Early Years
All of the DOE's tritium-producing reactors came on line between 1953 and 1955.[16] Their designs, long outdated, were a known liability for the weapons complex. The same ACRS that reviewed commercial reactor safety was also chartered to evaluate the safety of defense production reactors. For decades, the ACRS was highly critical of many features of the production reactors, first and foremost of which was the absence of a strong containment. As discussed in chapter 3, advocates of strong containment buildings for commercial reactors were successful with the AEC, but they lost the argument regarding the production reactors. Instead, the production reactors utilized relatively conventional building construction, supplemented by a "confinement system" that comprised large fans, ducts, and filters for removing radioisotopes from the building's atmosphere in the event of an accidental release from the reactor. And, of course, the sites were extremely isolated.

Still, the pressure from the ACRS and numerous other quarters had a cumulative effect that persuaded the DOE to develop plans to build a new facility for its long-term tritium needs. In the pre-1988 phase of this effort, the decision process for settling on a design and a location for the new reactor turned out to be much more complicated than it had been in the 1950s. Back then, a small cadre of closely knit nuclear leaders worked together under the tight security and intense time pressure that characterized the early years of the cold war. The only congressional oversight was by the highly cooperative Joint Committee on Atomic Energy. The reorganizations of the AEC in the 1970s, which eventually produced the DOE in 1977, distributed the jurisdiction of the weapons complex over at least seven separate congressional committees.[17] The official DOE historian of the NPR program, Rodney Carlisle, describes the resulting decision environment for site selection this way: "When a new production reactor was planned, political advocates of various sites had many more congressional venues for attempting to influence the choice of sites. Even after a site was chosen, advocates of other potential sites could use their representation in Congress to delay action and request further study. The number of senators and representatives directly affected by reactor siting had become quite large."[18] The choice of reactor technology was similarly politicized. Each of the competing design concepts was promoted by a different major corporate player who saw winning the contract as critical to the survival of its struggling nuclear division. Thus, the tritium supply decision involved a matrix of sites and technologies, each with its own insistent advocates and fierce opponents.

In the election of 1980, the Republicans gained not only the White House, but also both houses of Congress. Two powerful Republican senators, James McClure of Idaho and Strom Thurmond of South Carolina, ascended to key positions of power, and each would spend the next ten years maneuvering to get his state chosen as the site for the DOE's new tritium facility. They were joined for one battle or another by loose and changing coalitions of other members of Congress and corporate stakeholders.

The DOE attempted to make progress despite the growing influence of pork barrel politics by relying on independent panels of recognized technical experts. Carlisle recounts how this strategy ran aground:

Although the secretaries of energy hoped to get from prestigious experts objective and technical evaluations, the groups' reports themselves became politicized. ... If a group of experts advocated expenditure or planning without specifying site or technology, proponents of different reactor designs and locations could all agree upon the report as an argument for action. However, if members of a technical panel favored one choice over others, opponents criticized them as biased.[19]

To make matters worse, in the mid-1980s local and national antinuclear groups became more vocal and visible, insisting on community involvement and open decision processes. As a result of these barriers to progress, the DOE went through cycle upon cycle of new studies followed by preliminary decisions followed by political reaction followed by starting over again. Much paper was produced, but the nation continued its total reliance on the aging Savannah River reactors for its supply of tritium.

Phase 2: A New Urgency
The environment and safety crisis in the weapons complex following the Chernobyl accident brought a new sense of urgency to the tritium production issue and opened a new phase in the DOE's quest for a new facility to produce tritium. The cessation of all tritium production with the shutdown of the Savannah River reactors in 1988 signified to military planners that a clock was ticking: the tritium clock. The nation's reserve supply of the gas would be slowly consumed as each weapon was periodically recharged. Without a fresh supply, a time would come when some weapons would have to be decommissioned to provide tritium for others. This would force a kind of slow, unilateral nuclear arms reduction, a concept that a few brave thinkers[20] found appealing but was viewed with horror by most of the nuclear weapons establishment.

As noted in the previous section, James Watkins was brought in to run the DOE because of his reputation as a no-nonsense manager who could get things done in highly complex organizations. Although most of his energy would be taken up by the challenge of cleaning up the mess at the weapons production sites, he took very seriously the need to reestablish an adequate supply of tritium to replenish the nation's nuclear weapons. Taking note of the chaotic decision processes of the past, he brought in another outsider, Dominic Monetta, to run the now top-priority NPR program.

Monetta had no ties to any particular site or technology for the new production reactor, and in earlier encounters with Watkins in Navy programs he had demonstrated a strong and smart management style. His post was created at a level equivalent to that of the assistant secretary responsible for all other aspects of nuclear weapons, and his NPR program was designated as one of the top priorities of the department. These steps gave him the power he would need within the DOE to execute a successful program.

To avoid the pattern of failure of previous tritium programs, Monetta and his staff designed an elaborate process for selecting a technology and location for the new facility. This technology "beauty contest" would work in such a way that each major corporate player would continue to have a good a chance of winning well along in the process, thus avoiding early congressional interference with the program.

There were three design concepts in competition for the technology choice:

· the modular high-temperature gas-cooled reactor (MHTGR), an advanced concept that had been explored in demonstration reactors in the United States and Germany. It offered exceptional resistance to overheating accidents because it used fuel in the form of millions of small spheres encased in heat-resistant ceramic and because the coolant it used was gas, not liquid.

· the heavy-water reactor (HWR), an upgraded version of the tritium-producing reactors at Savannah River with modern, high-reliability systems, a strong containment, and advanced safety features.

· the light-water reactor (LWR), a concept whereby an unfinished commercial reactor in Washington state (WNP-1) would be purchased and modified to accept lithium targets.

There were also three contestants in the site competition: Idaho, Savannah River, and Hanford (the location of the unfinished WNP-1 plant). The site selection process had a key feature that diminished the intensity of the competitive environment: two plants would be built, each at a different site and each with a different technology. Hence, there would be only one losing site and one losing technology. Presumably, the political clout of the winners would help defend the outcome of the contest against the opposition of the losers.

In reality, the LWR option, under development at the DOE's Pacific Northwest Laboratory, near Hanford, was widely viewed as a long shot.

It is not entirely clear why that was so, but a cynic might point out that since this option was irrevocably tied to Washington state, it was guaranteed to be opposed by the two powerful congressional delegations from South Carolina and Idaho. Another insight comes from the massive draft environmental impact statement (EIS)[21] prepared by the DOE to evaluate all combinations of sites and technologies. A fundamental principle asserted in the EIS was that U.S. law and policy prohibited an NRC-licensed commercial reactor from producing tritium for nuclear weapons.[22] This restriction implied that if the LWR were selected, the DOE would have to complete the construction of WNP-1 at its own expense, operate it, and then sell the steam to local electric utilities (as the N reactor had done), rather than let a utility operate the dual-purpose plant. Thus, the LWR option was less attractive in this round than it would be in the third phase of the DOE's tritium quest, when the obstacles for producing tritium at NRC-licensed plants somehow disappeared (a development to be discussed in more detail later in the chapter).

The other two technology candidates, MHTGR and HWR, were seen as having a far better chance of being selected than the LWR approach. Only one bidder, a consortium of companies called CEGA, responded to the DOE's Request for Proposals for the MHTGR design, but two groups came in with HWR design proposals. One was a corporate team led by the prominent architecture/engineering company Ebasco, and the other was Westinghouse, a major reactor vendor. Thus from early on in the program, a competitive selection was needed only on the HWR side, not for the MHTGR or LWR.

In setting up the rules of engagement for the competition, Monetta demonstrated his understanding of how similar contests had failed in the past. First, he obtained substantial funding for all three major teams to develop detailed conceptual designs for the NPR, and a smaller amount for the LWR team at PNL to research key aspects of lithium targets. Second, he notified the two HWR teams that he expected the winning team to let the loser in on substantial parts of the design and construction work after the selection of a contractor was made. Thus there would be a piece of the pie for everyone, hence less incentive to flex congressional muscle after the DOE's decision.

Monetta also insisted on new rules for the DOE's national laboratories, such as Los Alamos, Argonne, and Sandia. He wanted no divided loyalties and no playing of one design concept against the other for the benefit of the laboratories.[23] For example, he insisted that each national laboratory work in support of at most one technology concept and that all activities at each laboratory be coordinated through a single point of contact. He also required each laboratory to set up a dedicated program office in Washington, D.C., so that coordination with DOE staff would occur naturally and frequently. In this and other ways, Monetta broke the traditional pattern of how the national laboratories worked with DOE headquarters. Reactions to the changes were mixed, as Carlisle notes: "As might be expected, his methods sometimes irritated long-term DOE staff members in established offices and some contractors who were used to a less demanding style and pace; others found the new approach refreshing."[24]

In 1990, the effectiveness of Monetta's approach to the beauty contest became clear when his office selected the HWR winner and afterward received no significant political interference. The Ebasco team won the day and proceeded to negotiate with the Westinghouse team to delegate to it some of the technical roles in the future program.

Both HWR design teams had submitted competent proposals, but an elaborate scoring process involving hundreds of reviewers from the DOE and the national laboratories ensured that the basis for the final selection was unassailable. One of the remarkable aspects of the winning proposal was the attention it paid to reactor safety. The head of the Ebasco team, Robert Iotti, believed that because of the importance of the tritium supply, the DOE should build a facility that went far beyond the safety requirements of commercial power reactors. He claimed that the Ebasco design would be "the safest reactor ever built."[25] The MHTGR team also made dramatic safety claims, based on the inherent integrity of their ceramic fuel and the benign properties of gas cooling. Such was the atmosphere three years after Chernobyl that both teams knew the image of an ultrasafe reactor would be received warmly by the DOE. Eight years later, in the third phase of the DOE's quest for a source of tritium, this emphasis on extraordinary safety would be strangely absent.

The Ebasco design was based on that of Savannah River's K reactor, which, like all the production reactors, had been shut down because of safety concerns. The Ebasco team realized that critics would expect convincing arguments that whatever problems existed with the original K reactor design were more than adequately dealt with in the new design. It also realized that, as with commercial reactors, the risk associated with operating the production reactors would lie almost entirely in the realm of low-probability, high-consequence accidents—that is, core melt accidents. Its approach to safety was therefore straightforward: anticipate severe accident scenarios early in the design stage and ensure that systems in the plant effectively mitigate the most important scenarios.

This design approach found great favor with the DOE and its review panels, and the idea of "designing out" severe accidents took strong roots in the Ebasco HWR project. In support of the design effort, the DOE sponsored research at Sandia, Argonne, and Savannah River on severe-accident phenomena. The research program drew strongly on the much broader activity in the NRC. Like the NRC's post-TMI program, discussed in chapter 3, it included experiments, computer code development, and probabilistic risk assessment.

Taking such a proactive approach to severe accidents in the HWR, however, presented a subtle danger for the DOE. The K reactor on which the Ebasco design was based was still undergoing massive retrofits to deal with the worst of its safety problems. Secretary Watkins's plan was to get the upgraded K reactor approved for operation, restart it for one tritium production cycle of a year or so, and then put the plant on standby as a backup in case a tritium supply was urgently needed before the NPR was ready. The HWR research on severe accidents might draw attention to some K reactor problems that could not be fixed with the ongoing refurbishment and thus generate resistance to Watkins's plan. Many in the DOE's reactor safety programs were inclined to follow the old proscription "don't turn over a rock if you are unprepared for what lies beneath." Some voices in the K reactor camp therefore called for caution in proceeding down the severe-accident research path.

The leaders of the HWR design program were sympathetic with this argument, but believed that since the K reactor restart was to be a brief demonstration run, not a long-term program of operations, a lighter standard of safety would be tolerated in the event that new problems were uncovered in the HWR research. Besides, they argued, the goal of a permanent and stable tritium supply was more important than the backup capability the K reactor would provide. Furthermore, the design team believed that if an aggressive and sincere effort was not made to understand severe accidents in HWRs and to design around them, gaining final approval for construction of the HWR plant might be very difficult. Underlying that concern was the lingering question of whether, in the long run, Congress would agree with Monetta's plan to build both the HWR and the MHTGR. A runoff between these two contenders would be brutal and intense, and both sides paid careful attention to how their actions might affect such a future competition.

So the proponents of the outdated K reactor feared getting into a damaging beauty contest with the modern HWR, and the two principal NPR contenders feared a final beauty contest against each other. In the tortured history of this second phase of the DOE's quest for tritium, both fears would come true. And in the end, each contestant in this strange three-way competition would lose.

One of the difficult things about conducting severe-accident research is that it is often easier to formulate accident scenarios and estimate their consequences than it is to calculate the probabilities that they will actually occur. Researchers therefore often explore an extreme scenario and later learn that its probability is so low that other scenarios are more important contributors to risk. For any progress to be made, however, studies must proceed in parallel down two tracks: consequence estimation and probability estimation. For that reason, the severe-accident analysts for the HWR studied a variety of events that might occur in hypothetical accidents without knowing for sure whether those conditions surrounding those events would ever be encountered. Many issues were explored, but two of them generated a great deal of anxiety because of the potential they presented for extremely energetic accidents similar to the one that occurred at Chernobyl.

The first issue was the concern that the fission processes in the reactor might "run away," as they do in a bomb. The difference between a nuclear bomb and a nuclear reactor is the following: in the chain reaction of a bomb, the rate of neutron multiplication increases exponentially until the device explodes into a hot plasma; in a reactor, the multiplication rate stays at precisely one, which is to say that, on average, only one neutron from each nuclear fission event succeeds in causing another fission event. There are numerous inherent mechanisms in reactor configurations that prevent the multiplication rate from exceeding one, and as a result the power produced in the reactor is steady, not escalating.

Commercial U.S. designs are exceedingly resistant to dangerous neutronic excursions that would occur if the multiplier increased above one for more than a fraction of a second. In contrast, the Chernobyl reactor had a severe design flaw: under some conditions the formation of steam bubbles due to boiling of water in the reactor core would cause the reactivity to increase above one, a trait that in nuclear engineering jargon is called a "positive void coefficient." In a reactor with a positive void coefficient, the increased reactivity that occurs with boiling will cause even more rapid boiling, making the problem worse. The escalating power generation due to a positive void coefficient destroyed the Chernobyl reactor in seconds. To U.S. reactor designers, positive void coefficients are anathema, and the HWR did not suffer from the design flaws that led to the positive void coefficients in the Chernobyl reactor. But it had a different problem: a potential for a runaway if fuel and target material separated from each other.

Normally the nuclear fuel (uranium) and the target material (lithium) in the HWR are packaged tightly together in a "fuel-target assembly" consisting of alternating concentric cylinders with gaps between them to allow cooling water to flow. Thus the uranium, where excess neutrons are produced, and the lithium, where they are absorbed, are always in close proximity. In a meltdown, however, portions of the target might become separated from the uranium fuel, resulting in excess neutron production in the regions that have too little target material—in other words, a local neutronic excursion. How serious this might be would depend on many unknowns, such as the extent of the separation between the fuel and target. If the neutronic excursion created a hot spot in the core that in turn increased the separation of fuel and target, the result would be another positive feedback situation, possibly resulting in a runaway of reactivity. Argonne[26] researchers calculated the reactor behavior in this scenario and found that the energy release might be modest or it might be very large—enough to launch the top of the reactor vessel as a missile that could strike and crack open the containment building.

The second issue that generated anxiety was the potential for explosive aluminum-water interactions. Because of experience in the aluminum industry, researchers at Sandia knew that under some circumstances mixtures of molten aluminum and water could spontaneously explode. Such explosions can be very violent, and despite decades of research by the aluminum industry and considerable effort to prevent them, many foundry workers have died from such accidents. Because the proposed HWR would use large quantities of aluminum in its target assemblies, a core meltdown might mix molten aluminum with water, causing an explosion. Sandia therefore conducted a research program to study what caused these violent reactions and what might prevent them. Experimenters set up a series of tests in the New Mexico desert to simulate worst-case conditions of melt-water interactions. Some of the tests resulted in explosions of surprising energy, in some cases destroying the test apparatus.[27]

Taken separately, each of these issues was a cause for concern, but an even more alarming possibility was that the two processes might occur simultaneously, one causing the other. For example, an aluminum-water explosion might cause a separation between fuel and target, or vice versa. As uncertain as each of these two phenomena was, the uncertainty became even greater when people started thinking about how the two processes might work together. Since completely overcoming this uncertainty was impossible, the DOE and its HWR designer had two possible avenues for dealing with the problem. They could carefully evaluate the probability of such events' occurring and demonstrate that the risk was acceptable, or they could design a containment building that would retain its integrity even if an extreme version of the event occurred. Reflecting the safety consciousness of the times, they chose to do both, starting with the containment design work.

Ultrastrong containments had been the subject of theoretical work at various institutes around the world, but particularly in Germany, where the political consequences of Chernobyl threatened the very life of the nuclear industry. When Ebasco decided to design a containment that could absorb the impact of an exploding reactor, it found that it could adapt the German designs, add its own concepts, and come up with a system that could withstand a very severe event. To answer the question "how severe?" the DOE commissioned a panel of experts who systematically evaluated the most extreme threats to the containment, including the possibility of a large section of the exploding reactor's striking the building from the inside.[28] With quantitative design requirements from this panel, Ebasco was able to develop a design for an ultrastrong containment that did not greatly increase the cost of the HWR plant. Thus, a potential safety problem with the reactor design was overcome early and at low cost, instead of later, when a solution might require expensive rework and retrofits. And the wisdom of studying severe accidents in the design phase was confirmed.

On the other side of the NPR contest, the MHTGR concept did not have the severe-accident vulnerability of the HWR, but it presented its own challenges. In particular, the tiny fuel spheres used in the MHTGR had to be manufactured to extremely close tolerances, because slight defects in their ceramic shells could cause leakage of tritium into the core during operation, forcing premature termination of production runs and time-consuming cleanup and refueling. The problem for the MHTGR team was that no manufacturer in the world then had the ability to fabricate spheres to these demanding tolerances. But the team worked assiduously at improving the technology for manufacturing the fuel pellets and expressed great confidence that it would achieve success within the time frame it was given. It was also aware, however, that the adept manner in which Ebasco had overcome its severe-accident disadvantage would make the HWR a more formidable competitor if there were ever to be a runoff between the two concepts.

In the third corner of the beauty contest triangle sat the K reactor. Watkins's goal of establishing the K reactor as a demonstrated backup capability consumed prodigious sums of money. Eventually $1.5 billion went to upgrades to various features of the reactor that had been the subject of criticism over the years.[29] But installing a strong containment building, much less an ultrastrong one, appeared impractical. Consequently, the dramatic results from the severe-accident research at Argonne and Sandia did not help the K reactor's image problems, since the analyses were as applicable to it as they were to the new design. Likewise, Ebasco's forthright engineering solution to the threatening accident scenario may have had the inadvertent effect of making the K reactor upgrades appear to be insufficient. These and other problems for the K reactor would come to the fore when a breakthrough in the nuclear arms race brought about the endgame of Phase 2 in the DOE's quest for tritium.

In 1991, dramatic progress in nuclear arms reduction talks with the Soviets led the U.S. government to rethink the proposed strategy of building two separate NPRs, despite Monetta's desire to avoid congressional conflict over siting. In February of that year, the DOE announced that there would be another selection, this time between the MHTGR and the HWR designs—just what the two sides had feared all along.[30] That change also implied there would only be one winning site, and within three months, the competition between Idaho and South Carolina reappeared in the form of an amendment to the 1992 defense budget virtually requiring that any NPR be built in South Carolina.[31] Clearly, Monetta's carefully fashioned management process was falling apart.

The competition between the two alternative technologies also began heating up, evidenced by a flurry of news stories in which the proponents of each approach took the six-billion-dollar contest public, boosting their own design and demeaning their opponent's. Also hitting the news were stories (many highly distorted) about how the accident scenarios discovered for the HWR were a potential safety problem for the K reactor.[32] With diminished priority assigned to the tritium program, Monetta found himself scrambling to protect his budget, an exercise that led to a bitter conflict with his erstwhile patron, James Watkins.

There are conflicting accounts of how and why Monetta's term as head of the NPR program was summarily ended in November 1991. The rapidly moving drama began in September when President Bush announced a plan to reduce the size of the nation's nuclear arsenal dramatically. The plan called for surplusing thousands of short-range weapons, so the effective inventory of tritium for recharging the remaining weapons instantaneously surged, and the perceived urgency of the DOE's efforts to restore a tritium supply simultaneously plunged.[33] At the end of October, the House-Senate conference committee on the 1992 defense authorization bill revised the budget by deauthorizing some $350 million from the K restart budget and tentatively earmarking it for the NPR program. Watkins was furious and believed that Monetta and NPR contractors had worked with Senator Sam Nunn and other committee members to fashion the change.[34]

At this point in Watkins's tour of duty at the DOE, the K reactor restart had taken on enhanced importance to him, because there was widespread belief that he would be replaced after the presidential election of 1992, regardless of whether the president won or lost his bid for reelection. The actual restart was scheduled for December 1991, and achieving that milestone would give Watkins's tenure at the DOE a much-needed success story. In contrast, the NPR program was unlikely to produce concrete achievements in the year or so left in Bush's first term. Clearly, Monetta would not share these same priorities, so the suspicion that he was working Congress behind Watkins's back had some plausibility.

The DOE was committed to choosing between the HWR and the MHTGR by the end of the year, at that point just two months away. Watkins responded to the conference committee's budget action by peremptorily postponing that decision for two years. He justified the delay on the grounds of the diminished urgency of the nation's tritium needs, but his action was widely seen as retaliation against congressional lobbying by Monetta and other NPR program stakeholders. The postponement was a hard blow to the NPR program, as it would remove much of the incentive for funding detailed design work during the intervening years. A few days after the announcement, Monetta resigned, reportedly at Watkins's request.[35] His carefully thought-through management system had succumbed to the same forces that had vitiated earlier DOE efforts to restore the tritium supply.

Ironically, the legislative language that had prompted Watkins's intemperate actions was eventually removed from the authorization bill. In any case, the brouhaha would have no effect on the scheduled restart of K reactor, which was slated for the last few days of 1991. Despite persistent questions from Senator Nunn and others about the aging reactor's safety and the need to bring it back into operation,[36] Watkins had no intention of halting the expensive program at the brink of success. Equally ignored was a petition opposing the restart that was circulated by the antinuclear group Greenpeace and signed by some 120,000 people.[37]

The restart was not to be stopped by opposition from outside the DOE, however; instead, failure was brought about by the very same internal problems of apathy and inattention to safety that all along were Watkins's principal challenge with respect to the weapons complex. During preparations for the restart of the K reactor, 150 gallons of highly radioactive water leaked from the reactor into the Savannah River over a two-day period.[38] Downstream citizens in Georgia and South Carolina were switched to alternative water supplies until the danger subsided, but the aftermath of the incident revealed grave lapses in the DOE's oversight of reactor facilities at the Savannah River site. First, it was revealed that a report in November of that year from a DOE-sponsored task force had warned explicitly about the type of leak that had occurred during startup preparations and that continuous monitoring was needed. These warnings had apparently been ignored.[39] Then it was reported that the leak was undetected for two days because the person in charge of authorizing transportation of the water samples to a nearby laboratory was out with the flu. In the world of reactor safety, such an event was unforgivable.

The leak at the K reactor caused the restart to be postponed, and soon lawmakers from both Georgia and South Carolina importuned the DOE to slow down the program or even terminate it.[40] Then another tritium leak in May 1992 captured great media attention, even though it was quite small. Undaunted, Watkins sparred with legislators on the K reactor question throughout 1992, repeatedly scheduling and rescheduling the restart as the year waned and the politics of the presidential election took center stage. In the end, the arguments against putting the old tritium plant back on line overcame the secretary's desire to do so, and he left office having failed to achieve his four-year ambition of restarting the K reactor. His successor in the Clinton administration, Hazel O'Leary, closed the program down in March 1993 and ordered the reactor to be placed on cold standby indefinitely.

In the meantime, the Bush administration had made further progress in strategic arms talks with the Russians. Seizing this progress for maximum benefit to the election campaign, President Bush announced in September that the entire NPR program would be terminated so that the funds could be directed to other needed activities—part of the "peace dividend" from the end of the cold war. The plan was to defer all further work until 1995, at which time the DOE would reassess the tritium needs of the nuclear arsenal and start anew the whole decision process about siting and technology.

In Bush's four years, over $3 billion had been spent to restore a tritium supply, but to show for it there was only an upgraded but inoperable K reactor and paper: mountains of design documents for the competing technologies. Strangely, in the next competition, the two technologies chosen as the front-runners by the DOE would include neither the HWR nor the MHTGR. In this and many other ways the nature of the third phase of DOE's tritium program would differ dramatically from that pursued in Monetta's tenure, so much so that it would seem more as if thirty years had passed than three.

From "Unreasonable" to "Reasonable" in the Blink of an Eye

With the election of a Democratic president, Bill Clinton, the Watkins phase of DOE's tritium quest ended, and the aftermath was not unlike that of a small war with no winners. For the leading combatants, the HWR and MHTGR consortia, the troops were demobilized, the wounded cared for, the lessons noted. Warehouses were stuffed with boxes of surplus, in this case, paper records. For the minor contestants, the two-year delay was an opportunity to revise strategies and lay the foundation for the competition to come. In the mid-1990s, two new leaders emerged that had been distant contenders in the earlier rounds: the accelerator production of tritium (APT) concept, and the commercial light-water reactor (CLWR) concept.

Starting with Ernest Lawrence's cyclotrons in the 1920s, high-energy particle accelerators were the most important research tools nuclear physicists had for studying the structure of atoms and subatomic particles. To probe deeper into the atomic nucleus, these exotic machines had to be made ever larger, and eventually they became so costly that only international collaborations could afford them. Costs for machines at the cutting edge of research became so astronomical that governments eventually pulled the plug on some projects, like the superconducting super-collider, in midconstruction. But the cost pressure also forced scientists and engineers to devise cheaper and more efficient accelerator designs. In the 1980s, scientists at Los Alamos National Laboratory and elsewhere began exploring industrial applications of particle accelerators. One of the most promising was the production of tritium without the use of a nuclear reactor.

Tritium production requires accelerators that, compared with today's powerful research machines, are of only modest energy and complexity. The Los Alamos concept (figure 6) uses a linear accelerator, consisting of a long, straight evacuated tube surrounded by electrical coils. Pro-

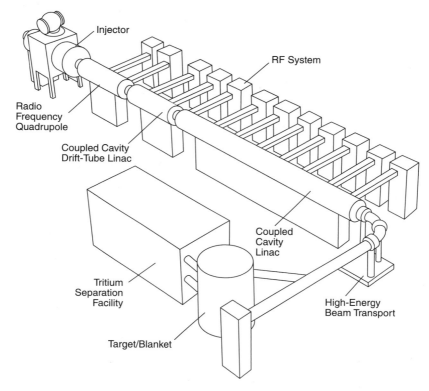

Figure 6
Conceptual diagram of the APT system. *Source:* Los Alamos National Laboratory (http://apt. lanl.gov/).

grammed pulses applied to the coils accelerate protons to very high energies, at which point they are diverted into a different building. There the protons collide with specially designed targets and produce great quantities of neutrons. Then, just as in a tritium-producing nuclear reactor, the neutrons collide with lithium atoms to produce tritium.[41] The principal advantages of this method over reactor production of tritium: very little nuclear waste and very little chance of a dangerous nuclear accident.

The APT concept was received enthusiastically in many quarters, including Watkins's office near the end of his tenure,[42] but it fared poorly in competition with the leading concepts because of its high cost and unproven effectiveness. One early study argued that an accelerator system large enough to satisfy the nation's annual tritium needs would require so much electricity that a dedicated nuclear power plant would have to be built nearby, thereby vitiating the concept's principal advantage.

For the third phase of the DOE's search for a new tritium source, the passage of time had helped the accelerator concept in two ways: first, the "goal quantity" of annual tritium production was reduced by a factor of five (assuming START-II compliance), and second, Los Alamos and its collaborators had convincingly demonstrated key aspects of the technology. By 1995, APT was the clear preference by the DOE's management, including Secretary of Energy Hazel O'Leary. In October of that year, a $3 billion contract was placed with the giant architecture/engineering firm Burns & Rowe to design and (possibly) build a tritium-producing accelerator system at the Savannah River site.[43]

O'Leary's decision was not, of course, without its detractors. Over the years a variety of concepts for producing tritium in commercial reactors had been floated, and various alliances of interested players had been forged. Reactor proponents had seen the NPR as the lifeline for commercial nuclear electricity: whoever got to build it would lead the entire industry when the inevitable resurgence of plant orders occurred.

By 1995, such aspirations had been greatly downsized, but supporters of reactor concepts had many friends in the government and warned against gambling the future of the weapons arsenal on an unproven technology. The secretary placated the congressional supporters of commercial reactor production of tritium by announcing a "dual-track" strategy for tritium production.[44] The APT was the preferred alternative and was to be heavily funded, but the CLWR track would continue to be studied as a backup in the event of a national emergency. The "national emergency" phrase reflected the widely held view that producing bomb material in civilian nuclear plants was contrary to U.S. nonproliferation policy. It is the same phrase found in the Hart-Simpson amendment to the Atomic Energy Act prohibiting production of plutonium in commercial reactors, *except in the case of a national emergency.*

Before the secretary's dual-track announcement, she had been assailed as "anti–nuclear power" by CLWR proponents, who cited as evidence her numerous appointments of antinuclear activists to key positions in the department. In response, her deputy secretary testified to Congress that O'Leary was by no means against nuclear power, but the country's strong antiproliferation policy dictated that CLWR be treated as a backup only for a national emergency or war.[45]

In the meantime, however, some little-noticed maneuvering by the DOE's CLWR camp was laying the groundwork for an assault on this policy.[46] The first stage of its campaign was to remove a barrier that had been created in the draft programmatic EIS for the government's tritium supply program.[47] A tough environmental law, the National Environmental Policy Act, a product of the country's growing environmental awareness and its distrust of government agencies, requires an EIS for all "major Federal actions significantly affecting the quality of the human environment."[48] The EIS serves as early notice to the public and other stakeholders, explaining the government's rationale for carrying out major projects.

The March 1995 draft EIS on tritium supply was a massive document discussing all the candidate technologies for the production, extraction, and recycling of tritium and all the possible sites for these activities. The CLWR option was considered technically viable but was deemed an "unreasonable alternative" because of the nation's well-established nonproliferation policy. In this regard, the 1995 draft EIS was completely consistent with the 1991 EIS on the NPR program.[49]

Normally, the DOE would produce a final EIS after it had digested comments obtained from public meetings and other outreach efforts, but in this case the department made a surprise move. In August, it announced that the comment period was being extended specifically for additional feedback about whether the commercial-reactor option should be considered reasonable or unreasonable.[50] Over the next few months, the DOE received numerous additional written comments, and in October the final programmatic EIS was published.[51] Astonishingly, the CLWR had been upgraded in the final EIS from an "unreasonable alternative" to a "reasonable alternative."

This surprising reversal was based on the thinnest of tissues. The final EIS noted that the DOE's extension of the comment period was "a result of public comments."[52] It also said that nonproliferation concerns were one of just two major issues raised in the extended comment period. By implication, public comments were the reason for changing the word "unreasonable" to "reasonable," since the final EIS gave no other explanation for the change.

Scant evidence exists to support the DOE's claim that public comments motivated the change in the CLWR's status. All public comments in response to the draft EIS are documented and catalogued in volume 3 of this massive report. Careful study (for details, see appendix A) reveals not only that in the period before the extension there were only four individuals offering comments on mixing civilian and military missions at nuclear facilities, but also that three of the four were *against* it. In the extended comment period, the views ran fifteen against dual use versus three in favor, and two of those three were executives of corporations standing to benefit from the change in policy. This evidence hardly constitutes a groundswell of public opinion, but it was apparently enough to transform an "unreasonable" alternative into a "reasonable" one.

Press reports, however, attributed at least some of the sentiment for the reversal to a consultant's study released in July, after the first comment period was over.[53] The study, which had been requested by O'Leary and produced over a very short time period, revealed unexpected interest in tritium production on the part of commercial electric utilities. Moreover, the cost of a dual-use approach using existing reactors appeared, according to the study, to be remarkably attractive. Encouraged by these findings, O'Leary apparently then directed the changes in the final EIS. Her motivations are not entirely clear at this point, but she had come to the government from the nuclear power industry and was at the end of her tenure (whether President Clinton won reelection or not). The actions of lame-duck cabinet chiefs are not always scrutable.

The public-comment phase of the programmatic EIS was managed by Steven Sohinki, a lawyer who had spent most his career with the NRC and who would eventually head up the CLWR program. Unlike most DOE program managers, he did not have a technical background, but rather an undergraduate degree in political science and a law degree from Georgetown University. Arguably, a background in politics and law was a more suitable preparation for the convoluted politics of tritium supply than any number of advanced degrees in science or engineering.

In January 1996, Sohinki met with representatives of electric utilities to promote the idea of tritium production in their reactors. He defended the reclassification of the commercial-reactor option with legalistic arguments, stressing that tritium is not classified by law as a "special nuclear material," but rather as a "by-product" of nuclear operations, like medical isotopes. Though this was a distinction appearing in a number of U.S. laws and international agreements, it was an unprecedented stretch to extend its implications to treating tritium as no more a nuclear weapons material than are the plastics and metals that make up a bomb's electronics.

The intent of most of the laws and agreements related to nonproliferation of nuclear weapons was to implement the spirit of Eisenhower's Atoms for Peace initiative: to foster the worldwide development of nuclear power without encouraging the spread of nuclear weapons. Considering that tritium in modern weapons participates fully in the nuclear events that occur when an H-bomb detonates and that, without tritium, the energy yield of these weapons would be reduced to a small fraction of the yield they are capable of producing with a tritium boost, it is hard to see why the gas shouldn't be considered nuclear weapons material. The NSG certainly recognizes the key role tritium plays in nuclear weapons: it includes the gas and its means of production on the list of materials and technologies subject to strict nonproliferation export control.[54]

Sohinki was to find that the broad utility interest in tritium production predicted by O'Leary's consultants never materialized, in part because of abiding doubts about the dual-use policy issue. But there was one exception: the TVA, which saw a golden opportunity to ease its awesome debt problems by selling its unfinished Bellefonte nuclear reactors to the DOE.

The TVA had begun construction of two reactors at the Bellefonte site in the mid-1970s, during the whirlwind phase of its ill-fated nuclear program (which chapter 6 details). By 1988 that program was in deep trouble and even deeper debt, so the TVA terminated construction at the Hollywood, Alabama, site. One of the reactors was 90-percent complete at the time construction was terminated.[55]

With the vision of turning a gigantic "stranded asset" into cash, the TVA was delighted with the new respectability that the tritium EIS change lent to the commercial-reactor option. In the two or three years following the DOE's reversal of its position on the CLWR, the giant public utility mobilized its considerable political influence to advance the cause in Congress and in the Clinton administration. Key congressional support came from the Alabama congressional delegation, but there was also widespread sympathy for the Bellefonte strategy throughout Congress.

Many members of Congress were intrigued by the plan under which the DOE would purchase one or more of the Bellefonte reactors, modify the design so that tritium could be produced, complete construction of the plant, and operate the new plant as part of the weapons complex. This approach was particularly attractive to members of Congress because of its economics. In the course of the tritium production campaigns, the DOE's new reactor would produce high-pressure steam that could be sold to a commercial utility for electricity production. The bottom line looked very good: a smaller capital investment than the accelerator option and the promise of a steady stream of revenue coming back to the federal coffers over the years.

Some in Congress cautioned that this arrangement would be a violation of the U.S. policy against dual-use nuclear facilities. But others pointed out that there was ample precedent, since the N reactor in Hanford, Washington, sold steam as a "by-product" of its plutonium operations for many years. They argued further that the no-dual-use policy banned commercial facilities from making weapons materials but did not ban military facilities from selling surplus goods to the private sector. Only the former activity raised clear nonproliferation concerns.

The uncertainty about the no-dual-use policy manifested itself in 1997 in legislative activities leading to the fiscal 1998 defense authorization bill.[56] The Senate version of the bill included a provision that cleanly removed the policy uncertainty. It amended the Atomic Energy Act to say that it was permissible to produce tritium in commercial reactors.[57] There was much opposition to this idea in the House, and its version contained no such provision. In the House-Senate Conference Committee deliberations, it was observed that there were different options for tritium production in commercial reactors, and that some seemed more benign, from a policy perspective, than others. For example, the Bellefonte option was consistent with precedent, violated no law, and appeared to be harmless from a nonproliferation perspective. What was needed, therefore, was a thoughtful and expert study of the policy implications of the various suboptions. So the conference committee deleted the Senate provision and directed the DOE to convene an interagency task force to review the relevant policy issues and report to Congress the following year.[58] The committee's report emphasized that the analysis was needed early enough in the following fiscal year to allow deliberations on any necessary amendments to applicable federal law.

The DOE's response to Congress's request was a remarkable document, *Interagency Review of Nonproliferation Implications of Alternative Tritium Production Technologies under Consideration by the Department of Energy*, submitted to Congress by Acting Secretary of Energy Elizabeth A. Moler in July 1998.* This report is unusual in many ways, including the fact that it was published only on the Internet and has no report number, no authorship, no issuing office, and no publicly available paper trail. The *Interagency Review* concluded that no law explicitly prohibited tritium production in a commercial reactor and that "although the CLWR alternative raised initial concerns because of its implications for the policy of maintaining separation between U.S. civil and military activities, these concerns could be satisfactorily addressed, given the particular circumstances involved."[59]

Considering the historical importance of the *Interagency Review*, it is a remarkably short report, by government standards (only ten pages long). It is an artful piece of advocacy, as effective in its purpose by what it does not say as by what it does. For example, the meaning of the term "commercial reactor" is left ambiguous, allowing widely different interpretations of what, exactly, was getting a green light from the review. The most widely held interpretation was a mild one: that the report was evaluating the option whereby the DOE would purchase the TVA's Bellefonte plant and make it a part of the weapons complex.[60] But the report was carefully worded to cover a much more extreme interpretation, that the tritium would be produced in a commercial reactor *owned and operated by an electric utility under license to the NRC*. These two interpretations differ profoundly in their policy implications, but the distinction is never discussed in the review.

The review's vagueness about distinctions between different "commercial" reactor concepts could hardly have been inadvertent. Congress's

---

* The *Interagency Review* is reproduced in appendix B, and a detailed critique is provided in appendix C.

request for the DOE's study was crystal clear on this point: "The commercial reactor track contains many sub-options for tritium production. As a practical matter, each of the different reactor sub-options has different legal and policy issues associated with it."[61] The heart of the conference committee's compromise on the FY98 National Defense Authorization Act was to get clarification on the policy distinctions among the suboptions so that Congress could decide whether legislation was needed for the commercial track to be pursued. But the *Interagency Review* provided no clarification on this issue at all. Indeed, the overall effect of the review was to generate confusion about the issues it was supposed to illuminate.

For example, the review paints the picture that the split between civilian and military uses of nuclear technology was never really an articulated and respected national policy, but rather a pattern of governmental actions that was not even followed consistently. Evidence is offered of supposed breaches in the policy, such as the fact that the TVA produced electricity for the uranium separation facilities in the Manhattan Project. Although true, this fact is ludicrously irrelevant—the no-dual-use policy is a proscription against making nuclear material for bombs in commercial nuclear plants, not against any commerce whatsoever between the military and civilian sides of the society. Another example offered as a breach is the fact that the military production reactors provided specialized isotopes for civilian scientific research and for the space programs. This example, like the sale of surplus steam from the N reactor, is relevant only to the mild interpretation of the term "commercial reactor," in which the reactor is viewed as part of the weapons complex, selling by-products of its weapons operations to the private sector. The no-dual-use policy proscribes the production of bomb materials in civilian reactors—just the opposite of the examples given. In the context of the extreme interpretation of the "commercial reactor" option for tritium, these arguments are egregious sophistry.

Nowhere does the document mention that in the NPR program, which was much larger in scope, production of tritium in civilian reactors was excluded for reasons of nonproliferation policy. Nowhere does it discuss the danger that the new technology could accelerate the transition from fission bombs to smaller and more deadly boosted weapons in countries like Pakistan and India. There is no discussion of potential conflicts between the plant's civilian mission, regulated by its NRC license and the electric utility's charter to serve its ratepayers, and its military mission, dictated by the needs of the nuclear arsenal and secret arrangements between the DOE and TVA. In fact, the issue of obtaining or amending an NRC operating license, a critical policy issue, is not mentioned once in the report.

The message of the *Interagency Review* was not well received in all quarters. Senator Strom Thurmond formally spoke out against it in session:

Some are claiming that because the Tennessee Valley Authority is a government agency that producing nuclear weapons materials in their reactors is consistent with U.S. policy. I can tell you that it is not. The Atomic Energy Act, which governs this policy, was never intended to condone the use of commercial-use facilities to produce nuclear weapons materials. . . . Anyone who is concerned about National Security and nonproliferation must acknowledge that designating a commercial-use reactor as the new tritium production source would signal to the world that it is now acceptable to use commercial-use reactors to produce materials for nuclear weapons. Let me say that one more time—it would tell the rest of the world that we believe there should be no distinction between civilian and military nuclear facilities.[62]

But the *Interagency Review* did not have to pass the test of obtaining the approval of Thurmond, a staunch APT advocate. In fact it had to pass no test at all. It was a pleading without a court, and it succeeded admirably in furthering the CLWR cause.

It is not unusual for government agencies to produce reports that are egregiously flawed and blatantly nonresponsive to their original charters. It is strange, however, for a report with the implicit endorsement of so many important federal agencies to be so profoundly flawed. The *Interagency Review* was characterized as the report of a "task force" of senior officials from the following federal agencies:

- National Security Council
- White House Office of Science and Technology Policy
- Office of the Vice President
- Arms Control and Disarmament Agency
- Nuclear Regulatory Commission
- Department of State
- Department of Defense
- Department of Energy

Obtaining feedback and concurrence from all these heavyweight agencies must have been an organizational nightmare, especially since the interagency phase of the work was accomplished in three months, according to the document itself.

The solution to the puzzle of how the *Interagency Review* coordinated the work of so many agencies in so brief a time is simple: many or most of the agencies listed appear never to have participated in the study. In response to Freedom of Information Act (FOIA) requests submitted for this book, the NRC has stated that it has no records of any meetings of an interagency task force on this subject and no records related to the *Interagency Review*. Likewise, the Office of Science and Technology Policy has stated that there are no records of its participation in the *Interagency Review*. The other agencies in the list above have been nonresponsive or are exempt from the FOIA.[63]

The FOIA responses of NRC and the Office of Science and Technology Policy flatly contradict *Interagency Review* statements about participation of their "senior officials." The level of participation of other agencies remains, at this time, uncertain. What is clear, however, is that the *Interagency Review* is not the kind of document one would like U.S. nuclear weapons policy to be founded upon.

The coordinator and principal ghostwriter of the *Interagency Review* was Joan Rohlfing, a senior DOE official and an expert on nuclear nonproliferation.[64] Interestingly, she was Hazel O'Leary's Director of National Security and Nuclear Nonproliferation when O'Leary directed the surprising change to the tritium EIS, the change that dismissed nonproliferation concerns about the commercial-reactor option. And here is something even more interesting: she was Bill Richardson's principal assistant on nonproliferation issues while he reviewed his tritium options in the fall of 1998.

Bait and Switch

In December 1995 DOE had committed to selecting a preferred tritium production technology within three years, and Congress later codified this commitment in legislation.[65] Thus in the last half of 1998 the competing factions in the tritium contest began to focus on the Secretary of Energy's December deadline for finally choosing among the various options under consideration. The politics of site selection was not generating as much heat as in past contests, since prevailing perceptions aligned sites with specific technologies. The APT facility would be built in South Carolina at the Savannah River site, and the site for CLWR was assumed to be the Bellefonte station in Alabama.[66] As the judgment day approached, a heretofore dark-horse candidate from Washington state made a sudden surge in DOE popularity: the Fast Flux Test Facility on the Hanford reservation, which proponents claimed could be converted to tritium production at a reasonable cost.[67]

Meanwhile, the technology partisans continued to strengthen their cases with research, demonstration, and detailed design work. The well-funded APT program continued to refine its target technology and system engineering. The CLWR program also made good progress in showing that tritium-producing targets could be successfully installed in conventional commercial reactors.

The design of the CLWR targets is exceptionally clever in that employing such targets enables a commercial reactor to be adapted to tritium production with rather little modification. Commercial reactor cores have, interspersed among their thousands of fuel rods, a smaller number of long, pencil-thin rods containing the element boron, a good neutron absorber. These absorber rods help stabilize the overall neutronic behavior of the core over the life of each fuel load. From an engineering perspective, what makes the CLWR option so simple is that (1) most of the locations for these absorber rods are vacant for any particular fuel load, and (2) lithium is also a good neutron absorber, so it could do some of the job normally assigned to boron in the absorber rods. Consequently, it is possible to place rods containing lithium into some of the unused absorber rod channels without significantly changing any other aspects of the reactor core. The difference is that when the lithium absorbs the neutrons, tritium is produced. Since the lithium is slowly depleted, or "burned," as tritium is produced, the device is known as a tritium-producing burnable absorber rod (TPBAR).

To be effective, TPBARs must satisfy two requirements: they have to fit exactly into the existing holes for the absorber rods, and they must be very well sealed, so the tritium gas generated in the lithium cannot escape into the reactor water. The DOE has studied a variety of design

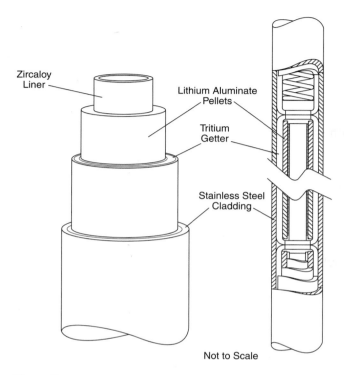

Figure 7
Tritium-producing burnable absorber rod. *Source:* Adapted from figure at DOE
Web site (http://www.dp.doe.gov/dp-62).

options for over fifteen years, and the current TPBAR design (figure 7)
is well thought-out.

The key technical demonstration needed to show the viability of the
CLWR concept was to actually install some of these TPBARs in a conventional power reactor for a full cycle of tritium production and then
demonstrate that the tritium could be extracted after the rods were
removed. The DOE, in collaboration with the TVA, began such a demonstration at the Watts Bar nuclear power plant in 1997. The irradiation
was completed the following year and was declared a success.[68] In the
context of the earlier discussion on the no-dual-use policy, it is interesting that both agencies emphasized that in no way did this experiment
compromise the policy, since the tritium produced would not actually be
used in weapons.[69]

As noted above, the TVA's cooperation in this effort was driven by the vision of selling one of the Bellefonte units and thereby making a dent in its crushing $26 billion debt,[70] a legacy from nuclear overexpansion and poor management in the 1970s and 1980s (discussed in chapter 6). The DOE encouraged the idea that some kind of Bellefonte deal was the logical way to implement the CLWR option and garnered strong support for the concept from the Alabama congressional delegation. Sohinki did allow, however, that there were other possibilities, saying at one point, "If Bellefonte weren't ready for some reason, TVA could use Sequoyah or Watts Bar."[71]

Thus came into view a darker version of the CLWR option: the idea that the DOE might lease "irradiation services" from a currently operating commercial electric power plant. In this scheme, the DOE would own the TPBARs and the commercial utility would, for a fee, allow them to be inserted into the core, absorb neutrons during the normal course of electricity production, and be removed for further processing at a DOE-owned tritium separation facility. Seldom explicitly discussed, this option was steadfastly maintained in the CLWR strategy.

Throughout its history, the CLWR program had been adamantly opposed by some who believed it was wrong to mix bomb making with civilian nuclear missions, with or without the "steam by-product" fig leaf. One such opponent was Edward Markey, a congressman from Massachusetts. Along with a colleague from the district where the APT would be built, Markey sponsored a successful amendment to the fiscal 1999 defense authorization bill prohibiting any use of commercial reactors for tritium production, except in case of war or a national emergency declared by Congress. It couldn't have been a simpler amendment, merely adding the two words "and tritium" to the list of fissile materials in the Hart-Simpson amendment. But the provision ran into trouble in the Senate, where Senator Jeff Sessions of Alabama inserted a countervailing amendment preserving the DOE's right to choose between the CLWR and the APT. The conflicting provisions in the House and Senate versions of the defense authorization bill virtually guaranteed that the prohibition would be removed in conference, and it was.[72]

When the TVA first responded to the DOE's 1997 request for proposals for a CLWR, the Bellefonte arrangement was at the heart of its offer, but it also indicated that the use of existing, operating reactors (such as Watts Bar) was a possibility. In part, this was intended to establish a strong position in the competition among the utilities that might respond to the government's solicitation of interest. But there were no other responders, and the TVA thus found itself in an uncomfortable position.[73] In reality, the TVA's management was interested only in a Bellefonte deal and soon withdrew the offer of its operating reactors.[74]

But the DOE's appetite had been whetted by the idea of leasing irradiation services in currently licensed reactors. The option would certainly look good from a cost perspective, blowing all competition from the APT out of the water, no matter what accounting magic the accelerator proponents tried. But perhaps even more important was the realization that a proposal for a CLWR that was the result of modifying existing reactors would find much smoother sailing with the NRC, since obtaining an operating license for a new plant would be orders of magnitude more difficult than obtaining a license *amendment* for an existing plant . . . assuming, that is, that the NRC chose not to take on the highly charged dual-use policy issue.[75] In January 1997, one NRC commissioner urged his colleagues to do just that, but the rest of the commission overruled him and took the position that it was of no regulatory concern that the requested modifications had nothing to do either with electricity or public safety.[76] At that point, the existing-reactor path looked enticing, indeed.

In April 1998 Secretary of Energy Federico Peña unexpectedly resigned, putting the schedule for the tritium decision in jeopardy. To meet the December deadline, prompt Senate approval of a replacement, followed by a steep learning curve by the new secretary, would be required. President Clinton wasted no time in nominating a strong candidate: Bill Richardson, a former congressman from New Mexico and the highly regarded U.S. ambassador to the United Nations. The Senate was agreeable, and the new secretary was sworn in on August 18, about four months before the tritium decision deadline.

When Richardson arrived at his new post, he encountered problems far more vexing than the tritium decision. For example, the DOE was facing a scandal that would threaten its very existence: the allegation of profound and damaging loss of secret nuclear weapons design information to the People's Republic of China (see chapter 4).[77] Richardson's first order of business was to deal with Presidential Decision Directive 61, which ordered sweeping changes in the DOE's counterintelligence programs. Under this order, the secretary owed the NSC a response to thirty-three specific recommendations for changing the way security was handled in the department and at the national laboratories. His response was already late the day he arrived on the job, but by the end of November he had carried out the necessary reviews and approved all the recommendations, also obtaining the concurrence of all the national laboratories.[78]

Against this background, the decision on the means of obtaining a tritium supply was hardly pressing, especially since whatever real urgency existed when Congress specified the December deadline had been dramatically dissipated by progress in arms control talks. Reductions in the planned size of the U.S. nuclear arsenal have two effects on the tritium supply question. First, fewer warheads means less annual tritium needed, thus reducing the size of the tritium production facility required. Second, reductions allow the date for startup of the new facility to slip, since warheads removed from the active inventory can be "mined" for their tritium to replenish the active weapons, a concept called "recycling." By the summer of 1998, breakthroughs in arms control negotiations with the Russians had relieved the time pressure on establishing a new supply, extending the date when new tritium would actually be needed by many years.

Nonetheless, Richardson wanted to impress Congress that the new man at the DOE was a man of action, not delay, and he fully intended to meet the deadline. He dutifully familiarized himself with the byzantine "political science" of tritium production and received numerous briefings by the competing teams at DOE headquarters. These briefings were essentially sales pitches, revealing an atmosphere that was in sharp contrast to Dominic Monetta's methodical, criterion-based evaluation of NPR options eight years earlier. An unmitigated adversarial relationship had developed between the CLWR and APT camps, and the competition was played out not only with ebullient assessments of their respective technologies, but also with the equivalent of negative political campaigning, each against the other, with leaked news stories and dustups in Congress and the press.[79]

Cost estimation was a source of frequent controversy. Over the years, charges and countercharges flew about unrealistic assumptions by one

Table 3
DOE's July 1998 cost estimates (in billions of dollars) for tritium production options

	Accelerator	Bellefonte	Irradiation services
Initial investment	3.4	2.4	0.6
Operation and maintenance	5.5	−0.9	3.4
Life cycle total	9.2	1.6	4.0

Note: Negative operations and maintenance costs reflect the sale of "steam as by-product" in the Bellefonte option. The life cycle total includes decommissioning costs (not shown). *Source:* Letter from acting secretary Elizabeth Moler to Senator Strom Thurmond dated July 31, 1998.

side or the other. In the interim between Peña's departure and Richardson's arrival, the Energy Secretary's office issued cost estimates for the leading tritium production options using a uniform set of economic assumptions. The results are shown in table 3.

At first glance, it would appear that the Bellefonte option was the most attractive from a life cycle cost perspective. But Richardson noted that the initial investment, coming straight out of the DOE budget while he was at the helm, was by far the lowest for the irradiation services option. Some might criticize that choice for its breach of the no-dual-use policy, but the *Interagency Review*, authored by his principal advisor on the subject, had said, essentially, "no problem." The only barrier to Richardson's choosing the irradiation services route was the TVA's recalcitrance.

Enter the DOE's lawyers, who found the needed leverage to gain the TVA's acquiescence in an old law known as the Economy Act. Dating back to the depression era, it was used primarily to coordinate activities of different federal agencies on a "noninterference" basis. It was typically invoked to allow one agency to pay another agency for the use of office space or vehicles that would otherwise be unused. But the DOE pressed a strong interpretation of the law, arguing that as a federal agency, the TVA was *required* to provide the requested irradiation services as long as there was no interference with its principal missions. Moreover, the services had to be provided to the DOE, according to its lawyers, "at cost."

This turn of affairs was deeply disturbing to TVA Chairman Craven Crowell, who had begun the negotiations with the DOE with a vision of turning the Bellefonte white elephant into positive cash flow on the account books. The TVA repeatedly submitted revised Bellefonte-related contract offers, trying to find a combination of up-front and operating costs and revenues that would interest the DOE.[80] But the Watts Bar/Sequoyah irradiation services path had broad appeal to Richardson. With it, he could keep initial expenditures low, achieve a high flexibility with respect to the amount of tritium needed, and keep in reserve a fallback option that would put the policy ball in Congress's court. That fallback, suggested by the wording of the Markey amendment, would be to defer tritium production at the civilian reactors *until Congress declared a "national emergency."* Thus the secretary could, if necessary, retreat to high ground on the policy issue, and Congress would be at fault if tritium reserves disappeared faster than the pace dictated by arms cuts.

It was important, of course, to get the TVA on board with this plan. Crowell's heart was set on a Bellefonte deal, but the TVA also had good reason to acquiesce to the Watts Bar/Sequoyah alternative, since it would provide potent protection from enemies in Congress who wanted to privatize the TVA (see chapter 6). It is not known what kind of pressure Richardson brought to bear on Crowell to finally bring the matter to a settlement. In the internal pecking order of federal agencies, the DOE is not top dog, but it certainly outranks the perennially besieged electric utility. In the words of savvy insiders at *Nucleonics Week*, an industry newsletter: "Though TVA was not legally bound by the Economy Act to accede to Richardson's wishes, in the 'real world' of Washington politics and policy, he made the federal utility an offer it couldn't refuse."[81]

Richardson got TVA's reluctant acquiescence in a December 8 letter from Crowell, who even then continued to insist that an arrangement involving the Bellefonte plant would have much lower life cycle project costs and would be better overall for everyone.[82] But Richardson would not be persuaded, and on December 22, 1998, he announced that the DOE's preferred path for reestablishing the tritium supply would be to lease irradiation services from the TVA at its Watts Bar unit 1. The two Sequoyah reactors would be available as backups in case additional capacity were needed. The DOE would provide the funds for altering the plants and pay for whatever quantity of tritium was produced. The APT would be the secondary path, and the DOE would continue with research on key aspects of that technology, but not with construction. And to the great disappointment of its proponents in Washington state, the Fast Flux Test Facility would play no role at all in the tritium strategy.[83]

In announcing his decision, Richardson acknowledged that concerns had been expressed about the country's long tradition of producing weapons material only at dedicated military facilities, but he pointed to the *Interagency Review* as reassurance that the concerns were manageable. When first requested by Congress, the review was intended to pave the way for the Bellefonte option, but instead it blurred the differences among the commercial-reactor suboptions, allowing instead the choice of Watts Bar and Sequoyah. Knowingly or not, Richardson thus pulled off one of the greatest bait-and-switch maneuvers in nuclear history.

Richardson's decision made a strange kind of sense in the dysfunctional environment he had inherited. With it, he fulfilled the DOE's 1995 commitment to make a concrete decision by the end of 1998, while minimizing the future bureaucratic burden on his department. In the near term, he would not be diverted by great battles over budget, because the only big-ticket item in the program was the construction of the $400 million tritium extraction facility at the Savannah River site.[84] For that, he could count on support from the powerful South Carolina delegation. Review of the safety of the modified nuclear plants was essential, but that responsibility lay with other agencies. As the licensee, the TVA would present and defend the proposal to amend its operating license, and the NRC would review it. The DOE would not even be a party to that process, except for paying the salaries on both sides (a sum that would be quite small in comparison with the kinds of numbers in table 3). Another benefit of the plan was that if the goal quantity of tritium were reduced because of START-II or for some other reason, he could slip the schedule for the whole program at little cost to the DOE. And if the criticism of the implied shift in nonproliferation policy were sufficiently persuasive, he could point to Congress as the place where a new "dual-use for national emergencies" policy could be crafted. Even if Congress took such a step, his program still made sense, and Congress would be left holding the bag on the issue of what really constitutes a "national emergency." Clever man.

In the real world, however, where the U.S. government's actions influence the future health and security of billions of people, it must be said that the secretary's tritium decision constituted an abandonment of responsibility. The separation of civilian and military uses of nuclear energy is a fundamental principle underlying a complex fabric of policies and institutions by which the weapons nations, with the United States as clear leader, have curbed the spread of nuclear arms. By comparison, making life in the federal bureaucracy easier for the Secretary of Energy and his staff by passing the buck to other federal agencies is of minuscule importance.

The contrasts between the tritium decision process during the Watkins phase and the one used by Richardson in 1998 are amazing:

· The earlier decision process was carefully crafted, formal, and traceable. This time it was hasty, adversarial, and virtually invisible.

· Then, the dual-use proscription was strictly respected, even though the cost savings from ignoring the policy would have been much greater, since the tritium goal quantity was much larger then than in 1998.

· The two technologies chosen as superior the last time around (i.e., HWR and MHGTR) were not even on the short list this time.

· The technology adversaries then competed intensely to offer the safest nuclear plant possible. This time around, safety was not even a minor factor in the decision.

· Then, the DOE committed to a higher standard of safety than was required of any existing commercial reactor. This time the attitude was that if the Watts Bar and Sequoyah plants were not safe enough, the NRC would have shut them down.

· Then, cost was a secondary factor compared to reliability and safety, even though federal budgets were very tight. This time, cost seems to have been the dominant factor, despite substantial budget surpluses.

What is so ironic about these contrasts is that in the earlier decision-making phase, the superpower confrontation was still a fundamental reality. By 1998, the urgency of the tritium decision should have been dramatically reduced because of the disengagement that had taken place. Yet the secretary wished to meet an arbitrary deadline and made a choice that, among the available options, must be considered the moral lowball.

In the months following Richardson's announcement, the TVA continued to bargain for a better position, delaying the formal interagency agreement needed to seal the deal. It pointed out that foreign nuclear fuel suppliers such as Canada and Australia were bound by their own national laws and international agreements not to provide uranium for any weapons-related use. So the DOE worked out an arrangement to create a pure domestic uranium supply specifically for the tritium-producing reactors.[85] The TVA then argued that the new fuel supply was outside the current market structure and that it had no right to expose its electricity production business to the associated risks. In response, the DOE found language to indemnify or compensate the utility for such risks. The TVA pointed out that its power plants used many components and subsystems purchased from suppliers in countries like Japan, which strictly forbids exporting products intended for any nuclear weapons manufacture. Integrated circuit boards were a particular concern, since Japan's vigorous nuclear industry had fostered a broad range of supporting companies that had become the suppliers of choice in the United States and elsewhere. Not to worry, the Departments of Energy and State said they would work out arrangements to obtain whatever components might be needed from countries having less-refined scruples about how their export products are used. And to compensate the TVA for these inconveniences, the DOE agreed to pay the TVA an extra $30 million over a ten-year period.[86]

What is wrong with this picture? The United States *invented* export control of nuclear weapons technology in the first place. Export control is the linchpin of the dual-path nuclear strategy first laid out by President Eisenhower. It is at the heart of the elaborate international system of nonproliferation controls that was developed during and following the Carter years. Now the federal government is working out clever ways to get around the export control laws of foreign governments? Clearly, something has gone wrong.

The DOE had no intention of letting the TVA escape its fate and looked to other agencies in the administration for support. For example, the Department of Defense (DOD) had long been a DOE ally in getting tritium production on a fast track. In the summer of 1998, the two agencies had teamed together in a blitz of correspondence to members of Congress about the *Interagency Review*'s finding that proliferation problems of tritium production in commercial reactors were "manageable."[87] Steven Sohinki was confident of the DOD's willingness to help persuade the TVA. For example, he openly told his staff and the TVA's point of contact that the Secretary of the Navy was prepared to tell TVA Chairman Craven Crowell that if the TVA did not cooperate, the Navy would requisition the Sequoyah plant on national security grounds.[88] This was truly interagency hardball.

It took a year for the agreement between the TVA and the DOE to be completed. The long delay reinforced concerns by some in Congress that the DOE's plan was weak.[89] Another source of consternation among members of Congress was the fact that soon after the secretary's announcement of his decision to pursue the irradiation services option, he cut the funding for the APT "backup" option by a factor of two, providing further evidence of how large a factor cost was playing in his thinking, an emphasis that seemed misplaced given the gravity of the issues involved.

One of those issues is the potential for spread to other countries of the tritium production technology employed in the TVA reactors. Given the current plans, it will be exceedingly difficult for the DOE to prevent classified details of its TPBAR designs from diffusing quickly to countries like India and Pakistan. For these borderline nuclear-armed countries, transformation of their arsenals into tritium-boosted weapons will be a strong temptation in the coming years. It should be a top priority within the U.S. government to erect barriers to such diffusion of nuclear secrets, but the DOE is proceeding with a remarkably sanguine attitude toward secrecy.

Despite a change in administrations since the 1998 decision, the U.S. government continues to pursue the plan to produce tritium in nuclear plants licensed by the NRC for commercial electricity production. This is particularly surprising since continued progress in nuclear arms reductions should be the basis for dramatic postponement of the need for new tritium. For example, in April 2000, the Russian Duma at long last approved the START-II treaty, which calls for mutual reductions in U.S. and Russian strategic arsenals by more than a factor of two. The math of radioactive decay then applies in a simple way: a reduction by a factor of two in the number of warheads allows a delay in the date when new tritium supplies are needed by about twelve years, the half life of tritium (because in the interim the tritium from decommissioned weapons can be used to recharge the ones that remain in the arsenal). START II is not yet in force as a formal treaty because the Bush administration has not pursued the steps needed to make it so (as of press time for this book).[90] But the important thing regarding the question "when will new tritium supplies be needed?" is that President Bush has endorsed the idea of nuclear arms cuts even deeper than those called in START II.[91]

The DOE's own analysis of a START-II-compliant nuclear arsenal puts the date when new tritium is needed at 2011, and that includes a five-year "reserve" against contingency. With less-conservative assumptions and reasonable guesses about reductions below START-II's 3,500 warheads, Frank von Hippel, at one time President Clinton's assistant director for national security, estimates that the date by which new tritium will be needed has slipped to 2029.[92] In November 2001, President Bush announced plans to cut the U.S. arsenal even more deeply than what von Hippel assumed for his 2029 estimate.[93] The DOE's continued insistence that new tritium from the TVA's reactors is needed by 2006 is thus completely unjustified by current perceptions of the size of the future U.S. nuclear stockpile.[94]

Nonetheless, the plan proceeds unmolested and virtually unnoticed. Perhaps what lies behind the DOE's routinization of nuclear proliferation issues is public apathy. Perhaps Americans see the START treaties and the end of the cold war as something to do with worries of the past, and not, in Jonathan Schell's words, "the gift of time," time that we must use to make the twenty-first century safer.[95] Even if that is so, the people entrusted with managing nuclear weapons technology have a responsibility to see more clearly.

The only remaining administrative hurdle for the government's new tritium plan is for the NRC to grant the TVA license amendments allowing the changes in hardware and procedures at the Watts Bar and Sequoyah ice condenser plants that are necessary to enable the plants to produce tritium. Chapter 3 discussed the serious safety problems of such reactors. The next chapter will show how those problems are exacerbated by a flawed safety culture at the TVA and will be exacerbated further by the conversion of its reactors to dual-use facilities. And it will also explain why the NRC's use of pre-TMI licensing procedures may allow it to ignore these issues and let the TVA and DOE have their way.

6
Tennessee Waltz

Is it possible that nuclear energy is too difficult for the American utilities? Nuclear energy will always be a demanding technology, one that requires a level of technical sophistication that American utilities generally do not possess.
Alvin Weinberg, 1994

Nuclear Misadventures at the Tennessee Valley Authority

The federal government's new tritium plan calls for the TVA to modify its reactors for tritium production and to operate them in the new dual-mission mode for as long as the DOE needs tritium. From the perspective of public safety, the TVA is probably the worst possible choice for this assignment. Its performance over the years in building and operating nuclear reactors is simply appalling, revealing it to be a fossilized, inefficient, unresponsive bureaucracy that is profoundly deficient in the management skills needed for such a complex and dangerous job.

These may sound like harsh words about an agency that many people associate with semiromantic notions of the New Deal's coming to the rescue of starving families in the 1930s. The problem is that, whereas the TVA's missions have changed over its sixty-five-year history, its management structure has not. And management structure, we now know, has a great deal to do with how safely nuclear reactors are built and operated.

In 1932, newly elected President Franklin Roosevelt felt he had to do something for the miserably poor people who lived near the Tennessee River, that great southern river that begins in the Great Smoky Mountains of Tennessee, wanders south into Alabama, then executes a 150-mile-wide U-turn to return to its home state and cross northward into Kentucky. Within a few months of his election, Roosevelt persuaded

Congress to create the TVA, partly a jobs program, partly a social experiment, partly a way to control ravaging floods and salvage unproductive land, and partly a way to bring electricity and prosperity to one of the poorest parts of the United States. Taming the river was seen as a central purpose, but tapping the river's energy to produce electricity as a by-product was also authorized.[1] Later, electricity production came to dominate the TVA's activities.

The Tennessee Valley Act established a three-person* board to run the TVA. Each board member was to be appointed by the president and approved by the senate, and each would serve a nine-year term. The president was to decide which of the three would chair the board.

Over the decades, the TVA's mission evolved. Many of the early goals, like flood control, were achieved, and others withered as the perceived need for them faded. To justify the TVA's continued existence, the board sought new missions or expanded old ones. Over time, electricity came to dominate all others. Well into the 1980s, the TVA followed a vision first articulated by David Lilienthal, one of its first board members: "There is no such thing as too much electricity. For electricity is a creater, a builder. Electrical energy creates its own market."[2] In the 1950s this vision translated into the belief that building more power plants would bring jobs and prosperity in two ways, first through the construction projects themselves, and second through the electricity-hungry industry that all that available power would attract into the region. It was a "supply-push" philosophy, one that seemed to be working in the postwar economic expansion. The TVA's growth plans were sometimes constrained, however, by interference from Congress or the Office of the Budget. So in 1959 the TVA board cut a deal with the federal government that would make the TVA the most autonomous electrical utility in the country. It was allowed to finance its power projects by issuing bonds instead of through congressional appropriations. In exchange, it would not sell power outside an invisible "fence" surrounding its market, which penetrated into seven southern states.

In comparison to other electric utilities, the TVA's level of autonomy was remarkable. The board could set the rates it charged for electricity without regulatory oversight. It needed no external approval to plan and

---

* It was strictly a three-*man* board from 1933 until 2000, when Skyla Harris, former chief of staff to Tipper Gore, was appointed to the board.

finance new power plants through bond issues, as long as its total debt did not exceed a limit set by Congress. And it enjoyed the freedom of not having to satisfy expectations of stockholders for a reasonable return on investment. This would have been an ideal arrangement if the members of the board were top corporate managers with an uncanny feel for the future, but they were just senior civil servants doing their best in a job most had been given as a reward for loyal service to the powers that be.[3] Far from being able to see into the future, they usually didn't know what was going on inside the gigantic organization under them.

By the mid-1960s TVA was a blind giant stumbling toward a disastrous nuclear future. When the hydroelectric potential of the Tennessee River had been largely tapped, the TVA began to build large fossil-fired steam plants to generate the electricity that its plans called for. But it was soon bitten by the nuclear bug. In 1966 the TVA announced plans to build seventeen nuclear reactors, far and away the most ambitious nuclear program in the country. In 1967 it started building the Browns Ferry plant in northern Alabama, which would be five times bigger than any commercial nuclear reactor ever operated.[4]

With Browns Ferry, the TVA made a fateful decision that probably seemed like no decision at all. It decided to build the plant itself. Other utilities saw themselves as producers and sellers of electricity. They turned to the great architecture/engineering firms like Stone and Webster for the job of building these complex industrial facilities. But at the TVA the tradition of creating local jobs and the belief that the TVA could build anything ran through the organization's blood. It began hiring and training what would become an army of specialized workers for its ambitious nuclear program.

The TVA's vastly expanded engineering and construction organization proceeded to design and build, bringing to the complex task of nuclear power plant construction a unique management approach that had evolved from decades of building dams and steam plants. It was an approach that emphasized great confidence in the TVA's way of doing things, unquestioned acceptance of line authority, an emphasis on keeping to the project schedule, if not budget, a tradition of improvising during construction, a strong sense of team loyalty, and a corresponding resentment of outside interference (with varying definitions of "outside").[5] This was the TVA way, and when applied to nuclear energy, it was a prescription for disaster.

A very serious accident at the Browns Ferry plant in 1975 was a harbinger of future troubles. Workers examining the shafts carrying huge trays of electrical cables into the reactor building used the tried and true method of a candle flame to detect air leaks, a gross violation of safety procedures. The candle ignited the cables' plastic insulation and the flames soon propagated out of the workers' reach. Because many of the burning cables were essential for controlling the reactor and running its cooling system, the potential for a core meltdown was very real. As hundreds of electrical cables became engulfed in the smoky blaze, the local fire department was called in. But the Browns Ferry plant manager ignored the advice of the local fire chief and refused to allow firefighters to use water on the blaze since he (mistakenly) thought that would cause more problems than they already had. The fire burned for over seven hours, and all systems, both normal and emergency, for circulating water throughout the reactor core were lost. Fortunately, plant engineers managed to get some flow of water through the reactor by means of crude workarounds, and a core melt accident was avoided. But the reactor was essentially out of control for several hours before firefighters prevailed, finally extinguishing the blaze with the water hoses the plant manager had forbidden.[6] It was the worst nuclear reactor accident in history, until it was eclipsed by TMI four years later.

The Browns Ferry fire and ensuing investigations of its cause revealed early symptoms of the clash between the TVA's way of doing things and what government regulators required in the way of quality assurance. Nuclear plant designers realized early on that the systems in these plants were so complex and so capable of causing harm to the public that they could be made safe only if extraordinary levels of attention were brought to bear on their construction and operation. Strict control was needed on drawings, materials, parts, and worker skills, and a system of checks and double checks had to be implemented. That system was called quality assurance (QA), and experts from both industry and government spelled out the minimum standards the QA program at each nuclear plant had to satisfy.

But the TVA was building dams according to its own management style when some of these QA gurus were toddlers. The people who had made it to positions of authority within the engineering and construc-tion ranks saw themselves as builders, not paper pushers. In grudging acquiescence to regulations, they tolerated QA staff within their projects, but only if everyone at the site understood that the QA employee's role was to satisfy the Washington bureaucrats and otherwise stay out of the way.

The TVA board was well insulated from these tensions. Over the decades the TVA's line organizations had developed a management style that filtered out negative information as it migrated upward, especially at the interface to the board itself. Board members seldom had engi-neering backgrounds, and by tradition and necessity they trusted the line organizations to carry out their responsibilities without interference from above. The board knew that the 1975 Browns Ferry fire was serious, but it was extinguished after all, and the board felt confident that the line organizations would get the plant back up and running as soon as possible.

The degree to which the TVA was out of touch with reality is revealed by two events occurring soon after the Browns Ferry fire: first, it requested and was granted construction licenses for its sixteenth and seventeenth nuclear reactors, and second, it promoted the Browns Ferry plant manager (who had been criticized by the NRC for preventing the fire department from extinguishing the fire) to head up all nuclear oper-ations, a position he held until 1983.[7] This was the TVA way in action.

What did make the board nervous was the financial impact of con-struction delays in the nuclear programs. To finance the capital-intensive construction of power plants, they had asked Congress for a series of increases in the authorized debt ceiling: from $1.75 billion to $3.5 billion in 1970, then up to $15 billion in 1976, and finally to $30 billion in 1979.[8] Congress obliged on each occasion with little comment. Thus unfettered, the TVA exercised with abandon its authority to issue bonds for nuclear power plant projects. By 1979 the TVA's nuclear program dwarfed that of any other utility in the country: three reactors were oper-ating, and fourteen were under construction.[9] But the TVA, along with the rest of the industry, was learning how hard it was to build these complex facilities on schedule and within budget. As the debt soared, the expected offsetting increase in electricity production did not occur. To make matters worse, fossil fuel prices skyrocketed in the 1970s. The board's only option was to raise rates to the TVA's customers, which it did reluctantly and often. By 1981, one third of the TVA's electricity revenues went to debt service.[10]

Rate increases were received poorly by the TVA's customers, and the board soon realized that freedom to set rates without oversight was a two-edged sword, since there was no public utilities commission to take the heat. The board, politically if not technically astute, responded with pressure on the line organizations to cut costs and get the remaining nuclear plants finished. In the definitive history of the TVA's management, Erwin Hargrove describes the board's dilemma: "This was a difficult bundle of problems. The increase in the debt limit was to be quickly absorbed by unanticipated costs of nuclear construction. There was pressure to get the plants up and working as soon as possible in order to limit costs from the stretched-out construction program. But this pressure was in implicit conflict with the need for making sure that the plants were built in accordance with the safety requirements for operation."[11] The TVA's board finally woke up and canceled plans for four nuclear reactors in 1982. But the troubles at the remaining plants were just beginning.

After TMI, NRC inspectors became more insistent that the TVA follow QA regulations. But managers at TVA headquarters and the construction sites continued to treat their QA staff with contempt and to prevent them from carrying out their functions. In one notable case, a QA supervisor, Dan DeFord, was reassigned to a job with no employees to supervise and given a desk with no telephone after TVA management discovered that he had revealed QA deficiencies to NRC inspectors. His humiliating treatment sent a strong message to employees who might be inclined to rock the boat.[12]

But anger and frustration ran deep in the TVA's ranks, and soon revelations of flagrant QA violations began surfacing everywhere, particularly with respect to the Watts Bar plant, which was scheduled to commence operation at the end of 1985. To fend off pressure from the NRC and congressional investigators, the TVA hired an outside QA firm to evaluate the allegations. To the surprise and consternation of TVA management, the firm's findings reinforced the message from Washington: there were thousands of violations and deficiencies at all of the TVA's plants, and some were very serious.[13]

In 1985, the head of TVA's Office of Power finally faced facts and ordered all five operating TVA nuclear plants shut down until thousands of violations could be remedied. He felt it would be impossible to satisfy the NRC's safety and QA requirements while the plants were still operating. After investing $14 billion in seventeen reactors, the TVA was not generating a single kilowatt of nuclear electricity. It would be years before it would.

In response to these shocking developments, a variety of panels and commissions delved into the root causes of the TVA's failure. Most of the findings were consistent with earlier studies of the structural defects of the TVA, which traced the root causes to the collective beliefs, expectations, and values that had developed within the organization over the decades. One study's conclusions pointed to the way the bureaucracy worked:

People spent their careers in one division and saw little of people in other units. Vertical movement up in rank was slow and dependent on retirements, and promotion was tied to length of service. The expansion of the work of divisions thus created career opportunities. One consequence was that TVA tried to do as much work in-house as possible in order to maximize the number of internal opportunities. Consultants were seldom used, and each division did its own troubleshooting. These practices reinforced TVA's sense of its own technical competence. Red Wagner [board chairman at the time the report was written] was quoted as saying: "We don't want to hire consultants who are the best experts. We want our staff to be the best experts available."[14]

But the TVA couldn't pay top dollar for the best people because of the salary caps for civil servants. The board had asked Congress repeatedly for an exception to the salary caps to attract and keep the best and brightest in the nuclear industry. But Congress would not grant the request.

Equally important contributors to the breakdown in QA were the isolation of the board of directors from operations, the autonomy of the operating divisions, and the long-standing rivalries among them. Clearly, these were root causes deserving of attention. But the board, caught flat-footed by the crisis and feeling out of its depth, embarked instead on a massive quick fix. First, it cancelled plans for four more nuclear reactors. Then it hired Admiral Steven White, recently of Admiral Hyman Rickover's nuclear Navy, and gave him czarlike power over all of the TVA's nuclear operations. There was virtually no limit to what it was willing to spend to solve the problems with the TVA's nuclear power operations, since $16 billion remained in their congressionally authorized line of credit. It threw money at the TVA's nuclear problems at a rate that would have been impossible for another utility in the same dire straits.

White's spectacular $355,000 salary was a source of great resentment among many of the old hands in the TVA's nuclear division. But he knocked heads and spent the TVA's money and slowly brought the reactors up to regulatory standards. He brought in many contractors from outside the TVA to oversee the work of correcting multitudinous design and construction errors and to bring QA records up to date. The costs were staggering: at one point the board approved outside contracts for 700 engineers at a cost of $170 million simply to correct existing problems at the unfinished Watts Bar plant.[15]

It took a little more than the planned two years for White to bring the TVA's reactors into compliance with regulations, but eventually four of the five reactors came back into service in the early 1990s: two at the Sequoyah plant and two of the three at Browns Ferry. Unit 1 at Browns Ferry, the TVA's first reactor, has never recovered from the 1975 fire and its repercussions. It probably never will.

White left the TVA in 1988, and most of the outside contractors left soon afterward. Although he had accomplished his mission, the underlying causes of the problems remained behind. As Hargrove explains, "[t]he organization could not be changed in two or three years. For one thing, White could not fire anyone. His announcement that he would only stay two years encouraged the career people to wait him out."[16] Put simply, White rode into the TVA with his huge team of high-paid consultants, fixed at enormous expense the myriad defects and noncompliances, and rode out a couple of years later. No great changes had been made at the root cause level, and the TVA's nuclear division was still a deeply flawed organization.

Hope for organizational renewal appeared when Marvin Runyon, head of Nissan USA, was persuaded to chair the TVA's board. It was understood that he would essentially operate as chief executive officer and apply his great organizational skills toward transforming the TVA into something resembling an efficient American corporation. In the face of stubborn resistance, he implemented a number of changes in the recalcitrant management structure, and things seemed to be moving in the right direction by 1992. But then in just the third year of his nine-year term, he left to become the Postmaster General of the United States. Runyon apparently had decided he would rather fix the Post Office than the TVA.

Loose Screws at the Watts Bar Plant

After Runyon left the TVA board, much of the energy behind reforming the organization subsided. A kind of normalcy returned, but some things had changed as a result of the upheavals from 1985 to 1992. One change, probably for the good, was that the nuclear building spree got pared down to just finishing the beleaguered Watts Bar Unit 1. Ground had been broken on the unit twenty years earlier, but progress on the plant was punctuated by many crises and shutdowns brought on by revelations of substandard fabrication, malfeasance, and outright falsifications to the NRC. Before it was finally completed in 1996, it became known as the world's most inspected and most expensive nuclear plant.[17]

A second change stemmed from the fact that the TVA found a way to deal with the salary cap. The concept was to pay annual bonuses to employees for achieving specific milestones. Bonuses were offered to low-level employees as well as to top managers, for whom the amounts of bonuses often exceeded their annual salaries. This change had mixed effects: better overall compensation no doubt attracted and retained better people, but excessive focus on milestones could compromise safety, as will be seen.

But a third change was clearly not a good thing for the TVA. It was the emergence of a veritable guerilla war between whistle-blowers on one side and the TVA's managers and lawyers on the other. Dan DeFord had shown that individuals who had been punished for revealing safety violations at nuclear plants could invoke the protections of the Energy Reorganization Act, take the TVA to court, and win. The TVA's managers saw such people as disloyal troublemakers, the kind that had brought on the troubles of the previous years. The huge stable of TVA lawyers simply viewed the lawsuits as excellent opportunities to demonstrate their mastery of labor law (Congress had wisely assigned to the Labor Department responsibility for evaluating violations of the whistle-blower provisions of the Energy Reorganization Act). The lawyers had plenty of practice: as of 1989, TVA employees had filed 90 percent of all whistle-blower cases at U.S. nuclear utilities.[18] The TVA's board was, as usual, impotent and irrelevant in the face of these fierce conflicts among specialists.

To make matters worse, the NRC was signaling that it had run out of patience with "the TVA way" and expected Watts Bar to be completed in strict accordance with requirements. In a 1991 letter to TVA nuclear chief Oliver Kingsley, NRC's executive director for operations, James Taylor, warned:

On numerous occasions over the years, the NRC has heard various TVA management teams describe both the weaknesses in past corrective action programs and the intent to address root causes in future programs. Nevertheless, major problems have continued uncorrected. . . . Because the continuing problems at WBNP [Watts Bar] are of very significant concern to the NRC, a significant civil penalty would normally be proposed. However, I am not persuaded that such an action can help bring about the necessary changes any more readily than the multitude of program changes TVA has unsuccessfully implemented at WBNP since the shutdown of its nuclear program in 1985. Therefore, after consultation with the Commission, enforcement discretion will be exercised in this case and neither a Notice of Violation nor a civil penalty will be proposed.[19]

Taylor was acknowledging here that fines had been found ineffective in changing this giant government corporation's behavior. He proceeded to threaten to withhold an operating license until the NRC staff was fully satisfied with the TVA's progress, concluding, "In order to provide that necessary level of assurance your future performance will require substantial improvement." These are unusually harsh words for formal correspondence between the NRC and one of its licensees.

QA seemed to be a skill the TVA could not acquire. For example, the workmanship on Watts Bar's safety-related electrical cables was so bad that the NRC required the TVA to replace 1.3 million feet of wiring.[20] In a 1994 interview the NRC's chairman complained about the Watts Bar QA program. "We've been very disappointed that time and time again TVA comes in and says systems are done when they are not," he said. "It's almost like denial on the part of management that they didn't take QA steps very seriously."[21]

Such was the institutional environment when the final push to complete the Watts Bar plant began. After numerous delays, the TVA finally set its sights on starting the plant up by the end of 1995. A generous bonus package was attached to this milestone, and everyone involved felt the schedule pressure.

Getting the ice condenser system completely ready for operations was a key step, since fuel could not be loaded until this major safety system was fully operational. The man responsible for bringing the great vault of ice-filled baskets up to operational readiness was a dedicated and capable engineering specialist, Curtis Overall. As he supervised the filling of the baskets with chipped ice in early 1995, he had no way of knowing he would soon be caught in the jaws of the great TVA machine that had ruined so many safety workers before him. Within months, his career, his health, and even his life would be jeopardized simply because he made the mistake of taking nuclear safety too seriously.

In Overall's story, which continues to this day, we can see the contradictions between pious official pronouncements about the TVA's commitment to public safety and the underlying forces motivating the organization's actions. It reveals the alarming reality that, despite extraordinary pressure applied by the agencies charged with regulating the TVA, there are some ways in which it will never change. That realization should be kept foremost in mind when the matter of whether the TVA should be getting into the nuclear weapons business is considered.

Overall's fateful encounter with the hypocrisy of the TVA's commitment to safety began in an ordinary enough way. After the ice baskets had been filled to the brim, he had to deal with the ice overflow, which had collected on the floor of the great ice condenser compartment. He had developed a method of vacuuming the overflow into a melting tank so the whole operation could be done neatly and efficiently.

The trouble showed up when Overall cleaned out the melt tank after all the water had been drained away. He found a large collection of steel screws and screw heads, over 200 at final count. He recognized them immediately as the type of screw that fastened the ice baskets to the containment's superstructure. He knew there shouldn't be loose screws in the melt tank, and certainly not screw heads, since these were specially manufactured to high standards and installed according to a clear QA procedure. On the other hand, he knew the ice baskets had been installed in the "bad old days" before QA problems had brought the TVA's entire nuclear program to its knees. So the presence of screws and screw heads in the melt tank could be a problem if it was a sign that there were large numbers of missing or fractured screws.

Overall was well versed in the procedures for such an "adverse condition," and he proceeded to prepare a problem evaluation report (PER) that would initiate a series of actions through which the TVA could evaluate the importance of the problem and decide what to do about it. He sent some of the screws and screw heads to the TVA's metallurgical lab to get a report on how and why they had failed.

The collection of broken screws Overall had found was a very small fraction, only 0.1 percent, of all the ice basket screws in the system. The relevant safety question was, how many more bad screws were there? Was his discovery a sign of a big problem, or of no problem? If only 0.1 percent of the screws were bad, safety analysts could probably perform calculations showing that the ice condenser system would be quite capable of performing its safety function, which was to absorb the heat and steam from a pipe break accident. But if a much larger fraction, say 10 percent or 20 percent, were defective, then the immense forces from the steam release could tear one or more ice baskets from the framework and hurl it upward toward the containment dome. Overall knew that just such an incident had occurred at a Westinghouse ice condenser test facility many years earlier, when a basket that had not been properly secured had been launched through the roof by the force of the test's steam release.

To answer the question of how many defective screws were involved, Overall developed a plan for inspecting a representative sample of locations throughout the ice chest, using video cameras for locations that were otherwise inaccessible. If the results came up favorable, the PER could be closed out, and the schedule for starting up Watts Bar would not be greatly affected. On the other hand, if a significant fraction of the sampled locations were missing screws, then that would mean trouble: the ice would have to be melted and drained, and a complete refurbishment of the ice baskets would be needed. The schedule for fuel loading and plant startup would then be shifted by six months or more. The end-of-1995 milestone would be missed, and bonuses, like Kingsley's $147,000, could be in jeopardy.[22]

With such high stakes, TVA management soon began to show an interest in Overall's findings. First, about six weeks after he initiated the PER, they transferred it to another organization, a virtually unprecedented step that isolated Overall from further involvement in the safety issue. Second, they insisted that the metallurgy department revise its report on the defective screws and delete most of its conclusions about the likely causes for failure. Third, they notified Overall that he was to be transferred from his present position to a group of "at-risk" employees—essentially people targeted for a layoff. All this happened less than two months after he had filed the PER. Before Overall joined the at-risk group, where he would spend his time writing proposals and sending out resumes, his managers at Watts Bar asked him to do just one last thing for them: train an inexperienced employee to take over his former job.[23]

With Overall out of the picture, TVA management soon closed out the PER without performing an inspection, video or otherwise. A year later, Overall was laid off. None of this was reported to the NRC.

It was a cruel blow to Overall's career. He had achieved a high level of responsibility through seventeen years of hard work at the TVA but had never completed all the courses he needed to get the bachelor's degree that would allow him to be called "engineer" and that would guarantee that his job skills would be marketable and portable. He tried for months to find work that used his hard-won skills, but he got nowhere. The best he could do was a factory job paying $7 an hour.[24] Finally, feeling abused and misused by his former employer, he filed suit against the TVA in January 1997, invoking the whistle-blower protection provisions of the Energy Reorganization Act.

The ruling in Overall's case took more than a year, and in the interim his dire financial situation required his son to drop out of college and his wife and daughter to take additional jobs. He suffered great emotional strain from the whole experience and went under the care of a psychologist. But in April 1998 Overall finally had cause to celebrate when the administrative law judge handed the TVA one more in a long string of defeats in whistle-blower cases. He ordered Overall reinstated to his old job, with back pay, legal expenses, and $50,000 in compensatory damages.[25]

But as with many of these cases the employee won on paper and lost in real life. The TVA appealed the case immediately, ensuring another long delay. At least, Overall thought, he had his job back, and the blow to his finances would be repaired. Little did he know that the "TVA way" was about to put his life in danger.

In August, the anonymous threats began. Notes arrived via interoffice mail or were left on his windshield or at the front door of his house. One threat contained just the word "Silkwood," referring to the nuclear whistle-blower who had died under mysterious circumstances in 1974. He was threatened in anonymous phone calls. Then one day, he returned to his truck after shopping at an office supply store and found a package that looked very much like a bomb, what local police called "a hoax device" made by a professional or highly skilled amateur.[26]

Shattered and suffering from chest pains, Overall was admitted into a hospital under an assumed name (at the suggestion of local law enforcement). It would be months before he would be able to return to work, but at least he was able to draw a paycheck from the employer he was still fighting in court.

The TVA lost its appeal of the Overall case in April 2001.[27] Again it had to pay Overall's legal costs, but no additional compensatory damages were awarded.* The TVA's next step was predictable: it appealed the case to the next level. It is now *TVA v. the U.S. Department of Labor.*

Forced into action by these ugly revelations, the NRC fined the TVA $88,000 for its discriminatory treatment of Overall in late 2001.[28]

The TVA's actions in this case may seem inexplicable. These legal rulings are not close calls. The judges have rejected the TVA's arguments with force, and one can even read in the rulings a degree of anger between the lines. But a review of the costs and benefits of the TVA's course of action reveals that, in the light of the organization's hidden agendas, every step taken makes sense.

By isolating Overall from the deliberations about the broken screws, TVA management was able to declare the ice condenser operable without having to perform the video inspections that he had proposed. It thus avoided the risk of discovering an unacceptably high fraction of damaged

---

* Overall has filed a separate suit aginst the TVA charging than it violated the Energy Reorganization Act by not providing a safe working environment for employees who raise safety issues. The suit refers to the threats against Overall and the TVA's failure to take action about them. The case is still before the Department of Labor's administrative law judge.

or missing screws, which it knew would cause the end-of-1995 startup milestone to be missed.

Then, by going to court against Overall instead of settling with him, the TVA accomplished another goal—it broadcast a strong, familiar message to all employees: cooperate with management on QA and safety issues or pay a high price. This is not to say that the TVA today is as contemptuous of QA as it was in the 1970s and 1980s. It is just that differences of opinion between staff and managers on QA matters are to be resolved quickly and quietly in the manner directed by management. It is a standard of behavior with roots deep in TVA's past, and it is illegal.

The logic behind the TVA's two appeals is similar. The more time that passes with Curtis Overall in limbo and living a life of discomfort and fear, the clearer is the TVA's message to problem employees. His health has suffered grievously from stress-related ailments. Few people at the TVA admire him; no one envies him. The anonymous threats indicate that there are some who hate him. This outcome is sad, but it strengthens the authority of TVA management over its employees immensely. No other explanation for TVA's actions fits.

These are potent benefits when viewed through the prism of the TVA's authority structure, but what about the costs? The fines against the TVA to date total less than $300,000, a miniscule amount to a government agency that services a $26 billion debt. The TVA no doubt sees as unfortunate the harsh criticism of some of its managers levied by the judges and the NRC. But part of the TVA way is to forgive its loyal soldiers for occasional excesses of zeal. Many of the managers who perpetrated the wrongs against Overall have received excellent promotions since he discovered the broken screws.[29] The lawyer who represented the TVA in the lawsuits is now general counsel, the TVA's top legal gun.

The TVA's nuclear division today is not the same organization it was when QA failures brought it to an embarrassing halt in 1985. For one thing it no longer builds reactors: Watts Bar was the last nuclear reactor completed in the United States, having taken twenty-four years and $7 billion to build, a record in both respects. For another thing regulators no longer routinely single out the TVA as a QA disaster: its five operating reactors have records of violations and achievements that are about average for U.S. utilities.[30] Clearly people at the TVA have learned that QA is not a joke and that following procedures for nuclear operations is not that difficult.

But as Curtis Overall's story shows, the TVA still marches to a different drum in many ways. It still enjoys remarkable autonomy, being regulated in limited respects only by the Department of Labor and NRC, whose punishments apparently do not sting. The three-person board remains isolated from nuclear operations and incapable of imposing its will on the divisions below it. The management consists largely of long-time employees who have paid their dues and who now demand respect and obedience in return. As an organization the TVA is inflexible, deeply resistant to reform, and, when threatened, quite capable of behavior that is contrary to the interests of the public it is supposed to serve. Yet this is the agency that now seeks the NRC's permission to modify the Watts Bar and Sequoyah reactors so they can make tritium for its partner bureaucracy, the DOE. It is an ominous prospect.

Visualize This

If the TVA and DOE have their way, there will be a time in the not too distant future when the nuclear reactors at Watts Bar and Sequoyah will operate slightly differently than they do now. The differences, though, will hardly be noticeable to workers at the plants or the people who live near them. But deep inside the reactor cores, hundreds of long, thin rods owned by the DOE will be undergoing a slow transformation caused by the storm of neutrons generated by the fuel rods only inches away. Slowly, the lithium layers in the rods will change to tritium, destined to recharge the hydrogen bombs of America's nuclear arsenal. Unfortunately there will in all probability be an additional invisible change: these workers and neighbors will be significantly more at risk from a serious accident at these reactors, an accident that would release massive amounts of deadly radioactivity into the atmosphere and the Tennessee River.

In its request to the NRC to amend its operating license to allow tritium production, the TVA claims that these plants will be adequately safe after the changes necessary to enable the plants to produce tritium are made.[31] Fortunately, experts at the NRC, who can either approve or reject the license amendment, must make an independent review of this claim. Their overriding concern in this review will be public safety.

But there is a problem. The NRC, like all government agencies, must follow a set of rules codified in federal law, and the current regulatory structure is not well suited to this unique nuclear safety situation. The peculiar history of commercial nuclear power has shaped today's regulatory environment, and the routine processes and procedures available to the regulators are poorly suited to an adequate evaluation of the proposed reactor changes. The problem is core melt accidents.

The old rules for getting an operating license for a nuclear reactor said applicants didn't have to consider the rare combinations of failures that might lead to core melt accidents. Then the accidents at TMI and Chernobyl caused regulators as well as nuclear reactor designers to rethink that philosophy. In the United States (and elsewhere) there emerged new concepts for "passive" reactors that factored resistance to core melt accidents into their designs. In parallel, the NRC developed new approaches to regulation allowing the licensee to use probabilistic risk analysis to claim credit for those aspects of the new designs that reduce risk to the public in innovative ways. But in a sense it was too late to correct the regulatory misconceptions of the past, since there have been no new nuclear plants ordered in the United States since TMI.

What to do about all the plants that were operating or under construction before the new appreciation of core melt accidents was thus the defining question for NRC and the nuclear industry in the 1980s and 1990s. Applying strict new rules like the ones worked out for future reactors would have forced many plants to shut down. Doing nothing was out of the question politically.

Eventually, a vast and complex compromise in the venerable spirit of grandfathering was worked out. The old licensing rules were allowed to stand, with slight modifications, and the plant owners took the initiative to upgrade their plants based on the findings of their own risk analyses (called "individual plant examinations"). Numerous plant changes, mostly voluntary, have resulted in a fleet of reactors that is probably much less likely to undergo core melt accidents than before. In contrast, the protection to the public afforded by the reactors' containment systems was not greatly improved, even for designs like the ice condensers at Sequoyah and Watts Bar.

This great compromise was rooted in the belief that nuclear reactors, even those designed according to the old rules, posed no undue threat to the public when built and operated properly and that the economic benefit of the electric power they generated outweighed their deficiencies with respect to core melt accidents. Now the NRC is faced with a licensee that wants to use its reactor for more than just electricity, a licensee that wants to get into a side business with its nuclear power plants. To make the NRC's dilemma worse, these plants are ice condensers, known to be marginal with respect to core melt accidents.

The changes proposed for the TVA's reactors are not trivial. They involve the reactor core itself, the heart of the beast. A higher degree of fuel enrichment will be needed for tritium production. A new machine will be installed in the refueling canal to pull the tritium-bearing rods out of the core and bundle them for transportation off-site. The expected concentration of tritium in the cooling system will be more than doubled, since some leakage from the tritium-producing rods is unavoidable. This means that these plants will leak more tritium into the Tennessee River (by as much as a factor of seven), since it is impossible to prevent the migration of tritium from the primary system into the river.[32] Since tritium is radioactive and poses health hazards even at low doses, increased leakage into the river means increased public risk.

The implications of these and many other changes will be difficult to assess. What is certain, however, is that the increase in risk to the public will be due almost entirely to core melt accidents. But the old licensing rules, only slightly modified since TMI, still apply to these reactors, and the TVA's license amendment requests don't mention core melt accidents.

For example, nowhere is it discussed what would happen if power to the plant from the electric grid was lost and the backup diesel generators that provide emergency electricity to the reactor coolant pumps also failed. The scenario is called "station blackout," and it is a dangerous event for most nuclear plants, because the pumps and emergency devices that keep the core from overheating must have electricity to work. Computer simulations performed for the NRC are generally consistent in their predictions for what would happen at Watts Bar or Sequoyah if the station blackout persisted for a day or more. The core would overheat, melt down to the bottom of the reactor vessel, and melt through the vessel. At that point, the only thing keeping the colossal quantities of radioactive smoke and gas from escaping to the outside environment would be the containment. But as discussed in chapter 3, ice condenser containments are so poorly suited to such conditions that they will almost certainly fail, releasing a massive and deadly cloud of radio-activity. People living within a hundred miles or so would then be at the mercy of the winds and the weather. Fatalities could be in the hundreds or thousands.

This is the kind of accident that deserves the attention of the safety analysts, but station blackout is not discussed in the TVA's license amend-ment requests. The old licensing rules assumed that simultaneous failure of access to the grid and on-site diesels was too unlikely to worry about. But the scenario could happen in real life. In 1990 the Vogtle nuclear power plant in Georgia experienced a station blackout for thirty-five minutes, not long enough to cause core damage, but long enough to be scary. In 1996 the Catawba plant, an ice condenser in South Carolina, lost off-site power for more than a day with only one of its two diesel generators working.[33]

Such events are "beyond the design basis," and the TVA offered no thoughts on them in its submittals to the NRC. But the effects on public safety of the proposed plant changes reside almost entirely in the realm beyond the design basis. For example, the changes will probably cause there to be more "outages," or reactor shutdowns, per year. It is widely believed that the risk of a core melt accident increases with the number of outages per year, an effect analogous to the heightened risk of airline accidents during takeoffs and landings.[34] This impact on public safety is not discussed in the TVA's submittals.

Another potential source of increased risk involves organizational factors. Increasing the complexity of the power plants' function (chang-ing from one mission to two) will create a cascade of effects on what are called "human factors." There will be changes in various probabilities having to do with workers forgetting or ignoring key steps in procedures or managers providing ambiguous guidance. Modern analysis tools for evaluating the effects of plant changes on human factors could be used to address these subtle but important issues, but the TVA's license amendment requests don't deal with these issues at all. Given the track record of the TVA as an organization, it is likely that it would adapt to the changed mission less effectively than most utilities would.

Nor do the TVA's submittals discuss the highly sensitive, but highly important, issue of sabotage. All of the facilities of the U.S. nuclear weapons complex are heavily defended against attacks from the outside, whether they be surreptitious attempts to penetrate the various layers of protection, armed assaults, suicide missions, or combinations of all three. Specially trained and equipped guard forces maintain an extraordinary degree of readiness with live-fire training exercises and continuous surveillance of boundaries and entry points. The DOE sites where nuclear weapons or weapon ingredients are handled or produced are located in remote, hard-to-reach, hard-to-penetrate places like the Savannah River site, where the tritium from the irradiated rods will be extracted. The remoteness of these sites serves the additional function of minimizing exposure of the public to hazardous materials in case the facilities are damaged by some kind of external attack.

In contrast, the Sequoyah and Watts Bar plants are only lightly protected and are not significantly isolated from civilian populations. They are power plants, not military installations. Fishermen troll the waters of Watts Bar Lake a stone's throw from the chain-link fences surrounding the nuclear power plant. Sequoyah is located in a highly populated region, just ten miles from downtown Chattanooga, Tennessee's fourth-largest city. The discovery in 2001 of detailed drawings of U.S. nuclear power plants at abandoned Al Qaeda caves in Afghanistan has sharply increased concerns about nuclear power plant security.[35] Recognizing the possibility that U.S. nuclear power plants could be future targets for terrorists, the NRC in 2002 decided to order upgraded security at all commercial reactors.[36] But it is highly unlikely that security at the Watts Bar and Sequoyah plants could ever be brought up to the level of the facilities of the nuclear weapons complex.

It seems reasonable to ask, therefore, whether the new mission of producing materials for nuclear weapons at these nuclear power plants might increase the likelihood of a terrorist attack on them and what hazards such an attack might pose to the nearby population. The way to analyze such issues is called "external events risk analysis," and it is a well-developed branch of probabilistic risk analysis. The old licensing rules, however, do not require such a study.

There is a way that the NRC could invoke probabilistic risk analysis even though these license amendment requests fall under the domain of the old licensing rules. Over the past fifteen years or so the NRC and the nuclear industry have developed a concept called "risk-informed decision making" to augment traditional safety analysis.[37] It is usually used when a plant owner identifies a way to reduce costs or improve production but can't implement the improvement because one or more NRC requirements stands in the way. So the licensee attempts to demonstrate with risk analysis that the requirement could be relaxed or modified with no significant impact on public safety. If the NRC agrees with the analysis, the relief is granted. Predictably, it is a very popular concept with the industry, and an often criticized one among antinuclear groups.

But the NRC's guidelines on risk-informed decision making also allow for the more unusual situation when the NRC staff sees the potential for increased public risk because of a requested change but the licensee has offered only traditional analysis.[38] Under those conditions, the guidelines authorize the staff to request risk-related information and analyses from the licensee. The language in the NRC procedures is guarded about this option, since the guidelines must respect the grandfathering compromise that requires the NRC to operate under the old licensing rules for all existing plants. Consequently, the procedures state that responding to the NRC's request for risk information is voluntary on the part of the licensee.

Given the high political stakes involved, and given how rarely the NRC has invoked its authority to evaluate non-risk-based amendment requests with risk-based analysis, it is unlikely that the TVA's request to convert its plants to tritium production will be denied on the basis of risk information.*

The fact that the safety review of the changes proposed for the TVA's reactors would occur within the traditional licensing framework was surely a factor in the DOE's decision in 1998 to pursue the commercial-reactor route for its tritium supply. Options involving a new nuclear facility might have been subject to much higher standards of safety review. Besides, it must be nice for the DOE to be off stage in this potentially contentious and highly visible situation. The TVA and NRC must play the lead roles, and all the DOE does is pay everyone's salary.

* The NRC's review of the TVA license amendment requests began in September 2001. At press time, the NRC's use of risk analysis in its ongoing review has been very limited.

That in itself is one of the strangest facts in a very strange situation. All NRC reviewers, all of the TVA personnel who have prepared and are defending their license amendment requests, and all the contractors each side hires to assist it are paid with DOE funds. It will amount to a lot of money, but to the DOE it is apparently worth it. It had only two other choices: build a brand new tritium-producing facility or admit that no tritium will be needed for fifteen years or more. The former would cost money and bring inevitable headaches, and the latter would cost a lot of political capital among the powerful constituencies that the DOE's nuclear weapons program must satisfy.

In the same vein, it is worth asking why the TVA would want to take on the tritium mission. The answer is not obvious until one looks beneath the surface, at the hidden agendas motivating its board of directors. There one will find that the board's greatest fear is the push to break the agency up and sell its power assets to private industry. The idea has been around for a long time. It was endorsed in a 1997 Congressional Budget Office report, and numerous congressmen from the Northeast and Midwest have campaigned long and hard for it.[39] Strong opposition from congressional delegations in the TVA's service area has beaten back these efforts so far, but adding a tritium mission to some of the TVA's reactors would create a lasting bulwark against the threat. With Watts Bar and Sequoyah churning out tritium along with their megawatts, privatization of the TVA would become greatly complicated. What other electric utility would want to take over these plants and their dual missions? If no one wanted them, would the DOE be willing to operate them as part of the weapons complex? It is highly unlikely.

Finally, there is the NRC. What hidden agendas motivate its decision makers? Its top people would have preferred, no doubt, that the TVA's request had never been made. That is one of the reasons that the DOE's claim, later found to be false, that the NRC participated in its *Interagency Review* seemed so inexplicable. High political sensitivity about severe accidents will play a role in the NRC's behavior with respect to the TVA's request. A dominant behavior pattern at all levels in the agency is avoidance of controversy, and core melt accident issues are intrinsically controversial. Because the probability of core melting is so low and at the same time so uncertain (ranging, for example, from 0.001 per year to 0.000001 per year), it is maddeningly difficult to resolve arguments about it. Recent history has shown that some in the NRC are quite capable of manipulating information for the purpose of minimizing the importance of severe-accident issues, as was shown in chapter 3.

The NRC will surely be hesitant to invoke its seldom-used authority to initiate a discussion about the risk implications of the TVA's requested license amendments, because doing so could unavoidably affect future licensing activities. Antinuclear activists could point to such an action as setting a precedent that should be followed in other cases. Similarly, the nuclear industry watches the NRC's actions closely for signs of "ratcheting," the slow tightening of regulatory oversight that occurs in small steps, one ruling at a time. The industry battled against ratcheting in the post-TMI era and remains highly sensitive about it today. Consequently, a rejection of the TVA amendments on the basis of severe-accident concerns is sure to elicit sharp criticism from the nuclear industry.

The fact that some aspects of the modified reactors' safety are classified casts further doubt on the vigor the NRC is likely to bring to bear in reviewing the TVA's request. Secrecy for some aspects of the NRC's review may be unavoidable for national security reasons, but it may also serve a secondary purpose: shielding an inadequate safety review from the public eye. The opposition between secrecy and protection of the public and the environment is seen clearly in the history of the DOE's nuclear weapons complex, as discussed in chapter 5.

These considerations lead to pessimism about how well the public's interests will be served as these three federal bureaucracies move forward on the new tritium policy. Each agency has a charter that prominently includes protection of the public from nuclear hazards, but for each there are powerful forces operating from within that can compromise how effectively that charter is carried out.

Grievous policy missteps concerning nuclear energy and nuclear weapons have occurred before. This book has described several such cases of institutional failure. But history has also provided examples of recovery from nuclear folly, such as Jimmy Carter's clear-sighted, though clumsy, redirection of U.S. plutonium policy (chapter 2). Flaws in the agencies charged with nuclear matters can be overcome by public awareness and the operation of checks and balances within the representative system of government. How that might take place in regard to the new tritium policy is discussed in the book's final chapter.

7

What's the Rush?

Chicago, February 27, 2002: Today the Board of Directors of the *Bulletin of the Atomic Scientists* moves the minute hand of the "Doomsday Clock," the symbol of nuclear danger, from nine to seven minutes to midnight, the same setting at which the clock debuted 55 years ago.
Bulletin of the Atomic Scientists, 2002

This has been a story about harm done to the public, but it is not a chronicle of dark deeds by scoundrels. It is a thoroughly modern account of institutions that are charged with looking after the public interest failing to do so, failing not through venality or corruption, but because nuclear arms issues are so complex and potent that individuals operating within the various nuclear bureaucracies lose perspective. It is difficult, year in and year out, to remain acutely aware of the awesome danger that nuclear weapons pose, and it is easy to allow complacency slowly to overtake concern.

In 1981, historian Michael Brenner reflected on the exceptional challenge of managing the two sides of nuclear technology: "The closer one looks at the intricate and varied terrain of the proliferation issue, the more one appreciates the requirements for an unusually high degree of policy integration across an exceptionally broad range of issues. Easy tolerance of a disjointed approach to nuclear energy questions can expose proliferation concerns to the vagaries of domestic energy politics, or to the parochial behavior of executive agencies."[1] Today, the same might be said about other emerging high-technology issues, like genetic engineering, the Internet, and health care, to name a few. The answer to these challenges should be not acquiescence, but insistence on the high degree of integration and responsibility that they require.

We could simply point the finger of blame at former Secretary of Energy Bill Richardson for abandoning the U.S. policy against the production of nuclear weapon materials in commercial power reactors, but the story presented in the book shows that he is not alone culpable. For example, the Bush administration continues to follow the tritium plan Richardson initiated, years after he departed the scene. And years before Richardson took the top job at the DOE much of the groundwork for the policy reversal was laid by others, as revealed in chapter 5. In 1995, proponents of the ailing nuclear power industry prevailed upon Hazel O'Leary, then Energy Secretary, to make a last-minute revision to a key EIS, changing the status of the commercial-reactor concept for weapons tritium from forbidden to on a par with all other options under consideration. Brazen spinners in her department explained that the change was due to public comment, an unsupportable distortion.

Three years later, but still before Richardson's arrival, top DOE staff penned a manifesto for abandoning the nation's long-standing no-dual-use policy under the guise of responding to a congressional request for a thorough multiagency examination of the policy. Rather than a balanced policy review, Congress got a vaporous and anonymous brief full of dodges and deceit.

These early events might never have been of great consequence, except for the fortuitous fact that the TVA desperately desired to unburden itself of a "stranded asset," the Bellefonte nuclear station. When the DOE solicited utility interest in its plan to make tritium in commercial reactors, the only bidder was the TVA, whose financial straits led to its offer of the Bellefonte plant for conversion to a tritium factory, arguing that the DOE's policy study legitimized the concept.

But the new Energy Secretary was Richardson, a savvy and confident leader, who pulled the rug out from under the TVA by insisting on a deal involving its operating nuclear power plants, not Bellefonte. Unaware of the deceptions and distortions in the *Interagency Review*, he believed it gave a green light equally to Bellefonte and existing, licensed plants. When the TVA balked, Richardson demonstrated his clout in the Clinton administration through an unusual invocation of the Economy Act, and after a year of pressure, the TVA finally conceded, giving Richardson what he wanted: the ability to make tritium for nuclear weapons in currently licensed electricity-producing nuclear power plants.

There is something peculiar, though, about the Economy Act story. A careful reading of the statute suggests that the DOE's claim that the act *required* the TVA to go along with its plan would very likely have failed in a court of law. A more plausible explanation of why the TVA eventually gave in to the DOE's demand is that the TVA's board, once it gave up on a Bellefonte deal, recognized, Brer' Rabbit–style, that being thrown into the briar patch of the nuclear weapons complex might not be so bad. Certainly, such a move might help thwart its enemies' attempts to privatize the beleaguered old New Deal agency.

This is indeed not a tale of dark deeds, but rather a narrative of bureaucratic gambits and countergambits, image management, and spin control, all against a background of, in Brenner's words, "vagaries of domestic energy politics" and "parochial behavior of executive agencies." It is about bureaucrats who have lost their compass.

Brenner also spoke of the government's disjointed approach on nuclear questions, a characteristic that also persists to this day. The disjointed nature of government responsibility for things nuclear is manifest, for example, in the fact that proponents of the new tritium plan appear never to have considered the safety problems of the three operating reactors targeted for conversion to weapons work. As discussed in chapter 3, these ice condenser plants are in a small class that NRC studies have identified as particularly vulnerable to core melt accidents. Their vulnerability is widely recognized throughout the reactor safety community, but the NRC has decided that these problems are not sufficient to require modifications or to shut the plants down. That decision is largely a reflection of the fact that there are only a small number of these plants in the United States and that after decades of conflict with the nuclear industry over severe accidents, the NRC has come to a "live and let live" compromise with nuclear utilities, allowing them to operate under the licensing rules first formulated in the early 1960s.

In its review of the TVA's requests to amend the Watts Bar and Sequoyah operating licenses, the NRC is assessing the safety of these plants, both as is and after modifications. There are many reasons to fear that this review will be superficial and biased. Over the past fifteen years the nuclear industry, through its relentless lobbying of Congress, has pressured the NRC to bring to an end its program of research on core melt accidents, a program prompted by the TMI accident in 1979. Today the regulatory agency is well chastened by that pressure and is strongly inclined to take a narrow view of its responsibilities, as explained in chapter 3. It has already gone on record that it is of no regulatory concern that the plant modifications have nothing to do with electricity production or public safety.

A thorough and objective assessment of safety issues is made even less likely by the tangle of vested and conflicted interests among the players in the safety review: the DOE, the TVA, Westinghouse (the TVA's contractor for safety analysis), and the NRC. The DOE can bring enormous pressure within the administration on the NRC, meeting any NRC delays in approving the license amendment with accusations that the regulatory agency is jeopardizing the viability of the commercial nuclear industry *and* national security. As for the TVA, the license amendment review puts that beleaguered federal utility in the position of defending not just the modifications of the three reactors it operates at the two plants, but also their safety as they are currently configured and operated. Any rock overturned in the safety review could result in costly shutdowns and backfits just to be able to continue producing and selling electricity. Westinghouse is in a similarly compromised position; since it designed all nine of the virtually identical ice condenser plants in the United States, it will be strongly motivated to avoid questions about their vulnerability to core melt accidents. And finally, the NRC has learned a simple fact of life about regulating the declining nuclear industry: controversy leads to budget cuts.

All these parties will be well served, at least in terms of their own interests, if the NRC just takes a legalistic approach to the license review, following the old procedures of safety analysis that were the basis on which the original operating licenses for the three TVA reactors were granted, forgoing the modern procedures based on risk analysis it now has at its disposal. The temptation for the NRC to rely solely on the old procedures will be strong, despite the fact that these traditional analysis methods are blind to core melt accidents, the most important source of public risk from nuclear reactors.

Then there is the problem that some aspects of the redesigned nuclear core will now involve classified information, resulting in greatly reduced public access to the NRC's safety review. As discussed in chapters 4 and

5, the history of nuclear secrecy in the United States yields four important insights:

• The machinery of classification and secrecy often screens government operations from external scrutiny, leading to shortcuts where protecting the public and the environment is concerned.
• It is impossible to prevent the diffusion of scientific and engineering concepts through a system of secrecy imposed within an open society.
• In the absence of a sense of national urgency, it is difficult to achieve scrupulous adherence to classification procedures in civilian organizations.
• Failures of the secrecy system generally lead to stricter controls rather than more realistic assessments of the possibility of preventing leaks.

What these insights mean for the commercial tritium option is, first, that the imposition of secrecy will erode, to an unpredictable degree, the checks and balances that have been implemented to ensure that the public is protected from nuclear reactor accidents, and second, that implementing the new technology for producing tritium in commercial reactors will doubtless lead to the dissemination of that technology to other countries. Neither of these concerns seems to have been considered in the government's plan for tritium production.

If the stakes in this matter were not so high, we could tolerate these errors of judgment. Poor decisions and wrong-headed policies are rife in the federal government, so much so as to provide an endless supply of humorous anecdotes. But we are not talking about subsidies to beekeepers or pork-barrel water projects. In this transition period between the old cold war and a new world of shifting alliances energized by virulent international terrorism, control of production and distribution of tritium should be viewed as being as important as control of fissile materials was in the past.

The spread of advanced manufacturing technology, the broad availability of information about nuclear weapon design, and the very real potential for the diversion of weapons-grade plutonium or uranium from Russia's poorly guarded stores all mean that the technical barriers to upgrading a fission weapon to a deuterium-tritium-boosted weapon has been dramatically reduced. This means the likelihood that a proliferator will acquire H-bomb capability soon after acquiring A-bomb capability is much greater than before, especially if tritium is easy to obtain or to produce. And an H-bomb arsenal is many times more dangerous and more deliverable than the equivalent arsenal of pure fission weapons.

These developments call for enhanced vigilance about the availability of tritium and the technology for producing it. But with its new tritium policy, the DOE is inexplicably moving in the opposite direction, risking worldwide dissemination of the new technology for producing tritium by using commercial facilities that were never designed to protect classified information. At the same time, the new policy on tritium production undermines the symbolic potency of the long-standing U.S. policy whereby it voluntarily imposes the same restriction on its own commercial nuclear industry that the NPT imposes on non–weapons states.

This long bill of charges invites the obvious question: "why?" Richardson said the new policy of producing tritium for military weapons in commercial reactors would save money, but as discussed in chapter 5, the amounts likely to be saved are small compared to the annual operating costs of the nuclear weapons program. Besides, there is another obvious question not addressed by the budget savings justification. That question is "why now?" What is the rush?

Highly credible experts put the date when new tritium would be needed to replenish the decaying stock in the U.S. arsenal as late as the year 2029,[2] assuming only modest reductions in the active stockpile relative to START-II levels (see chapter 5). The Bush administration is today planning arms reductions much greater than those assumptions, implying an even later date before new tritium is needed. *What, possibly, can be the justification for throwing aside a cherished nonproliferation tradition in order to have a supply of new tritium thirty or more years before it is needed?*

At one level there is a plausible answer to this question, one that is consistent with the cynical game playing that has so often characterized the federal government's actions regarding nuclear technology. The nuclear weapons complex has an embarassing twenty-year history of trying and failing to decide about its long-term source of new tritium. An easy path was presented to it when Richardson set aside the dual-use prohibition and chose the commercial-reactor option for producing the tritium. Old cold warriors in the government surely see the desirability of taking the last few steps along this path: getting the NRC licenses for the three TVA reactors amended and carrying out at least one complete irradiation and extraction cycle. Postponing those steps to a future in which the public might be more engaged and opposition stronger surely would seem unwise to them. It is almost certainly for that reason that the DOE schedule for when new tritium is "required" is still based on START-I stockpile levels, not those of START-II or the even lower levels recently announced by President Bush.

But at another level, the heart of the answer to the question "why?" is that the leaders and bureaucrats who have taken on the responsibility of managing the country's nuclear programs and policies have lost their perspectives and consequently cannot carry out their duty to the public. They no longer can fairly judge what is important.

The deeply flawed U.S. tritium policy has been justified in large measure by a false assertion of crisis about the need for new tritium, with the DOE establishing 2006 as the date by which new supplies have to be available. This brings to mind a parallel series of events in 1974, when bureaucrats in the Nixon administration created an artificial crisis in uranium enrichment services through a series of legalistic ploys and tricky deals. As explained in chapter 2, that crisis did immediate and lasting damage to the interests of the United States and the people of the world by creating a strong incentive for other countries to obtain enrichment technology on their own, in exact opposition to the U.S. government's policy on nonproliferation.

In chapter 2 the remarkable parallels between the artificial enrichment crisis of the 1970s and the unwise new tritium policy of the 1990s were delineated. Brenner has chronicled the irreparable damage done to U.S. interests by the manipulations of Nixon-era nuclear bureaucrats. Opportunities to prudently manage the dual sides of nuclear technology were lost in the ensuing international crisis. Also irreparably damaged was the reputation of the United States as a fair world leader in nuclear affairs and as an honest negotiator. These consequences were vastly out of proportion to the benefits envisioned by the perpetrators of the crisis. Today, the world is far more complex than it was in the 1970s, and the potential damage from such shortsighted nuclear policy excursions is correspondingly greater.

The U.S. government plans to begin irradiation of tritium-producing rods at the TVA's Watts Bar reactor (or one of the Sequoyah reactors) by the year 2006. It is still possible that this plan will be abandoned, either through White House recognition of its folly or as a result of pressure from Congress or the public. Public awareness of the dangers of weapons of mass destruction has been elevated by the terrorist attacks of September 11, 2001, and their aftermath. Perhaps this heightened awareness will manifest itself in a more critical attitude toward the government's nuclear weapons policies. Exactly how pressure might be brought to bear as a result of this greater awareness depends on the outcome of events in the near future.

One possibility that could alter the DOE's commercial-reactor tritium production plan is that the NRC will rise to the occasion and apply probabilisitic risk assessment techniques in assessing the TVA's license amendment requests. Such a step would bring into sharp focus the impact of the proposed reactor conversions on the safety of the surrounding populations. Not the least of these impacts is the increased likelihood of terrorist attacks on these plants after they have been converted to be, effectively, the most vulnerable elements of the nuclear weapons complex. Risk analysis might even cause the NRC to deny the TVA's requests, though the typical outcome of contentious license amendment proceedings is that the licensee withdraws the request when defeat seems inevitable.

Such an outcome would force the DOE to revise its schedule for when new tritium is needed. In the decades made available by such a reassessment, there would be plenty of time to design and construct a dedicated tritium production facility within the weapons complex proper.

Another way the government's new tritium plan might be redirected is through presidential involvement, just as Jimmy Carter reversed the U.S. commitment to a plutonium economy in the 1970s. George W. Bush's personal involvement in negotiations on nuclear arms reductions with the Russians may expose him to the glaring contradictions between the current tritium production schedule and the size of the planned nuclear arms cuts. Like his father before him (chapter 5), Bush can win points from all sides by simply deferring further expenditures on a new source for tritium until there is an actual need. But instead of slipping the schedule by just five years as his father did, Bush can probably afford ten to twenty years.

Congress might be the place from which sanity is injected into the government's tritium production program. An amendment to declare tritium a "special nuclear material" whose production would be illegal in commercial reactors passed in the House but failed in the Senate in 1998. With awareness of nuclear weapons proliferation much elevated today compare to then, such a legislative solution might succeed before the TVA reactors are converted.

In the worst case, even if such redirection of policy does not occur and tritium is finally produced at Watts Bar or Sequoyah, the compromise to the U.S. nonproliferation posture might still be mitigated. Given the sharp reductions in the nuclear arsenals now planned by the Bush administration, the weapons complex will by then be awash in tritium recovered from nuclear warheads removed from the active stockpile. If any sanity prevails when the TVA tritium becomes available, perhaps a renewed commitment to the principle of isolating civilian nuclear power from nuclear weapons work could be demonstrated simply by segregating the TVA-produced tritium from the military inventory. By abstaining from the use of this tritium in nuclear weapons, the United States might salvage some shred of symbolism about its nonproliferation stance.

The sad thing is that even such a feeble gesture would probably encounter opposition from nuclear warriors in the U.S. government, people who have developed an eerie kind of bureaucratic bravado about nuclear weaponry, confusing as wisdom their own desensitization to the dangers of nuclear war.

Managing the risk of nuclear war is surely one of the greatest challenges the United States faced in the twentieth century, and it will continue to be so in the twenty-first. But the nature of the challenge has changed, and an adequate response will be impossible if overall directions and specific decisions are left to the professionals and experts in the nuclear weapons enterprise. The real experts on the best interests of the nation are its citizens and their representatives. Without their informed and active involvement, the risk is high that instead of experiencing a peaceful and prosperous future, the nation and the world will be ravaged and unraveled by pointless and avoidable nuclear conflicts.

Appendix A. Analysis of Public Comments on the DOE's Programmatic Environmental Impact Statement on Tritium Supply and Recycling

The National Environmental Policy Act (NEPA) is a powerful tool created by Congress to force Federal agencies to disclose to the public their intent to build or modify major facilities. Before significant engineering effort can be expended, any agency planning such an undertaking must issue a draft EIS that explains the purpose of the facility or change and lists the alternative approaches being considered (always including "no action"). The law then requires that the EIS be made available to the public through a variety of channels and that the public be offered abundant opportunities to comment on the various options. Though NEPA is an environmental law, it recognizes that government decisions must balance environmental impact against a variety of other considerations, such as cost, safety, and the public interests served by the project. Thus the EIS lays out the agency's thinking about the relative costs and benefits of each alternative approach under consideration, inviting comment on all types of impacts, not just environmental ones.

NEPA does not impose any litmus test for environmental impact per se; rather, it requires the agency to demonstrate that it has factored environmental impacts into its decision process, that it has disclosed to the public the basis for its preference, and that it has obtained public comment. The agency is under no obligation to take account of the public's response to its disclosures in any other way than publishing each comment along with the final version of the EIS, though it is customary to offer commentary on the public input. Citizens, of course, can take any complaints they may have to their representatives or invoke processes defined by other environmental laws; NEPA's primary role is to provide early information that allows such recourse to occur before an agency incurs major costs in pursuing the project.

A federal agency preparing an EIS is not required to assess all conceivable alternatives for its actions, only "reasonable alternatives." Other alternatives may be dismissed peremptorily because of one or more fundamental obstacles like cost, technical feasibility, existing law, or longstanding policies. These "unreasonable alternatives" may be listed, along with the basis for rejecting them, at the beginning of the EIS so that the public is aware of the how the alternatives were narrowed down to a reasonable few. Clearly, the rationale for categorizing an alternative as unreasonable must be compelling.

During James Watkins's tenure as secretary of energy, the DOE carried out a sizable program (the NPR program, discussed in chapter 5) to generate preliminary designs of what were expected to be two large tritium production facilities. The annual tritium output of the two facilities was referred to as the "goal quantity," tied to the size and makeup of the vast U.S. nuclear arsenal before START-I was signed, with a generous margin for even further growth. It was anticipated that the two plants would cost the government $10 billion or more to build and many times that over the life of the plants.[1] Clearly, the option of using some of the currently licensed nuclear power plants to produce the needed tritium had the potential of saving billions of dollars. Yet the CLWR option was summarily rejected in the programmatic EIS for the NPR program. In contrast to the ambiguous position taken later, this EIS was very clear about what was being rejected and why: "The production of nuclear material for defense purposes by commercial power reactors licensed by the U.S. Nuclear Regulatory Commission would be contrary to the longstanding national policy to separate commercial nuclear power generation from the nuclear weapons program."[2] Because of that peremptory rejection, the DOE did not present in the EIS an analysis of the environmental impacts of the CLWR approach to tritium production.

By 1995, arms control measures had caused the goal quantity to be reduced by more than a factor of four.[3] Consequently, the DOE had to undertake a completely new EIS for its proposed commercial tritium production facilities. The draft EIS was superficially consistent with the 1991 report in rejecting CLWR as an unreasonable alternative, giving two reasons: "The production of tritium for defense purposes in nuclear reactors that generate electricity for commercial sale would be contrary to the long-standing policy of the United States that civilian nuclear facilities should not be utilized for military purposes. Such use of commercial reactors would make the United States' nonproliferation efforts much more difficult because other countries could demand equal footing."[4] This time, however, the DOE's rejection of the commercial reactor option was somewhat less complete than in 1991, since the EIS now included a substantial technical analysis of environmental impacts for the CLWR option, apparently just in case minds changed about the no-dual-use policy. With the dramatically reduced size of the required facility, the cost savings that would result from using commercial reactors to produce tritium would be substantially decreased compared to five years earlier. But apparently supporters of the commercial-reactor option had gained influence in the department since 1991, and they had set the stage for overcoming the no-dual-use policy barrier.

The draft EIS was published in March 1995. As explained in chapter 4, when the final version came out in October, the CLWR alternative had been deftly reclassified from "unreasonable" to "reasonable." Conveniently, the environmental analysis had already been performed for the draft report. Thus no further changes (other than promoting the alternative to the status of "reasonable") were needed to put the CLWR on an equal footing to all the other reasonable alternatives—quite a coup!

The DOE explained this reclassification as having been prompted by public comment, a claim that can be put to the test by examination of volume 3 of the final EIS, where detailed information on public comment is published, including comments received at the various public meetings held by the DOE as well as other communications such as letters and faxes. Normally, the information on the public meetings is based on a transcript prepared by court reporters, accurately conveying the words of the citizens that chose to speak at these meetings, along with their names. But for this EIS, the DOE introduced an innovation that unfortunately had the effect of dissociating opinions from individuals. The lead DOE staffer for dealing with public comments was Steven Sohinki, later to become the director of the DOE's overall tritium program. Instead of just taking comments and questions from individual citizens, Sohinki organized the people attending each meeting into "breakout sessions" that brainstormed particular aspects of the EIS, then produced a list of ideas on the assigned topic. This technique is widely used in business situations or in efforts to forge community alliances, but it is singularly inappropriate for capturing the independent opinions of concerned citizens. The information provided in volume 3 of the final EIS concerning these meetings consists of high-level summaries of what subjects were raised, without regard to whether it was DOE personnel, DOE contractors, or private citizens raising them. We simply cannot know what was said by whom.

The written comments do not suffer from these problems; each is reproduced in volume 3 of the EIS. These statements by citizens make possible a quantitative evaluation of the DOE's claim that public comment caused the change in the eligibility status of the CLWR alternative. Such an assessment shows that the facts do not support the claim.

Recall from the main text that there were actually two periods of public comment. First, there was the normal period of two months during which comments were received at the public meetings and by way of mail and other communications. Then, after the end of the comment period, the DOE took the unusual step of soliciting additional public comments specifically on the no-dual-use policy and on whether the CLWR should be reconsidered as a reasonable alternative.

In the written comments from the first comment period, only three individuals offered opinions on the policy allowing tritium production in commercial reactors. Two were against it, and a third favored it. The person who favored it was Christopher Paine, a spokesperson for the Natural Resources Defense Council, an organization generally considered to be antinuclear. Paine's eleven-page letter is deeply critical of the EIS, claiming that it was so deficient as to violate NEPA. On the no-dual-use policy, he maintained that there is no policy that prohibits an arrangement whereby DOE would own the reactor and operate it as a defense facility, while selling the steam to an electric utility to offset operational costs. He cites the N reactor arrangement as precedent. Thus the comments in the initial comment period were two to one against allowing CLWR, and the one endorsing its eligibility was discussing the DOE ownership version of the plan, not the irradiation service option.

In the extended comment period there were many more written comments, which is not surprising, since the DOE's unusual request for additional comments on the policy issue had gotten a lot of attention. A survey of these comments shows fifteen individuals arguing against changing the no-dual-use policy and three supporting it. Two of those three were executives of nuclear companies who would gain directly from allowing the CLWR option. One was a manager from the TVA, who argued the merits of the DOE's purchase of TVA's Bellefonte plant (see chapter 5). The other was George Davis, a manager from ABB, an international reactor manufacturer lobbying hard for a new multipurpose reactor that would make tritium, burn excess weapons plutonium, and generate electricity. Davis was the project manager for this "triple-play" reactor proposal and naturally supported the designation of CLWR as "reasonable," claiming at the same time that the ABB concept should be added to the list of reasonable alternatives. Interestingly, he also chastised the DOE for the way it had finessed the policy issue:

DOE has not provided justification for a last minute change, to allow existing reactors to be included in the final PEIS [programmatic EIS]. The Draft PEIS's nebulous reference to concerns about the "policy issues" related to production of tritium in a commercial reactor were never explained or justified. The Federal Register Notice does not provide any explanation as to why or how the previous concerns have suddenly disappeared. Although we agree with the conclusion, the resulting decision to add existing reactors as a reasonable alternative, at the very last moment, seems suspicious. At the least, it creates the appearance that DOE may have waited until the very last moment, and, then, provide only a very limited public comment period, as a means to limit public input to the NEPA process.[5]

Thus a rough count of support for an interpretation of policy allowing the CLWR as a reasonable alternative is four in favor, seventeen opposed, with much of the support compromised by caveats and conflict of interest.

There is no reason the DOE should make its decisions based solely on a majority opinion from its citizen commentors; certainly NEPA has no such requirement. But the story of the DOE's change of heart about the no-dual-use policy suggests that the public comment process of that law was used as a smokescreen to obscure the real reasons for the reversal.

Appendix B. *Interagency Review of the Nonproliferation Implications of Alternative Tritium Production Technologies under Consideration by the Department of Energy*

The following document was obtained from DOE's CLWR Web site: <http://www.dp.doe.gov/public/> in March 2000. Paragraph numbering has been added to facilitate the critique provided in appendix C. (Since it is an HTML document and only available on the Web, page numbering depends on the computer that downloads the file.)

INTERAGENCY REVIEW OF THE NONPROLIFERATION IMPLICATIONS OF ALTERNATIVE TRITIUM PRODUCTION TECHNOLOGIES UNDER CONSIDERATION BY THE DEPARTMENT OF ENERGY

* * * *

A Report to the Congress
July 1998

Introduction
This report to Congress is provided in response to the direction set forth in the National Defense Authorization Act for Fiscal Year 1998 (P.L. 105–85) Conference Report. The report directs the Secretary of Energy to utilize a senior level, interagency process to review and assess the issues associated with the commercial reactor option for tritium production.

The Department of Energy (DOE) must establish a new source of tritium to maintain the U.S. nuclear weapon stockpile. Currently, the Department is pursuing a dual-track strategy for tritium production: (1) use of a commercial light water reactor (CLWR), and (2) development of a proton accelerator for tritium production. In addition, the

Department is evaluating whether an existing research reactor, known as the Fast Flux Test Facility (FFTF) should play a role in the Department's tritium production strategy. Although the congressional direction required the Department to report only on the issues associated with the commercial reactor option, the Department chose to evaluate the non-proliferation issues associated with each of the options under consideration. This report reflects the Administration's views on all of the technologies.

The report outlines the findings of the review and summarizes the conclusions of Executive Branch agencies developed in the course of the review.

THE NONPROLIFERATION IMPLICATIONS OF ALTERNATIVE TRITIUM PRODUCTION TECHNOLOGIES UNDER CONSIDERATION BY THE DEPARTMENT OF ENERGY

Summary of Conclusions of DOE Review and Results of Interagency Evaluation

I. Background

1.   The Department of Energy (DOE) must establish a new source for producing tritium needed to maintain the U.S. nuclear weapon stockpile. Tritium, a radioactive isotope of hydrogen, is required for all U.S. nuclear weapons to function as designed. The United States has not produced tritium since 1988, when the last of the defense production reactors at DOE's Savannah River Site was shut down. Tritium decays at a rate of about 5.5 percent per year, thus it must be replenished in all U.S. weapons on a routine basis. Since the U.S. nuclear weapons stockpile has been reduced consistent with the Strategic Arms Reduction Treaty, the United States has been able to fulfill its ongoing tritium needs since 1988 by recycling tritium from weapons that have been withdrawn from the stockpile. However, given projected force requirements, the size of the existing tritium stockpile, and tritium decay rates, the United States must establish a new production source by 2005 in order to maintain the reliability of the enduring nuclear weapon stockpile.

2.   It is important to note at the outset that tritium is not a fissionable material capable of sustaining a nuclear reaction. Thus, it is not classi-

fied as a special nuclear material and is therefore not subject to the prohibition in the Atomic Energy Act of 1954, as amended, on the use of such materials for nuclear explosive purposes if produced in a commercial light water reactor.

3.   In December of 1995, DOE, in consultation with the Department of Defense (DOD), decided to pursue research and development of two tritium production technologies: (1) a commercial light water reactor (CLWR), and (2) a proton accelerator. In January 1997, Secretary Hazel O'Leary directed that a third technology, an existing DOE test reactor, known as the Fast Flux Test Facility (FFTF), also be evaluated for its potential role in tritium production.

4.   While resolution of any nonproliferation policy issues is important in making a final determination on a future tritium source, it should be noted that the nonproliferation issues identified in this report represent only one of a range of factors that the Department must take into account in making the tritium production technology decision. The Secretary of Energy must also consider cost, technical risk, legal or regulatory challenges, compatibility with the requirements established in the Nuclear Weapons Stockpile Memorandum, and environmental impacts associated with each option in making his final selection. In particular, it should be recognized that there can be a wide divergence in the relative attractiveness of the various options depending upon which selection criterion is being considered.

5.   DOE analyses have estimated, for example, that the investment cost of the commercial light water reactor option could be as low as $613 million over the next seven years, while the cost of building an accelerator for tritium production is currently estimated to be in the range of $3.4–$4.4 billion over a similar timeframe. A second critical factor in making the selection of a tritium production technology will be the ability of the respective technologies under review to fulfill DOD's stockpile needs in a timely and reliable manner. In this respect, the CLWR option promises to meet all these requirements, and an appropriately-sized accelerator option is also capable of meeting the production requirements. The FFTF, at best, appears able to meet a substantial portion, but not the full requirements, of projected total tritium demand. The current production goal for tritium is 3 kilograms (kgs) per year,

assuming a START I–sized stockpile. If U.S. stockpile requirements are revised in the future to reflect a START II–sized force structure, we estimate the annual production goal could be reduced to as low as 1.5 kgs.

6.   A final decision will not be made exclusively on the basis of nonproliferation considerations, but must be taken in the broader context of the best overall technology after all factors have been thoroughly weighed.

7.   In accordance with the direction provided in the Fiscal Year 1998 National Defense Authorization Act Conference Report, DOE undertook a two-phased review of the nonproliferation issues associated with the three tritium production options. In the first phase of the review, the Department solicited contributions from elements within the Department, as well as from outside experts recognized in the field of nonproliferation. The DOE assessment developed findings and issues that were presented for discussion within the broader interagency context during the second phase of the review, which consisted of a series of meetings and discussions with senior officials of other agencies, beginning in April, 1998.

8.   Participants in those meetings included high-level representatives from the National Security Council, the Department of Defense, the Department of State, the Arms Control and Disarmament Agency, the White House Office of Science and Technology Policy, the Office of the Vice President, and the Nuclear Regulatory Commission.

9.   After an extensive and interactive review, the Administration has concluded that the nonproliferation policy issues associated with the use of a commercial light water reactor are manageable and that the Department should continue to pursue the CLWR option as a viable source for future tritium production.

10.   With respect to the FFTF, the review concluded that the plutonium-fueled option for the FFTF was undesirable, because, after an initial period, it would be necessary to begin fueling the FFTF with plutonium that the President had declared excess to defense needs and never to be used for nuclear arms. High enriched uranium (HEU) could be used as an alternative fuel source for the FFTF, but the use of HEU fuel would run counter to U.S. policy to minimize the use of this fuel globally and

would reduce the tritium production output of the FFTF to levels below those required for the stockpile, even under a reduced START II–level requirement.

11. Finally, the review concluded that the accelerator option raised no significant nonproliferation policy issues, assuming export control measures covering this area are maintained.

II. Summary of Review
12. Commercial Light Water Reactor.

13. With respect to the nonproliferation impacts of the CLWR option, the DOE review determined that the principal impact was that this option had potential implications for the U.S. policy of separating civilian and military nuclear activities. The review concluded, however, that the use of CLWRs for tritium production was not prohibited by law or international treaty; that, historically, there had been numerous exceptions to the practice of differentiating between U.S. civil and military facilities; and that several factors would mitigate the possible impact of the selection of this option on U.S. nonproliferation policy. On this basis, the Administration has concluded that the nonproliferation policy issues associated with the use of a commercial light water reactor are manageable and that the Department should continue to pursue the reactor option as a viable source for future tritium production.

14. It should be noted that, if enacted into law, the Markey Amendment to the House-passed version of the FY 1999 National Defense Authorization Act would be the first legally binding restriction on the use of CLWRs for the production of tritium for defense purposes and would effectively eliminate all CLWR options.

15. **Background.** One of the key issues associated with the CLWR option is the potential impact on U.S. nonproliferation policy of using a civil reactor to produce an essential material for U.S. nuclear weapons. The civil/military separation in U.S. nuclear energy programs evolved gradually during the 1950s and 1960s, as the non-defense component of the U.S. nuclear program grew. The separation facilitated the development of the commercial nuclear power industry, both here and abroad, by insulating that industry from any direct connection to nuclear weapons production. In addition, the civil/military distinction enabled

the United States to demonstrate that a significant portion of U.S. nuclear activities were not contributing to the production of nuclear weapons. The bifurcation of the U.S. nuclear program has also facilitated U.S. exchanges with non–nuclear weapon states on the peaceful uses of nuclear energy and supported the basis for U.S. leadership in the International Atomic Energy Agency (IAEA) and other multilateral organizations involved in civil nuclear activities.

16. Over the years, the policy of distinguishing between military and civilian activities was made more explicit. In 1983, for example, the Hart-Simpson Amendment to the Atomic Energy Act expressly prohibited the use of special nuclear material (SNM) derived from commercial reactors for nuclear arms. Similarly, at the 1985 and the 1990 Nuclear Nonproliferation Treaty Review Conferences, U.S. interagency-cleared issue papers supported the civil/military dichotomy.

17. Absence of Legal Prohibitions. Notwithstanding this background, U.S. policy does not specifically prohibit the production of tritium for defense purposes in a CLWR, nor is this prohibited by U.S. law or by any international agreement to which the United States is a party. The sole legal prohibition against the use of a commercial reactor for defense purposes relates to a ban on the use of SNM produced in a commercial reactor for nuclear explosive purposes. Tritium is not classified as a special nuclear material under the Atomic Energy Act, and it is not a fissionable material capable of sustaining a nuclear reaction. Under that law, tritium falls within the definition of a byproduct material. Section 11(e) of the Atomic Energy Act defines byproduct material as (1) any radioactive material (except SNM) yielded in or made radioactive by exposure to the radiation incident to the process of producing or utilizing SNM and (2) the tailings or wastes produced by the extraction or concentration of uranium or thorium from any ore processed primarily for its source material content.

18. Exceptions to Policy. The civil/military separation has never been absolute. The Department's Hanford N Reactor, for example, was built to produce plutonium for nuclear weapons, but simultaneously generated steam that was in turn sold to a commercial vender for the production of electricity. In addition, the Department's production reactors at the Savannah River Site were also used to create plutonium-238 for

NASA's civilian programs, and, over the years, the defense side of the U.S. nuclear program was the primary source of many radio-isotopes, including cesium and californium, used for civilian applications. Indeed, DOE sold tritium produced in U.S. defense production reactors for civilian uses on the U.S. market until the early 1990's (when it became apparent that the U.S. would not restore a tritium production capability within the near future).

19. Similarly, the U.S. uranium enrichment infrastructure produced enriched uranium for both military and civilian purposes for decades. It should also be noted that a significant proportion of the electricity produced at several U.S. commercial nuclear power plants owned by the Tennessee Valley Authority (TVA) has been purchased by the U.S. Government to operate uranium enrichment plants at Oak Ridge, whose output, in turn, has been used in the production of nuclear weapons and naval propulsion fuel. Since the mid-1960s, however, no U.S. commercial nuclear power reactor has produced materials for use in nuclear weapons, and today, with the U.S. Enrichment Corporation limited to civilian purposes and the N Reactor shut down, there are no major dual-use nuclear facilities in the United States.

20. **The Nonproliferation Treaty (NPT) and U.S.–International Atomic Energy Agency (IAEA) Voluntary Offer Safeguards Agreement.** No restriction in the NPT would prevent the use of U.S. CLWRs for production of tritium for defense purposes, because the United States is a nuclear weapon state party to that treaty. For this reason, the United States is not prohibited by the treaty from manufacturing nuclear weapons or producing the materials needed for their production. This, in turn, means that the United States is not required to accept IAEA inspections (known as "safeguards") on its nuclear facilities to ensure that they are not being used for weapons purposes. The NPT thus presents no barriers to the CLWR option for tritium production.

21. Similarly, the U.S.-IAEA Safeguards Agreement does not ban the production of tritium in U.S. CLWRs. In 1980, the United States agreed to make all of its non-defense nuclear facilities, including all U.S. commercial nuclear power plants, eligible for IAEA safeguards to verify that special nuclear material in inspected facilities is not removed from IAEA oversight, except in accordance with the terms of the agreement—in

effect, a pledge that materials under inspection are not being used for nuclear arms. Through the agreement, the United States sought to reduce the perceived discriminatory nature of the Nonproliferation Treaty regime, which requires all non–nuclear weapon state parties to accept such safeguards on all of their nuclear installations. The U.S. initiative is also known as the "Voluntary Offer," because, as noted above, the United States is a nuclear weapon state party to the NPT and is therefore not required to accept any IAEA inspections. In practice, at the present time, the IAEA has chosen not to inspect any U.S. commercial nuclear power plants under the Voluntary Offer, but remains empowered to do so.

22. The IAEA, it should be emphasized, safeguards materials directly usable for nuclear weapons, such as high enriched uranium and plutonium, and other materials in the nuclear fuel cycle, such as low enriched and purified natural uranium, that can be transformed into direct-use materials. It does not, however, apply safeguards to tritium, which does not fall into these categories, and which, as noted above, is a byproduct material.

23. The IAEA Secretariat has indicated that a U.S. civilian reactor providing irradiation services for tritium production would not have to be withdrawn from the Eligible List under the U.S.-IAEA Safeguards Agreement. After consultations with IAEA officials, representatives of the U.S. Mission to the IAEA in Vienna reported that the IAEA stated that it "does not see a legal impediment to the possible U.S. production of tritium in a facility that is eligible for IAEA safeguards." In addition, the IAEA "confirmed that neither the material being irradiated nor that being produced would be subject to safeguards under the terms of the Voluntary Offer."

24. Nuclear Suppliers Group. The United States is a member of the Nuclear Suppliers Group (NSG), an organization whose thirty-five member countries have agreed to implement uniform export regulations requiring strict nonproliferation controls on transfers of nuclear equipment and material. Under guidelines issued by the NSG, tritium and tritium production equipment cannot be exported unless the recipient government provides assurances that they will not be used in any nuclear explosive activity or in any nuclear fuel-cycle activity not subject to IAEA safeguards. Before embarking on a tritium production mission in a CLWR, DOE would provide assurances that none of the tritium production equipment had been imported from any NSG country.

25. Bilateral Agreements. Certain U.S. bilateral agreements for nuclear cooperation prohibit the use of fuel and equipment imported under those agreements from being used for nuclear explosives. In pursuing the CLWR option, DOE would assure its trading partners that no foreign nuclear fuel or equipment supplied that was subject to such restrictions was being used for tritium production in a CLWR.

26. CLWR: Mitigating Factors. A number of factors associated with the CLWR option help mitigate any potential concerns about using a "commercial" facility for tritium production.

27. First, the review noted that under the 1980 U.S.-IAEA Safeguards Agreement, all U.S. CLWRs are eligible for IAEA safeguards and that the IAEA, which does not monitor the production of tritium, had advised the U.S. Government that the use of any CLWR to produce this material would not prevent the IAEA from applying safeguards at such facility. The interagency review concluded that should the decision be reached to produce tritium at a CLWR, the United States should maintain the facility on the list of installations eligible for IAEA inspection, which, if applied, would provide assurance that no special nuclear material at the facility was being used in nuclear weapons.

28. The review further concluded that to minimize divergence from the military/civilian dichotomy, the Department should fuel such a reactor exclusively with U.S. low enriched uranium fuel that was unencumbered by peaceful use pledges, thereby precluding the possible use of fuel derived from excess high enriched uranium that the President has pledged will never again be used in nuclear weapons.

29. In addition, the review noted that at present, the Tennessee Valley Authority (TVA) is the sole utility to bid for the contract to produce tritium through the use of CLWRs. Because TVA is an instrumentality of the United States Government, if its bid were accepted, the particular CLWRs to be used for this mission would be wholly owned by United States Government, rather than by a private sector entity. Moreover, TVA was chartered in its authorizing statute to serve both the nation's civilian and national security needs. In fulfillment of this mission, for decades, TVA provided the power essential for the production of enriched uranium for the nation's nuclear arsenal. Thus, if a TVA reactor were used to produce tritium, the review concluded, the activity would be, in effect, extending the past practice of using government-owned facilities simultaneously for civil and military purposes rather than setting a precedent.

30.   Also, to reinforce the special nature of the TVA facility, DOE could mandate that DOE employees would participate in all tritium handling activities at TVA facilities. In the case of a TVA reactor, only U.S. Government employees would be involved as TVA is a U.S. government-owned and operated organization/instrumentality.

31.   Finally, it was noted that the actual extraction of the tritium gas from the target rod material would not take place at the reactor site, but rather would be performed at a DOE defense facility, i.e., at a location entirely separate from the CLWR.

32.   On balance, the review concluded that, although the use of a CLWR to produce tritium for nuclear weapons raised initial concern about keeping military nuclear activities separate from civilian ones, this concern would be satisfactorily addressed by ensuring that the reactors would remain eligible for IAEA safeguards, requiring tritium production activities be performed by DOE defense program personnel, and using only unencumbered fuel in the facilities. Moreover, if the reactors used for the tritium mission were owned and operated by the U.S. Government, their use for the tritium production mission would be roughly comparable to past instances in which government-owned facilities were used for dual-purpose missions. Given the essential requirement for tritium to maintain the U.S. nuclear weapon stockpile and the flexibility, technological maturity, and cost-effectiveness of the [commercial] light water reactor option, the review concluded that DOE should continue to pursue the reactor option as a viable option for future tritium production.

33.   **Fast Flux Test Facility (FFTF).**

34.   The FFTF is a DOE, rather than a commercial, facility. Originally built as part of the DOE civil nuclear program, the FFTF has been placed

on the list of U.S. nuclear facilities eligible for IAEA inspection. If used to produce tritium for nuclear weapons, however, the FFTF's civil status could be readily changed, and it could be declared to be a part of the DOE defense complex. It could then either be removed from the IAEA-safeguards Eligible List or kept on the list as a unique exception to the rule that limits the list to non-defense facilities.

35.   The FFTF can be fueled either with plutonium or high enriched uranium (HEU). Virtually all plutonium available for this fuel, however, except for an initial supply that would last for about eighteen months, is encumbered by pledges made by President Clinton, Secretary of Energy O'Leary, and/or Secretary of Energy Peña that this material will never be used in nuclear arms and by the characterization of this material as "excess to U.S. defense needs."

36.   In declaring 200 tons of U.S. fissile material (including the subject plutonium) to be "excess to defense requirements," the President stated in March 1995 that the material would "never again be used to build a nuclear weapon." Similarly, the thrust of Secretary Peña's address to the IAEA General Conference in September 1997 was that the 52 tons of HEU and plutonium he was making eligible for IAEA inspections had been "removed from military use."

37.   Technically, it is true that using the material to produce tritium *for* nuclear weapons is not the same as using the material *in* such weapons. The use of the material for a clearly military purpose, however, would appear to require its removal from its current classification as "excess material." As a practical matter, using such plutonium to produce tritium for nuclear weapons could be perceived as running counter to these undertakings and would raise serious questions internationally about U.S. arms control commitments.

38.   The second fuel option for the FFTF would be the use of HEU fuel, material that would be enriched to approximately 60 percent U-235. (Uranium enriched to more than 20 percent U-235 is classified as high enriched uranium.) While not weapons-grade, uranium that is 60 percent U-235 is weapons-usable and is in the category of nuclear materials requiring the highest level of protection under DOE regulations. The United States has enough unencumbered HEU to permit the FFTF to operate without the use of material declared excess to defense needs. The

review also noted, however, that the use of HEU-fuel would reduce the tritium output of the reactor by approximately 20 percent thus further increasing the gap between the total production capacity of the reactor and projected tritium requirements.

39.   Operation of the FFTF on HEU, however, would run counter to the longstanding U.S. policy of minimizing the civil use of HEU. While FFTF would not be a "civil" facility if used for the tritium production mission, it would nonetheless represent the first new use of HEU in a reactor in the United States since 1978, when the Reduced Enrichment for Research and Test Reactors (RERTR) program was launched, under which the United States took a more active role in minimizing the global commerce in HEU. Use of HEU in the FFTF would undercut the RERTR program and would also erode parallel U.S. efforts to persuade Russia to avoid the use of HEU in several Russian nuclear reactors used for district heating. As a mitigating factor, however, it was noted that the Department of Energy and the Department of Commerce continue to operate five other non-power reactors that are fueled with HEU, even as the United States has pursued, with considerable success, its efforts to reduce the use of HEU globally. It was therefore not clear that the use of HEU to fuel the FFTF would have an unacceptable impact on this aspect of U.S. nonproliferation policy.

40.   On balance, the review concluded that because the use of plutonium to fuel the FFTF would require the reversal of U.S. commitments regarding material declared excess to defense needs, this option appeared unattractive. The nonproliferation impacts of the HEU option, while not insignificant, were more difficult to measure. However these impacts need not, in themselves, preclude further study of the HEU fuel alternative, if after assessment for flexibility, technological maturity, and cost-effectiveness, this option continued to receive consideration.

41.   Accelerator.

42.   The tritium production accelerator would be built as a DOE defense facility and thus does not raise any of the proliferation concerns associated with the options discussed above.

43.   However, the accelerator system does involve the deployment of technology sufficiently powerful to produce special nuclear material in

quantities of proliferation concern. For this reason, the accelerator technology would be controlled under Part 810 of the Code of Federal Regulations, Volume 10. Under Part 810, an authorization is required by the Secretary of Energy for the export of any technology that directly or indirectly could contribute to the production of special nuclear material.

44. It should also be noted that it is possible that a DOE tritium-producing accelerator could be a dual-use facility, producing radioisotopes for use in the civilian medical community.

45. In view of these considerations with regard to the accelerator option, the interagency concluded that the APT project does not pose proliferation risks.

46. Conclusions.

47. Overall, the interagency review of the nonproliferation aspects of the Department's selection of a tritium production technology reached several important conclusions.

48. First, it found that although the CLWR alternative raised initial concerns because of its implications for the policy of maintaining separation between U.S. civil and military nuclear activities, these concerns could be satisfactorily addressed, given the particular circumstances involved. These included the fact that the reactors would remain eligible for IAEA safeguards, and the fact that if TVA were the utility selected for the tritium mission, the reactors used for tritium production would be owned and operated by the U.S. Government, making them roughly comparable to past instances of government-owned dual-purpose nuclear facilities. Given the essential requirement for tritium to maintain the U.S. nuclear weapon stockpile, and the flexibility, technological maturity, and cost-effectiveness of the [commercial] light water reactor option, the review concluded that DOE should continue its pursuit of the reactor option as a viable source for future tritium production.

49. With respect to the FFTF, there was general agreement that the plutonium-fueled option for the FFTF was undesirable, because under this option, in order to use the FFTF to produce tritium for nuclear weapons, it would be soon be necessary to use plutonium that had been declared by the President to be "excess to defense needs." High enriched uranium could be used as an alternative fuel source for the FFTF, but the use of HEU fuel would run counter to U.S. efforts to minimize the use of this fuel globally. In addition, the use of HEU fuel would reduce the tritium production output of the FFTF to levels below those required for the U.S. nuclear weapon stockpile, even under a reduced START II–level requirement.

50.   Finally, there was general agreement that the accelerator project does not pose proliferation risks, assuming export control measures covering this area are maintained.

Appendix C. Critique of *Interagency Review*

Background

In the summer of 1997, the House-Senate conference committee on the fiscal 1998 defense authorization bill (which would become Public Law 105–85) needed to resolve differences between the House version and the Senate version of the bill in regard to production of tritium in commercial nuclear reactors. The U.S. policy against making fissile materials (uranium or plutonium, also referred to as "special nuclear materials") was clearly codified in the law by the Hart-Simpson Amendment to the Atomic Energy Act, which stated that no nuclear reactor licensed by the NRC would be allowed to make special nuclear materials for use in weapons. The definition of special nuclear materials was inherited from a much older portion of the 1954 law (Section 2014. Definitions). The relevant wording is as follows: "The term 'special nuclear material' means (1) plutonium, uranium enriched in the isotope 233 or in the isotope 235, and any other material which the Commission, pursuant to the provisions of section 2071 of this title, determines to be special nuclear material."[1] Thus the commission (at first the AEC, later the NRC)[2] had the authority to add other materials to the list. But it has not added tritium, largely because of a commercial market for very small quantities of tritium as illumination in exit signs, on runways, etc. Moreover, each succeeding presidential administration had studiously followed a policy that tritium for weapons should be produced only in military reactors, so neither a commission ruling nor a provision in law ever established the policy formally.

Lack of formal specification resulted in ambiguity when it came to practical choices. For example, as a cost saving, the government's N reactor in Hanford, Washington, was designed to divert the high-pressure steam produced in cooling its plutonium-producing core to a nearby generator facility operated by an electric utility. From this, the government received a steady revenue stream. This kind of civilian benefit as a by-product of a military facility did not seem at the time a cause for concern. There are numerous analogous ways the nonmilitary side of the nation enjoyed benefits from the by-products (or surplus) of the military.

Sensitivity would arise, however, if the benefit flowed the other way, that is, if the nonmilitary nuclear reactor produced materials for nuclear weapons. Such sensitivity would derive chiefly from the asymmetric nature of the NPT, which imposed virtually no constraints on the bomb-producing activities of the five weapons states but set strict restrictions on the other signatories. Some countries, like India, found this asymmetry so offensive that they refused to sign the NPT and opposed it whenever international forums gave them an opportunity to do so.

To soften the impression that the system imposed under the NPT was unfair and thus strengthen the international non-proliferation program, the United States follows a policy of voluntarily abiding by many of the same rules to which the non–weapons states are subject. This policy manifested itself, for example, in the so-called Voluntary Offer, whereby the United States agreed to IAEA inspections at all commercial power plants, just as if the United States were a non–weapons state. (This offer has until now been largely symbolic, since the IAEA has only rarely chosen to invest its limited resources on following through with inspections.) Another example is the aforementioned Hart-Simpson Amendment, again putting the United States on a par (albeit self-imposed) with the non–weapons states.

The Bellefonte option, whereby the DOE would have purchased the TVA's unfinished commercial reactor and make it a tritium-producing element of the nuclear weapons complex, enjoyed broad support in the Senate. If the DOE ran the tritium operation and sold the excess steam to the TVA for producing electricity, the parallel to the N reactor precedent would be exact, and there seemed not to be a policy issue. On the other hand an NRC-licensed commercial utility producing tritium in the course of its electricity production would be at the other extreme; if that didn't violate the no-dual-use policy then nothing would.

The Senate resolved the ambiguity by simply amending the Atomic Energy Act and stating in the defense authorization bill that the DOE was allowed to make arrangements with NRC-licensed utilities to obtain tritium produced in their reactors.[3] The House conferees, however, opposed this policy reversal. Because some versions of commercial-reactor production of tritium seemed so much more benign than others, the conferees agreed to get clarification from the experts in the agencies involved. The Senate was agreeable, no doubt expecting that the experts would find the Bellefonte option unobjectionable, whatever they thought of the option at the other extreme.

The conference committee report therefore chartered the DOE to lead a high-level policy study to shed light on the issue. In its charter, the committee noted the difference between a policy that is formalized in law and one that is followed as a matter of the best interests of the nation:

While questions exist as to whether or not current law prohibits production of tritium in a commercial facility, and because concerns have been raised regarding the effect that a decision to produce tritium in this manner would have on U.S. non-proliferation strategy, the conferees believe the policy, legal, and regulatory issues that have been raised must be addressed in a comprehensive manner prior to passage of any amendments to facilitate such a choice.

It is also important to note that the committee recognized different commercial reactor suboptions:

Utilizing the dual-track strategy since [1995], the Department has been pursuing the two most promising tritium production technologies: (1) the purchase of an operating or partially complete commercial light-water reactor, or lease of a completed reactor, or the purchase of irradiation services from the owner or operator of such a reactor; and (2) the design, construction, and testing of critical components of a proton accelerator system for the production of tritium.[4]

And the need to compare the policy aspects of the different commercial reactor approaches was clear: "As a practical matter, each of the different reactor sub-options has different legal and policy issues associated with it. The conferees believe that it would be helpful to the effort to secure necessary legislative changes if DOE could identify the preferred commercial reactor sub-option in advance of the final tritium production technology decision, preferably by March 1, 1998." Therefore, Congress directed the DOE to lead an interagency review:

The conferees believe that it is essential for DOE to identify and assess any policy issues associated with the various reactor sub-options in conjunction with other federal agencies including the Nuclear Regulatory Commission, the Department of Defense, and the Department of State arms control offices. The conferees direct the Secretary of Energy to utilize a senior level, interagency process to review and assess the issues associated with the commercial reactor option.

To carry out Congress's challenging charter, a great deal of work would be needed to coordinate a review that involved all these agencies. The final report of such a review should include supporting papers, records of meetings, lists of individuals supporting the effort, short biographies to support the fact that these people were indeed "senior level," and so on.

What a contrast this description is to what was actually produced. What Congress got was a rambling ten-page Internet document that named no authors or contributors and simply ignored the charter laid out so clearly in the conference report. No report number is given, nor is there an issuing office in the DOE (it was transmitted via a cover letter from Acting Secretary of Energy Elizabeth Moler). No supporting reports are cited, and the degree to which concurrence was obtained from the participating agencies is not discussed. It is hardly the kind of product one would think would exert a strong influence on U.S. nuclear weapons policy. But it did.

It is possible that the deficiencies in the *Interagency Review* were driven by schedule problems. The interagency portion of the work (whatever it consisted of) did not start until April 1998, a month *after* Congress's deadline for receiving the DOE's recommendations for needed legislation. It was at about that time that Secretary Peña announced his resignation, an announcement that surely created turmoil among senior DOE aides like Joan Rohlfing, who was responsible for producing the *Interagency Review*. Presumably, requesting more time for a report of this importance would not be a good way to burnish one's reputation at this critical junction. But in the absence of concrete information from the DOE on its internal processes (the agency has been unresponsive to FOIA requests to obtain documentary information), any discussion of motivations must remain purely speculative.

FOIA Reveals Interagency Myth

In the course of researching this book, several FOIA requests for information on the *Interagency Review* meetings were made to key agencies listed as participants (paragraph 8). The requests went to the NRC, the Department of State, the White House Office of Science and Technology Policy, and the DOE. The Office of the Vice President and the National Security Agency (also stated participants) are exempt from FOIA. The only participant to which a FOIA request was not sent was the DOD, because FOIA is managed in the DOD at the service level, and the *Interagency Review* did not specify which service(s) participated in the meetings.

These FOIA requests were made in July 2000. Technically, responses are due from federal agencies within twenty working days of such requests, but that deadline is seldom achieved. The NRC and the Office of Science and Technology Policy, however, provided reasonably timely responses.

Astonishingly, both of these agencies found no records of any participation in the *Interagency Review* meetings. The NRC's finding is of particular importance, since the agency is affected in numerous and important ways by the findings of the review, not only by the policy issue in general, but also by any licensing activities that might emerge from the DOE's decision. The NRC is a scrupulously meticulous agency when it comes to interagency meetings and issues of licensing policy, and it is virtually inconceivable that "high-level" representation could have occurred at *Interagency Review* meetings without there being ample evidence in the files. The conclusion is simple and astounding: the *Interagency Review* says the NRC participated when it did not.

At the time this book was published, the State Department and the DOE had not provided any information in response to the FOIA requests. The extent of interagency participation in the *Interagency Review* therefore remains highly uncertain at this time.

Below, the failings of the DOE *Interagency Review of the Nonproliferation Implications of Alternative Tritium Production Technologies under Consideration by the Department of Energy* are discussed, starting with the all-important category of issues *not* discussed, and proceeding to problems appearing in the document itself.

Issues Not Addressed

The *Interagency Review* is a very short document, and some of it ventures into issues (such as costs) beyond what was requested by Congress. The actual substantive discussion of the no-dual-use policy is limited to six or seven pages. Of more importance than what is discussed, however, is what is ignored.

The Suboptions

The principal reason that Congress asked for expert clarification of the no-dual-use policy in commercial reactors was that some suboptions under consideration by the DOE seemed to be worse than others. But the *Interagency Review* studiously avoids mentioning the suboptions. Virtually all earlier discussions of the DOE's dual-track strategy describes the CLWR track in the same words the House-Senate conference committee report used: "(1) the purchase of an operating or partially complete commercial light-water reactor, or lease of a completed reactor, or the purchase of irradiation services from the owner or operator of such a reactor."[5] Throughout the *Interagency Review*, that three-part description has been collapsed into a single phrase, "commercial light water reactor." The effect, no doubt intentional, was to blur the distinctions that Congress wanted sharpened.

Impact on Threshold States

As discussed above, the driving motivation underlying much of U.S. policy on nonproliferation is the need to encourage non–weapons states to abide by the terms of the NPT. To make such compliance attractive, the government has gone to great lengths to adhere voluntarily to elements of the NPT that apply to non–weapons states. In particular, those states forswear production of plutonium in their commercial nuclear reactors and allow IAEA inspectors to verify compliance with this principle. Under the Atomic Energy Act, the United States follows the same policy. The rationale for this is laid out clearly in the *Interagency Review* (paragraphs 15 and 21). The U.S. decision to produce tritium in commercial plants, however, is a signal to non–weapons states that tritium production in their commercial reactors would not be looked upon with disfavor. That is the sense of Senator Strom Thurmond's testimony quoted in chapter 5. The amazing thing is that this ramification of the change in the tritium production policy, which should have been at the heart of the policy analysis, is not even mentioned in the *Interagency Review.*

Technology Proliferation

Throughout the beauty contests, the DOE has been generous in sharing information about TPBARs with the other tritium-producing contestants. The whole world now knows that tritium can be produced in commercial electricity-producing reactors with little basic change to their designs. It knows that thin, multilayered rods inserted in the existing absorber rod positions can piggyback on electricity production with little effect on commercial operations. Some details have so far been kept secret, but how long would that secrecy succeed when hundreds of workers from all trades and all backgrounds are exposed to the technology in the course of running the TVA reactors? Those facilities are not designed to protect secrets, and the U.S. experience on civilians keeping secrets during peacetime is not reassuring (as discussed in chapter 4). How safe is the classified design information if the TPBARs are manufactured by a foreign-owned company, one of the options the DOE is currently pursuing? Is this one of the risks that is "manageable," according to the *Interagency Review* authors? It is impossible to say, since the subject is not discussed, except for a vague suggestion that the DOE "could mandate that DOE employees would participate in all tritium-handling activities at TVA facilities" (paragraph 30).

Conflicts for the NRC's Roles

In many ways, the NRC is caught in the middle of this change in tritium production policy. For one thing, the agency is forbidden by law (42 USC 7272) to expend funds for the purpose of regulating "any defense activity or facility of the Department of Energy." This issue is not mentioned in the *Interagency Review.* Had a "high-level" official from the NRC actually been present during the review, one would think the issue would have been raised, but of course, the FOIA results indicate there was no such person from the NRC participating. Similarly, there is no discussion in the report of the possible complications deriving from the NRC's implicit authority to halt operations at the plants, thus giving the civilian agency control over a military operation. Both questions were subsequently raised in the General Accounting Office's critique of the new DOE policy.[6] Another issue not mentioned is the fact that the NRC apparently has the authority to add materials to the list of what are considered special nuclear materials, an authority that has direct implications on the question of what the U.S. policy is or should be.

Previous DOE Acknowledgment of the Policy
Very capable people in the DOE's tritium programs in the Bush administration, and then later in the Clinton administration, produced draft EISs that explicitly excluded the possibility of commercial-reactor production of tritium on policy grounds. When the tritium goal quantity was much larger, the amount of savings that could be achieved by the use of existing commercial reactors was proportionately larger, but the government considered the commercial track unacceptable then from a policy stand point (as disscussed in chapter 5).

In a less formal context, there is other evidence that the belief that the no-dual-use policy applied to tritium as well as to plutonium was widely held in the government. For example, at a conference in 1988, Troy Wade, who was the top person in DOE's nuclear weapons program, pointed to a major difference between the Soviet Union and the United States with regard to tritium production by saying that "the United States does not have the comparable flexibility to use its civilian reactor programs as does the Soviet Union."[7] At the same conference, the top person in Los Alamos National Laboratory's arms reduction treaty verification program said, "Soviet policy does not now prohibit the use of civilian power reactors . . . to produce tritium, while U.S. policy does."[8]

It seems strange that there is no discussion of the earlier perspective in the *Interagency Review*, except for the vague words "although the use of a CLWR to produce tritium for nuclear weapons raised initial concern about keeping military nuclear activities separate from civilian ones" (paragraph 32).

Deficiencies within the Report

Although the greatest problems with the *Interagency Review* lie in its silences, there are also numerous important problems in the material presented.

Misleading Precedents

The *Interagency Review* places a great deal of emphasis on past examples of "exceptions" to the policy of separating commercial and military uses of nuclear technology (paragraph 18), but all such examples it cites are cases of military production operations providing benefits to the nonmilitary side of the nation. This is true of the sale of steam-as-by-product from the N reactor, production of special isotopes for scientific research, and production of special forms of plutonium for NASA's space reactors. These examples are irrelevant to the question of producing weapons materials in a nonmilitary reactor. The example of the TVA providing electricity for the Manhattan Project (paragraph 19) is particularly ludicrous. Why not mention the farmers of the New Mexico providing milk and eggs to Los Alamos? Further confusion is caused by treating the civil-military separation as a government-nongovernment distinction (paragraph 29). It is irrelevant that the TVA is a government utility. Many other electric utilities are also government operations, though most are not federal. The TVA is a civilian federal agency, and its reactors are civilian power plants. The no-dual-use policy is about making nuclear weapons material in such reactors.

Cost-Benefit Analysis

The *Interagency Review* is supposed to be an assessment of nonproliferation policy issues. An unsupported and unreferenced discussion of costs for the different technologies (paragraph 5) seems out of place here.

FFTF and APT Discussions

Though it was not requested, the *Interagency Review* includes a brief analysis of the APT (paragraphs 41–45) option (with which it found no non-proliferation problems) and a substantial discussion of the policy issues related to the Fast Flux Test Facility (paragraphs 33–40). There is nothing particularly objectionable to this added material, but what is interesting is that the FFTF is given quite short shrift on the policy issue. The points raised in the review are valid and represent a good analysis of why the FFTF should not be used for tritium production. If the CLWR discussion had been equally objective, the finding with respect to it might have been the same.

Appendix D. Glossary

ACRS   Advisory Committee on Reactor Safeguards, a congressionally mandated group that advises the NRC and the DOE on technical aspects of reactor safety.

AEC   Atomic Energy Commission, the federal agency responsible for both the development and regulation of atomic energy (both military and civilian) from 1954 to 1975, when it was disbanded. The DOE and the NRC now carry out its functions.

APT   Accelerator production of tritium, one of two DOE "tracks" for producing tritium.

CLWR   Commercial light-water reactor, one of DOE's "tracks" for producing tritium. The CLWR includes the possibility of using a dedicated DOE-owned reactor of a commercial design, or a reactor owned and operated by a commercial utility.

CONTAIN   Computer code created for the NRC that simulates events occurring in the containment of a nuclear reactor during a core melt accident.

corium   Molten mixture of reactor fuel and metal from support structures in the reactor core.

CPI   The NRC's Containment Performance Improvement program, carried out in the late 1980s.

DCH   Direct containment heating, a severe accident scenario in which molten corium is sprayed under high pressure into the containment building when the reactor vessel fails.

deuterium   A rare isotope of hydrogen, containing one neutron in addition to the normal proton in the nucleus. Together with tritium, it is an important explosive material for modern hydrogen bombs.

DOD   Department of Defense.

DOE   Department of Energy, the federal agency with the responsibility for manufacturing and maintaining nuclear weapons, as well as many other responsibilities related to energy supply.

EIS   Environmental impact statement, a report required by NEPA to inform the public of the federal government's intention to engage in any project that could affect the environment.

FBI   Federal Bureau of Investigation.

HWR   heavy-water reactor, which is cooled and moderated by heavy water, or deuterium oxide.

IAEA   International Atomic Energy Agency, the international body that carries out the inspection and monitoring terms of the NPT.

ice condenser   A type of nuclear power plant designed by Westinghouse Electric Company that utilizes beds of chipped ice in the containment building of the plant's reactor to absorb the steam and heat from a reactor accident.

INFCE   International Fuel Cycle Evaluation, a multinational review of policies related to development of atomic power and control of nuclear weapons proliferation in the late 1970s.

LWR   light-water reactor, which uses ordinary water (as opposed to heavy water) for cooling and moderating. All U.S. commercial reactors are LWRs.

Manhattan Project   The vast, secret U.S. programs to build the first atomic bombs during World War II.

Mark I   General Electric's first version of its suppression pool reactor, which absorbs the heat and steam from a pipe break accident by forcing the steam through a pool of water.

MHTGR   Modular High-Temperature Gas-cooled Reactor.

NEPA   National Environmental Policy Act.

NPR   New Production Reactor, the U.S. program in the 1980s and early 1990s to build a new nuclear reactor to produce tritium.

NPT   Nuclear Non-Proliferation Treaty, the international accord that restricts possession of nuclear weapons to the five original "weapons states": the United States, Russia, Great Britain, France, and China.

NRC   Nuclear Regulatory Commission, charged since 1975 with the responsibility for regulating civilian uses of nuclear technology, including nuclear reactors.

NSG   Nuclear Suppliers Group, consisting of those nations that can produce advanced equipment and materials that can be used in nuclear weapons.

NUREG-1150   NRC report entitled *Severe Accident Risks: An Assessment for Five U.S. Nuclear Power Plants*, applying risk methods to analysis of nuclear reactor operations.

plutonium   Radioactive heavy metal produced by neutron bombardment of U-238, with isotopes varying in atomic weight from 239 to 242. Suitable for atomic bombs or reactor fuel.

START Strategic Arms Reduction Treaties, by which Russia and the United States agree to reduce the number of strategic (i.e., deliverable at long range) nuclear warheads in their arsenals. START I is in force as a formal treaty obligation in both countries. START II was signed by the presidents of Russia and the United States and ratified by the U.S. Senate (in 1996) and the Russian Duma (in 2000). The Bush administration has indicated support for the arms reductions called for in START II but has not pursued the steps required to bring it into force as a formal treaty (*Source*: Amy F. Woolf, *Nuclear Arms Control: The U.S.–Russian Agenda*, Congressional Research Service report IB98030, October 15, 2001).

TMI Three Mile Island nuclear power plant, unit 2 of which experienced a core melt accident in 1979.

TPBAR Tritium-producing burnable absorber rod.

tritium A very rare isotope of hydrogen, containing two neutrons in addition to the normal proton in the nucleus. It is a critical explosive material for modern hydrogen bombs.

TVA Tennessee Valley Authority, a large federal electric utility providing electricity generated from hydropower, fossil fuel, and nuclear reactors in the mid-South.

U-235 Uranium-235, the isotope in natural uranium that is fissile, or easily split by neutrons, and is therefore suitable as an atomic bomb material.

U-238 Uranium 238, the nonfissile and dominant (99.3 percent) component of natural uranium.

UCSB University of California at Santa Barbara.

uranium Naturally occurring mineral that can be used as the explosive component of an atomic bomb if its U-235 component is enriched to a high fraction compared to its U-238 component, or as the fuel of nuclear reactors with lesser degrees of enrichment.

Notes on Epigraphs

Preface Senator Daniel Patrick Moynihan, Cable News Network presentation *Evans, Novak, Hunt & Shields*, aired December 24, 2000. After a successful academic career at MIT and Harvard University, Moynihan served in four successive administrations before being elected to four successive terms as U.S. senator from New York.

Chapter 1 Bernard Baruch, "The Baruch Plan," presented to the United Nations Atomic Energy Commission, June 14, 1946. Baruch was the first U.S. representative to the UN Atomic Energy Commission and presented the U.S. proposal to turn all nuclear weapons over to international control.

Bill Richardson, "Remarks by Secretary of Energy Bill Richardson: National Security Decisions," December 22, 1998. Richardson served as Energy Secretary to President Clinton from August 1998 to December 2000. Before that he was the U.S. Ambassador to the United Nations and a U.S. congressman from New Mexico.

Chapter 2 Enrico Fermi (1944), quoted by Alvin Weinberg in *The First Nuclear Era: Life and Times of a Technological Fixer*, 1994, p. 41. Fermi, a renowned Italian physicist, emigrated to the United States to escape Fascist persecution of his Jewish wife. He was the leader of the Chicago contingent of the Manhattan Project and led the design and construction of the world's first nuclear reactor.

Chapter 3 John Kemeny, in *Report of the President's Commission on the Accident at Three Mile Island*, 1989, p. 7. Kemeny was codeveloper of the BASIC computer programming language. He was president of Dartmouth College at the time of the TMI accident and headed a commission appointed by President Jimmy Carter to study the causes of the accident.

Chapter 4 Jonathan Schell, "The Unfinished Twentieth Century: What We Have Forgotten About Nuclear Weapons," *Harper's Magazine*, January 2000, p. 44. Schell was a columnist and editor of *The New Yorker* for twenty years. He is a prominent writer about nuclear disarmament issues.

Chapter 5 *Draft Environmental Impact Statement for the New Production Reactor*, April 1991. No final EIS was published, because the program was canceled in 1992.

Chapter 6   Alvin Weinberg, in *The First Nuclear Era: Life and Times of a Technological Fixer*, 1994, p. 184. Weinberg participated in the Manhattan Project and later became director of the Oak Ridge National Laboratory between 1955 and 1973. He was a prominent architect of the U.S. nuclear fuel cycle.

Chapter 7   "It's seven minutes to midnight," *Bulletin of the Atomic Scientists*, vol. 58, no. 2 (March/April 2002):4. Founded in 1945 by prominent scientists of the Manhattan Project, the *Bulletin* is one of the nation's leading magazines on global security and the threat of nuclear war.

Notes

Preface

1. I was personally and professionally involved in a number of the events and issues discussed in this book. In the interests of full disclosure, here is a summary of the connections. I was heavily involved in the NUREG-1150 project discussed in chapter 3, primarily as a manager of a technical group at Sandia National Laboratories that performed computer simulations of severe reactor accidents. My group also provided calculational support to the Nuclear Regulatory Commission's (NRC's) Containment Performance Improvement program, including studies of the performance of ice condenser containments in the late 1980s. In 1989–1993, I coordinated the Department of Energy's (DOE's) multilaboratory research program to factor severe accidents into the design of a heavy-water reactor to produce tritium for the weapons complex, described in the section entitled "Phase 2: A New Urgency" in chapter 5. At various times over the past twenty years, David Williams, the protagonist in the section "Shoot the Messenger" of chapter 3, reported directly to me, but not at the time the conflicts over the Zion report were occurring. I later came to be his manager again when he was trying to get satisfaction from Sandia's ethics organization and when his technical report on direct containment heating was finally suppressed by the NRC. I was a coauthor of the report sponsored by the NRC about ice condenser containment performance in severe accidents. This report is discussed in the part of chapter 3 entitled "Ice Condensers, the Little Containments That Don't." Finally, in 1999 I managed Sandia's work supporting the DOE program to study production of tritium in commercial reactors, briefly mentioned in the section called "Bait and Switch" in chapter 5. Sandia's role in that program was very limited, and my personal involvement was even more so. I retired from Sandia in the fall of that year.

2. John Keeble, *Out of the Channel; The Exxon Valdez Spill in Prince William Sound*, 2nd ed. (Spokane, WA: Eastern Washington University Press, 1999).

Chapter 1

1. For literal-minded scientific readers, these statements may seem imprecise, but they are substantially accurate. By "fuels," I mean uranium and plutonium,

regardless of isotope. By "physics," I mean the physics of cross-sections, neutron flux, nuclear fission, and chain reactions, not details of the neutron spectrum or the hydrodynamics of inertial confinement.

2. TVA's power program is self-financed, but its much smaller nonpower programs, such as regional economic development, are federally financed.

Chapter 2

1. Richard Rhodes, *The Making of the Atomic Bomb* (New York: Touchstone, 1986), p. 745.

2. Ibid, pp. 734, 740.

3. Paul Kennedy, *The Rise and Fall of the Great Powers* (New York: Vintage Books, 1987), p. 343.

4. Richard G. Hewlett and Jack M. Holl, *Atoms for Peace and War* (Berkeley and Los Angeles: University of California Press, 1989), p. 72.

5. David Lilienthal, *Change, Hope and the Bomb* (Princeton: Princeton University Press, 1963), p. 103.

6. The liability limits specified by the Price-Anderson Act have changed since its implementation in 1957. Today, each reactor must be covered by a $200 million liability insurance policy for an accident involving that reactor, but if an accident at *any* reactor exceeds that amount, *all* reactor owners must contribute to the excess damages, up to a maximum of $88 million per reactor owned. The government assumes responsibility for any costs incurred above that point. Since there are currently 104 operating reactors, the government would to have to step in only if the costs of a reactor accident exceeded $9.4 billion ($200 million plus $88 million times 104 reactors). Web site of the American Nuclear Insurers (http://www.amnucins.com).

7. Hewlett and Holl, *Atoms for Peace and War*, p. 516.

8. Elizabeth S. Rolph, *Nuclear Power and the Public Safety: A Study in Regulation* (Lexington, MA: Lexington Books, 1979), p. 56.

9. Ibid., p. 93.

10. Michael J. Brenner, *Nuclear Power and Non-proliferation* (New York: Cambridge University Press, 1981), p. 19.

11. Ibid., p. 30.

12. Brenner (ibid.) makes this point forcefully: "*The crisis that flared in June 1974 with the blocking of enrichment orders was in fact planned*" (p. 37, italics in original). He then provides ample evidence to back up the statement.

13. Ibid., p. 36.

14. Ibid., p. 52.

15. Ibid., p. 57.

16. Ibid., p. 61.

17. Ibid., p. 14.

18. Ibid., p. 70.

19. Energy Secretary Hazel O'Leary announced this fact at a press conference on June 27, 1994, according to Institute of Energy and Environmental Research, *Physical, Nuclear and Chemical Properties of Plutonium*, available on the institute's Web page at <http://www.ieer.org/fctsheet/pu-props.htm>.

20. President Gerald Ford, *Statement on Nuclear Policy*, October 28, 1976, quoted in Brenner, *Nuclear Power and Non-proliferation*, p. 115.

21. Ford Foundation Nuclear Energy Policy Study Group and Mitre Corporation, *Nuclear Power Issues and Choices* (Cambridge, MA: Ballinger, 1977).

22. Harald Müller, David Fischer, and Wolfgang Kötter, *Nuclear Non-proliferation and Global Order* (New York: Oxford University Press, 1994), p. 52.

23. Four countries today continue efforts toward plutonium-based reactor operations: France, Great Britain, Russia, and Japan. These programs have had virtually no impact, however, on the commercial electricity sector.

Chapter 3

1. This point is made clear in Rolph's discussion of standards: "And even by 1966 only six commercial plants were in operation, all 265 MW or less. . . . In spite of the obvious obstacles, for political reasons, the AEC had little option but to try, all the while arguing the standards should be general and flexible" (*Nuclear Power and the Public Safety*, p. 65).

2. Ibid., p. 61.

3. George T. Masuzin and J. Samuel Walker, *Controlling the Atom* (Berkeley and Los Angeles: University of California Press, 1984), pp. 219 ff.

4. Rolph, *Nuclear Power and the Public Safety*, table B-1.

5. Mazuzan and Walker, *Controlling the Atom*, p. 198.

6. "Nonetheless, the AEC devised no specific standard incorporating the relationship between distance and containment, and it continued to judge the site for each power reactor application on a case-by-case basis" (ibid., p. 219).

7. Rolph, *Nuclear Power and the Public Safety*, p. 68.

8. Donald W. Stever, Jr., *Seabrook and the Nuclear Regulatory Commission*, (Hanover, NH: University Press of New England, 1980), p. 45.

9. This discussion focuses primarily on the design criteria for containment strength. Actually, at least one other design criterion implicitly assumed core melting. The criterion for containment leak-tightness started by postulating a certain amount of radioactivity in the containment and then required the calculated dose to a human at the site boundary to be less than a certain value. The amount of radioactivity postulated for use in this calculation was so high that the only way it could occur would involve core uncovery. It is probable that despite its inconsistency with respect to other design criteria, this approach was chosen because using a design basis accident to determine the amount of radioactivity in the containment would have resulted in allowing leak rates to be so large

that they would have been in intuitive conflict with the idea of a "leak-tight" building.

10. Charles Perrow, *Normal Accidents* (Princeton, N.J.: Princeton University Press, 1999), p. 30 (first published by Basic Books, New York, 1984).

11. "Three Mile Island: A Chronology," *Washington Post*, March 28, 1989, available at <http://www.washingtonpost.com/wp-srv/national/longterm/tmi/stories/chrono032889.htm>.

12. Nuclear Regulatory Commission, *Issue 155: Generic Concerns Arising from TMI-2 Cleanup*, NUREG-0933, Rev. 2 (Washington, DC, 1992).

13. Perrow, *Normal Accidents*.

14. Memorandum adopted by the participants of "Lessons of Chernobyl" conference, April 22, 1996, Kiev, Ukraine, available at the Web site of the Nuclear Information and Resource Service, Washington, DC (http://www.nirs.org/confstat.htm).

15. United Nations Scientific Committee on the Effects of Atomic Radiation, *Sources and Effects of Ionizing Radiation: UNSCEAR 2000 Report to the General Assembly, with Scientific Annexes, Volume 2: Effects* (New York: United Nations, 2000).

16. International Nuclear Safety Advisory Group (INSAG), *The Chernobyl Accident: Updating of INSAG-1*, (INSAG-7) (Vienna International Atomic Energy Agency, 1992), p. 24.

17. In 1955, for example, a government test reactor called EBR-I underwent a partial core melt accident. Mazuzan and Walker, *Controlling the Atom*, p. 127.

18. Atomic Energy Commission, *Theoretical Possibilities and Consequences of Major Accidents in Large Nuclear Power Plants*, AEC/DOE WASH-740 (Washington, DC, March 1957).

19. Glenn Seaborg, quoted in Rolph, *Nuclear Power and the Public Safety*, p. 49.

20. Nuclear Regulatory Commission, *Reactor Safety Study—An Assessment of Accident Risk in U.S. Commercial Power Plants*, WASH-1400, NUREG 75/014, 1975.

21. Rolph, *Nuclear Power and the Public Safety*, p. 149.

22. Nuclear Regulatory Commission, *Severe Accident Risks: An Assessment for Five U.S. Nuclear Power Plants*, NUREG-1150 (Washington, DC, 1989).

23. The early conditional containment failure probability (CCFP) measure for Mark Is was lower than that for ice condensers, but the corresponding core damage frequency (CDF) had the opposite ranking. The product of the two is the probability of an early release, and the ice condenser had the largest value of the five plants studied.

24. These counts are based on reactors operating as of 1988 and are taken from Nuclear Regulatory Commission, *Nuclear Information Digest*, NUREG-1350,

vol. 9, appendix A. With the start-up of Watts Bar Unit 1 in 1996 the total number of ice condenser plants operating in the United States was brought to nine.

25. Nuclear Regulatory Commission, *Mark I Containment Performance Improvement Program*, SECY-89-017 (Washington, DC, January 23, 1989); also "Installation of Hardened Wetwell Vent," Generic Letter 89-16, Washington, DC, September 1, 1989.

26. Nuclear Regulatory Commission, *Individual Plant Examination Program: Perspectives on Reactor Safety and Plant Performance, Part 1: Final Summary Report*, NUREG-1560 (Washington, DC, 1997), vol. 1, pp. 4–13.

27. Nuclear Regulatory Commission, *Integration Plan for Closure of Severe Accident Issues*, SECY-88-147, May 25, 1988.

28. Nuclear Regulatory Commission, "Completion of the Containment Performance Improvement Program and Forwarding of Insights for Use in the Individual Plant Examination for Severe Accident Vulnerabilities," Generic Letter 88-20, Supplement 3, Washington, DC, July 6, 1990.

29. Based on the NRC's list of licensed plants. Nuclear Regulatory Commission, *NRC Information Digest*, NUREG-1350 (Washington, DC, 1997), vol. 9, appendix A.

30. Nuclear Regulatory Commission, *Revised Severe Accident Research Plan*, NUREG 1365, Rev. 1 (Washington, DC, December 1992).

31. Transcript from "Briefing on Severe Accident Research Program," Tuesday, October 26, 1993 (available at NRC's Public Document Room).

32. This and subsequent elements of the Zion report chronology are from Dave Williams's "Chronology," in his internal memorandum to N. R. Ortiz, July 8, 1994.

33. Internal memorandum from D. A. Powers et al. to N. R. Ortiz, December 17, 1993.

34. Letter from Brian Sheron, U.S. Nuclear Regulatory Commission, to N. R. Ortiz, Sandia National Laboratories, February 4, 1994 (available at NRC's Public Document Room).

35. Internal memorandum from Williams to J. E. Kelly, Sandia National Laboratories, May 16, 1994.

36. Nuclear Regulatory Commission, "Implementing Research Projects," RES Office Letter No. 6, Rev. 1, Washington, DC, November 26, 1993.

37. Letter from C. J. Tinkler, U.S. Nuclear Regulatory Commission, to K. D. Bergeron, Sandia National Laboratories, February 7, 1996 (available at NRC's Public Document Room).

38. Internal memorandum from D. C. Williams to C. M. Tapp, both Sandia National Laboratories, September 19, 1996.

39. In a detailed e-mail dated April 21, 2001, Williams explained to me the reasons for his belief that Sandia was at least as responsible for the problems as was the NRC:

It was Ortiz's responsibility to insist that technical differences between the lead Sandia author of the study and other staff, including Williams, be resolved internally, and he failed to do so. It was Ortiz who ignored Williams' repeated pleas that the conflict between his results using the CONTAIN code and the simplistic Issue Resolution models be brought to the attention of the NRC and the external peer reviewers at an early stage, when corrective action could have been taken without greatly disrupting the program. It was Ortiz who decided Williams would not be allowed to present his results to the external peer reviewers. It was Ortiz who made the decision that Williams' report on the CONTAIN analysis of the DCH experiments would not be published: Sandia's contract with the NRC explicitly allowed Sandia to proceed with publication at Sandia's expense without the sponsor's endorsement. (Indeed, this contract provision had been included to cover precisely this situation, i.e., to allow Sandia to preserve its integrity by publishing research that might yield results displeasing to the sponsor.)

40. "DCH Issue Resolution for Ice Condenser Plants," memorandum from Ashok Thadani, Director of the Office of Nuclear Regulatory Research, to Samuel J. Collins, Director of the Office of Nuclear Reactor Regulation, June 22, 2000 available at NRC's Public Document Room, ADAMS Accession Number ML003725995.

41. M. M. Pilch, K. D. Bergeron, and J. J. Gregory, *Assessment of the DCH Issue for Plants with Ice Condenser Containments*, U.S. Nuclear Regulatory Commission, NUREG/CR 6427 (Washington, DC, April 2000), p. 109.

42. However, the NRC has not entirely ignored the vulnerabilities of ice condensers as revealed in NUREG/CR 6427. In 2001 NRC established a "Generic Issue," GI-189, regarding the vulnerability of ice condensers and GE's Mark III containments to failure from hydrogen combustion during station blackouts. The costs and benefits of improved igniter reliability for these containment types is a subject of ongoing research at the NRC. NRC, "Staff Plans for Proceeding with the Risk-Informed Alternative to the Standards for Combustible Gas Control Systems in Light-Water-Cooled Power Reactors in 10 CFR 50.44," SECY-01-0162, August 23, 2001.

Chapter 4

1. Harvard Nuclear Study Group, *Living with Nuclear Weapons* (Cambridge: Harvard University Press, 1983), p. 215.

2. Rodney W. Jones and Mark G. McDonough, *Tracking Nuclear Proliferation* (Washington, DC: Carnegie Endowment for International Peace, 1998).

3. United Nations, "Review Conference of Parties to NPT Opens at Headquarters; Much Disarmament Machinery Has 'Started to Rust,' Secretary-General Warns," Press Release DC/2692, United Nations, New York, April 24, 2000.

4. There is a second, overlapping export control group called the Zangger Committee with a somewhat less comprehensive program of control.

5. Federation of American Scientists, "Membership of Zangger Committee and Nuclear Suppliers Group," available at the federation's Web site

(http://sun00781.dn.net/nuke/control/nsg/member.html). Note that China, though not in the NSG, is a member of the parallel Zangger Committee but does not agree to international safeguards on its nuclear-related exports. This is believed to be because of its sponsorship of Pakistan's nuclear program, according to Jones and McDonough, *Tracking Nuclear Proliferation*, p. 309.

6. International Atomic Energy Agency, "IAEA Information Circular INFCIRC/254/Rev.3/Part 2," Washington, DC, February 24, 1998. The annex of this circular contains the list of controlled dual-use exports.

7. Mitchell Reiss and Robert S. Litwak, eds., *Nuclear Proliferation after the Cold War* (Baltimore: Johns Hopkins University Press, 1994), p. 344.

8. Gary Samore, in Reiss and Litwak, *Nuclear Proliferation after the Cold War*, p. 16.

9. Müller et al., *Nuclear Non-proliferation and Global Order*, p. 144.

10. Tim Weiner, "U.S. and China Helped Pakistan Build Its Bomb," *New York Times*, June 1, 1998, p. A6.

11. Peter R. Lavoy, Scott D. Sagan, and James J. Wirtz, *Planning the Unthinkable* (Ithaca, NY: Cornell University Press, 2000), pp. 125 (India), 166 (Pakistan). Some of these tests are known to have involved the use of thermonuclear materials, for example, deuterium and tritium, but it is not known what degree of boost was achieved.

12. John Tagliabue, "A Warning from an Official about an Increased Possibility of Nuclear Terror," *New York Times*, November 2, 2001, p. B1.

13. The most powerful hydrogen bombs have two stages: a primary, which is a boosted fission weapon like that illustrated in figure 1, and adjacent to it, a secondary, which uses lithium deuteride and uranium as fuel and achieves a much higher fraction of its energy from fusion reactions than the boosted primary does. In a two-stage device, the primary ignites the secondary.

14. Jones and McDonough, *Tracking Nuclear Proliferation*, p. 29.

15. Matthew Bunn, *The Next Wave: Urgently Needed Steps to Control Warheads and Fissile Material* (Washington, DC: Carnegie Endowment for International Peace and Cambridge: Harvard Project on Managing the Atom, April 2000), p. 10, available at <http://ksgnotes1.harvard.edu/BCSIA/Library.nsf/pubs/Nextwave>.

16. Jones and McDonough, *Tracking Nuclear Proliferation*, p. 5, provides the inventories and critical masses for enriched uranium and separated plutonium that lead to this figure.

17. Jones and McDonough, *Tracking Nuclear Proliferation*, p. 18.

18. Matthew Bunn, "Enabling a Significant Future for Nuclear Power," in *Proceedings of Global '99: Nuclear Technology—Bridging the Millennia*, Jackson Hole, WY (La Grange Park IL: American Nuclear Society, 30 August 1999), available at <http://ksgnotes1.harvard.edu/BCSIA/Library.nsf/pubs/.mb-nuclearfutr.htm>.

19. Bunn, *The Next Wave*, p. 18.

20. John McPhee, *The Curve of Binding Energy* (New York: Ballantine, 1973).

21. For example, see Carey Sublette, *Nuclear Weapons and Nuclear Arsenals*, Web document version 2.19, February 20, 1999, available at <http://www.fas.org/nuke/hew/Nwfaq/>.

22. Mark Dean Millot, "Facing the Emerging Reality of Regional Nuclear Adversaries," *Washington Quarterly*, vol. 17, no. 3 (1994), p. 41.

23. Bunn, *The Next Wave*, p. 1.

24. Matthew Bunn et al., "Retooling Russia's Nuclear Cities," *Bulletin of the Atomic Scientists*, vol. 54, no. 5 (September/October 1998), p. 44.

25. Müller et al., *Nuclear Non-proliferation and Global Order*, p. 157.

26. U.S. Department of Energy, Commercial Light Water Reactor Project Office, *CLWR Project Overview* (Washington, DC, 2000), obtained from <http://www.dp.doe.gov/dp-62>.

27. Sublette, *Nuclear Weapons and Nuclear Arsenals*, vol. 7.

28. Lavoy et al., *Planning the Unthinkable*, p. 166.

29. Roger Molander and Peter Wilson, "Anticipating Nuclear Proliferation," *Washington Quarterly*, 17, no. 3 (1994), p. 16.

30. Reiss and Litwak, *Nuclear Proliferation after the Cold War*, p. 347.

31. Albert Narath, chairman, *Report of the Fundamental Classification Policy Review Group*, Department of Energy (Washington, DC, January 15, 1997).

32. Rhodes, *Making of the Atomic Bomb*, pp. 454, 479.

33. Narath, *Report of the Fundamental Classification Policy Review Group*, In the section entitled "Protectability of Information," the distinction is made between "subjective" information, which is unconditionally protectable, and "objective" information, which cannot be made unconditionally protectable. Scientific information falls in the latter category.

34. Robert Oppenheimer, quoted in Rhodes, *Making of the Atomic Bomb*, p. 449.

35. Daniel Patrick Moynihan, *Secrecy: The American Experience* (New Haven: Yale University Press, 1998), p. 149.

36. Select Committee of the U.S. House of Representatives (the Cox Committee), *PRC Theft of Nuclear Warhead Design Information* (Washington, DC, January 3, 1999).

37. Walter Pincus, "China Spy Gains Overvalued, Two Former Lab Directors Say," *Washington Post*, May 30, 1999, p. A10.

38. John Diamond, "Nuclear Weapons Labs More Secure," *Chicago Tribune*, January 26, 2000, p. 6.

39. President's Foreign Intelligence Advisory Board, *Science at Its Best, Security at Its Worst* (the "Rudman Report") (Washington, DC: U.S. Government Printing Office, June 1999), p. 3.

40. Ibid., p. 2.

41. The quote is from the indictment itself. David Johnston and James Risen, "The Los Alamos Secrets Case: The Overview," *New York Times*, December 11, 1999, p. A1.

42. Stephen Schwartz, quoted in William J. Broad, "Friends Rally Support for Los Alamos Scientist," *New York Times*, December 21, 1999, p. F1.

43. Pervez Hoodbhoy and Martin Kalinowski, "The Tritium Solution," *Bulletin of the Atomic Scientists*, vol. 52, no. 4 (July/August 1996), p. 41.

44. Editorial, "Mayday! and May Day," *New York Times*, May 1, 1986, p. A26.

Chapter 5

1. Thomas B. Cochran, William M. Arkin, Robert S. Norris, and Milton M. Hoenig, *Nuclear Weapons Databook, Vol. II: U.S. Nuclear Weapons Warhead Production* (Washington, DC: Ballinger, 1987), p. 18.

2. Rachel Carson, *Silent Spring* (Boston: Houghton Mifflin, 1962).

3. Ralph Nader, *Unsafe at Any Speed* (New York: Grossman, 1965).

4. The moderator in a nuclear reactor serves to slow neutrons down without capturing them. The slowed-down neutrons are more likely to cause fission when they strike the nucleus of a fissile atom. The coolant is the fluid that carries the heat away from the core, just as water or antifreeze keeps an automobile engine cool. In light-water reactors, ordinary water serves as both the moderator and coolant, whereas in the RBMK and the N reactors, solid graphite was the moderator and heavy water was the coolant.

5. Bennett Ramberg, in *Hidden Dangers: Environmental Consequences of Preparing for War*, ed. Anne H. Ehrlich and John W. Birks (San Francisco: Sierra Club Books, 1990), p. 60.

6. National Academy of Sciences and National Research Council, Safety Issues at the Defense Production Reactors (Washington, DC: National Academy Press, 1987).

7. Rodney Carlisle with Joan M. Zenzen, *Supplying the Nuclear Arsenal* (Baltimore: John Hopkins University Press, 1996), p. 189.

8. Katherine Probst and Adam Lowe, *Cleaning up the Nuclear Weapons Complex: Does Anyone Care?* (Resources for the Future, Washington DC, 2000), p. 2, available at <http://www.rff.org/proj_summaries/99files/probst_nucweapcleanup.htm>.

9. Steven Blush, *New Directions in Nuclear Safety Management and Organization*, Department of Energy, Office of Nuclear Safety (Washington, DC, April 1993).

10. Ibid., p. 13.

11. John B. Roberts II, "Nuclear Secrets and the Culture Wars," *American Spectator*, vol. 32, no. 5 (May 1999), 34.

12. Probst and Lowe, *Cleaning up the Nuclear Weapons Complex*, p. 3.

13. Blush, "New Directions," p. 14.

14. Probst and Lowe, *Cleaning up the Nuclear Weapons Complex*, p. 2.

15. Ibid.

16. Carlisle, *Supplying the Nuclear Arsenal*, p. 226.

17. Ibid., p. 167.

18. Ibid.

19. Ibid., p. 174.

20. In particular, J. Carson Mark, former leader of Los Alamos's theoretical division, among others, championed the idea of letting the radioactive decay set the pace of international nuclear arms reduction. See *The Tritium Factor: Tritium's Impact on Nuclear Arms Reductions* (Washington, DC: Nuclear Control Institute and the American Academy of Arts and Sciences, 1989).

21. Department of Energy, *Draft Environmental Impact Statement for the Siting, Construction and Operation of New Production Reactor Capacity* (DOE EIS-0144D) (Washington, DC, April, 1991).

22. Ibid., vol. 1, p. S-5.

23. Carlisle, *Supplying the Nuclear Arsenal*, p. 208.

24. Ibid.

25. Ibid., p. 211.

26. Argonne National Laboratory Project Staff, *HWR-NPR Severe Accident Sequences and Phenomena-Neutronic-Thermal-Hydraulic Coupling Assessment*, ANL/NPR-90/004, Argonne National Laboratory (Argonne, IL, October 1989).

27. D. F. Beck and M. J. Rightley, *FCI Test NPR-1 Preliminary Report*, SAND90-2715, Sandia National Laboratories (Albuquerque, NM, 1990).

28. K. D. Bergeron, S. E. Slezak, and C. E. Leach, "Proposed Deterministic Severe Accident Criteria for the Heavy Water Reactor—New Production Reactor Containment," *Nuclear Safety*, vol. 34, no. 1 (January–March 1993), p. 20.

29. Thomas Lippmann, "Savannah River Reactor to Stay Shut," *Washington Post*, March 31, 1993, p. A14.

30. David Kramer, "Technologies in Contest for NPR Award," *Inside Energy*, April 8, 1991, p. 1.

31. Thomas Lippman, "Panel Picks Reactor Location in Advance of Hearings," *Washington Post*, May 10, 1991, p. A4.

32. William Sweet, "Severe Accident Scenarios at Issue in DOE Plan to Restart Reactor," *Physics Today*, November 1991, p. 78. Also Danialle Weaver, "SRP: Nuclear Time Bomb?" *Energy Daily*, March 18, 1991, p. 1.

33. Keith Schneider, "Arms Cut Leads White House to Question Plan for A-Plant," *New York Times*, October 4, 1991, p. A1.

34. "Secretary Watkins Fired Monetta, Sources Say," *Energy Daily*, November 12, 1991, p. 4.

35. Ibid.

36. Letter from Senator Sam Nunn to James Watkins, November 14, 1991. Also Matthew L. Wald, "U.S. Hopes to Start Old Atom Plant to Make Bomb Fuel," *New York Times*, December 6, 1991, p. A14.

37. Dannialle Weaver, "Greenpeace Petitions to Keep Department of Energy Weapons Plants Closed," *Energy Daily*, December 8, 1991, p. 4.

38. Peter Applebomb, "Anger Lingers after Leak at Atomic Site," *New York Times*, January 13, 1992, p. A12.

39. R. Jeffrey Smith, "Energy Dept. May Step up Safety Changes," *Washington Post*, January 19, 1992, p. A11.

40. Ibid.

41. Targets composed of helium-3 are also under consideration.

42. Jim Clarke, "Watkins Studies Accelerator for Possible Tritium Production," *Energy Daily*, April 7, 1992, p. 1.

43. "Burns & Roe to Lead DOE Effort on Tritium-Producing Accelerator," *Nucleonics Week*, September 9, 1996, p. 9. The $3 billion figure would be achieved only if the accelerator concept went to construction.

44. Department of Energy, "Record of Decision on Tritium Supply and Recycling," *Federal Register*, vol. 60, no. 238 (December 12, 1995), p. 63877.

45. "DOE to Build Accelerator for Tritium," *Inside Energy*, October 9, 1995, p. 1.

46. Kenneth Bergeron, "While No One Was Looking," *Bulletin of the Atomic Scientists*, vol. 57, no. 2 (March/April 2000), p. 42.

47. Department of Energy, *Draft Programmatic Environmental Impact Statement for Tritium Supply and Recycling*, DOE/EIS-0161D (Washington, DC, March 1995).

48. Ehrlich and Birks, *Hidden Dangers*, p. 38.

49. Department of Energy, *Draft Environmental Impact Statement for the Siting, Construction and Operation of New Production Reactor Capacity*.

50. Department of Energy, "Tritium Supply and Recycling Environmental Impact Statement," *Federal Register*, vol. 60, no. 165 (August 25, 1995), p. 44327.

51. Department of Energy, *Final Programmatic Environmental Impact Statement for Tritium Supply and Recycling*, DOE/EIS-0161 (Washington, DC, October 1995).

52. Ibid., p. ES-10.

53. "DOE Seeks More Public Comment on Reactors as Tritium Source," *Nuclear Fuel*, August 28, 1995, p. 12.

54. International Atomic Energy Agency, Communication Received From Certain Member States Regarding Guidelines for the Export of Nuclear Material, Equipment and Technology, INFCIRC/254/Rev.3/Part 2, Vienna February 24, 1998.

55. Michelle Williams, "Bomb Material Test May Be Key for TVA's Bellefonte Nuclear Plant," *Associated Press*, October 21, 1997.

56. FY98 National Defense Authorization Act (P.L. 105–85).

57. Section 3139 of Senate Bill 936 of the 105th Congress.

58. House of Representatives Report 105–340 (1997), p. 910.

59. Department of Energy, *Interagency Review of Nonproliferation Implications of Alternative Tritium Production Technologies under Consideration by the Department of Energy* (Washington, DC, July 1998), obtained from <http://www.dp.doe.gov/dp-62> and reprocduced in appendix B.

60. For example, David Ace, "Interagency Task Force Urges Pursuit of Bellefonte as Tritium Source," *Associated Press*, July 17, 1998.

61. House of Representatives Report 105–340, p. 910.

62. Senator Strom Thurmond, quoted in *Congressional Record* (1998), p. S12861.

63. The FOIA requests that were made for this book were directed to the DOE, the Department of State (which absorbed the Arms Control and Disarmament Agency after the *Interagency Review* was completed), the NRC, and the Office of Science and Technology Policy. Only the NRC and the Office of Science and Technology Policy responded to the request within a reasonable time period (not within the mandated twenty working days, but reasonably promptly). The Department of State and DOE requests were first submitted in July 2000. As of March 2002, no response has been received despite numerous inquiries. The Office of the Vice President and the National Security Council, both of which are cited as participants in the *Interagency Review*, are exempt from FOIA. No FOIA request was made to the Department of Defense, since such requests are handled at the service level, and the *Interagency Review* did not specify which service participated in the task force.

64. Interview with William Bishop by the author on August 14, 2000. Bishop was in charge of DOE's Office of Accelerator Production at the time the *Interagency Review* was written.

65. Department of Energy, "Record of Decision: Tritium Supply and Recycling Programmatic Environmental Impact Statement," *Federal Register*, vol. 60, no. 238 (December 12, 1995): 63877, and "Fiscal Year 1998 National Defense Authorization Act," P.L. 105–85, Sec. 3135.

66. For example, Strom Thurmond, in *Congressional Record* (1998), p. S12681, or Michelle Williams, "Bomb Material Test May Be Key."

67. *Inside Energy*, December 8, 1997, p. 1.

68. Department of Energy, *CLWR Project Overview* (Washington, DC, February 8, 2000), obtained from <http://www.dp.doe.gov/dp-62>.

69. "Reactor to Produce Bomb Material," *Associated Press*, September 15, 1997.

70. Michelle Williams, "Bomb Material Test May Be Key."

71. "Fight over Tritium Production Pairs Pork and Proliferation," *Nuclear Fuels*, July 13, 1998, p. 13.

72. "Senate Agrees to Retain Reactor as Option for Tritium Production," *Inside Energy*, June 29, 1998, p. 3.

73. Pam Sohn, "Tritium Question Cloudier," *Chattanooga (TN) Times*, November 18, 1998.

74. "At Richardson's Urging, TVA Revives, Revises Tritium Options," *Nucleonics Week*, December 10, 1998, p. 6.

75. In his 1998 press briefing, Richardson explicitly said that one of the problems with Bellefonte was the concern over how long it would take to get a license for Bellefonte. "Richardson Faces Resistance from Congress over Tritium Decision," *Inside Energy*, December 28, 1998, p. 3.

76. "NRC Punts on Policy Issues Raised by Tritium Production," *Nuclear Fuels*, January 13, 1997, p. 6.

77. Report of the Select Committee of the U.S. House of Representatives (the Cox Commission), *PRC Theft of U.S. Nuclear Warhead Design Information*.

78. Ibid.

79. Bill Loveless, "Thurmond Accuses DOE Officials of Campaign Against Accelerator," *Inside Energy*, September 7, 1998, p. 3; also Tarun Reddy, IG Finds no Basis for Tritium Charges, *Inside Energy*, December 14, 1998, p. 1.

80. "At Richardson's Urging, TVA Revives, Revises Tritium Options."

81. "DOE Decision on Tritium Production Bitter Pill for TVA, Nuclear Critics," *Nucleonics Week*, January 7, 1999, p. 8.

82. "At Richardson's Urging, TVA Revives, Revises Tritium Options."

83. "Remarks by Secretary of Energy Bill Richardson: National Security Decisions," Washington, DC, December 22, 1998, obtained from <http://www.doe.gov/news/speeches98/decss/natsec.htm>.

84. U.S. Department of Energy, "Energy Secretary Bill Richardson Breaks Ground for New Tritium Extraction Facility at Savannah River Site," Press Release, July 27, 2000. Available at <http://www.energy.gov/HQPress/releases00/julpr/pr00200.htm>.

85. John Harmon, "TVA to Make Key Bomb Component," *Atlanta Constitution*, December 9, 1999, p. 3A.

86. *Interagency Agreement between the United States Department of Energy and the Tennessee Valley Authority for Irradiation Services*, Interagency Agreement No. DE-AI02-00DP00315 (Washington, DC, January 1, 2000).

87. "Fight over Tritium Production Pairs Pork and Proliferation," p. 12.

88. The basis for the DOE's threat to ask the Navy to requisition the TVA's reactors is an obscure clause in the Tennessee Valley Act authorizing the TVA's board "upon the requisition of the Secretary of War (now Army) or the Secretary of the Navy to manufacture and sell at cost to the United States explosives or their nitrogenous content." The clause dates from the time when the TVA used its hydroelectric power to produce fertilizer and explosives, two closely related chemicals. Wesley Loy, "DOE Tritium Contract No Prize for TVA," *Knoxville (TN) News-Sentinel*, January 10, 1999, p. A1.

89. "The House Commerce Committee Has Asked DOE for More Details," *Inside Energy*, March 15, 1999, p. 13.

90. Amy F. Woolf, *Nuclear Arms Control: The U.S.–Russian Agenda*, Congressional Research Service report IB98030, October 15, 2001. Available at the Web site of the National Library for the Environment (http://www.cnie.org/NLE/CRS/).

91. David E. Sanger, "The Bush-Putin Summit: The Accord," *New York Times*, November 14, 2001, p. A1.

92. Charles D. Ferguson and Frank von Hippel, "U.S. Can Begin Cutting Its Tritium Needs and Arsenal without STARTing," Letter to the Editor, *Physics Today*, May 1999, p. 11.

93. Frank von Hippel's calculation was based on a reduction from START II levels of only about 20 percent. The reductions announced by President Bush in November 2001 are between 37 percent and 51 percent.

94. The original 2005 schedule that was tied to START-I levels has been slipped to 2006, largely because of the year-long delay in negotiating the Memorandum of Understanding between DOE and TVA.

95. Jonathan Schell, *The Gift of Time* (New York: Metropolitan Books, 1998).

Chapter 6

1. Erwin C. Hargrove, *Prisoners of Myth* (Princeton, NJ: Princeton University Press, 1994), p. 21.

2. David Lilienthal, in a 1944 talk to TVA distributors, quoted in Hargrove, *Prisoners of Myth*, p. 125.

3. Daniel Ford, *Meltdown* (New York: Touchstone, 1986), p. 241.

4. Ibid., p. 242.

5. For example, see Hargrove, *Prisoners of Myth*, chapter 9, pp. 242 ff.

6. Ford, *Meltdown*, p. 220.

7. Ibid., p. 243.

8. Hargrove, *Prisoners of Myth*, pp. 188, 223.

9. Government Accounting Office, *Tennessee Valley Authority: Financial Problems Raise Questions About Long-term Viability*, GAO/AIMD/RCED-95-134 (Washington, DC, August 1995), p. 2.

10. Hargrove, *Prisoners of Myth*, p. 225.

11. Ibid., p. 227.

12. DeFord fought back in court, citing the Energy Reorganization Act of 1974, which forbids retaliation against nuclear employees who reveal safety problems. After a five-year legal battle, he won, gaining reinstatement, back pay, legal fees, and compensatory damages (U.S. Department of Labor Case No. 81-ERA-1, available at <http://www.oalj.dol.gov.public.wlblower/decsu/81era01c.htm>).

13. Ford, *Meltdown*, p. 257.

14. Marc J. Roberts and Jeremy S. Blum, summarized in Hargrove, *Prisoners of Myth*, p. 167.

15. Ibid., p. 271.

16. Hargrove (paraphrasing Sandra Seeley), ibid., p. 272.

17. Peter N. Spotts, "Doubts Still Dog World's Most-Inspected Nuclear Plant," *Christian Science Monitor*, June 11, 1996, p. 1.

18. Rebecca Ferrar, "TVA Tops List of Informing by Workers," *Knoxville (TN) News Sentinel*, October 12, 1989, p. A1.

19. Letter from James M. Taylor, U.S. Nuclear Regulatory Commission, to Oliver D. Kingsley, Tennessee Valley Authority, August 26, 1991 (EA 91-019) (available at NRC's Public Document Room).

20. Nuclear Regulatory Commission, *Meeting Summary—Meeting with Members of the Public Regarding Watts Bar Nuclear Plant*, TAC M72494 (Washington, DC, November 3, 1995), p. 10.

21. Ivan Selin, quoted in "Selin Says NRC 'Disappointed' in Recurrence of QA Problems at Watts Bar," *Inside NRC*, November 28, 1994, p. 7.

22. Duncan Mansfield, "Turn of the Screws: Twisted Fate Met TVA Whistleblower," *Memphis Commercial Appeal*, January 31, 1999, p. C5.

23. Department of Labor, *Curtis C. Overall v. Tennessee Valley Authority*, Case No. 97-ERA-53, *Recommended Decision and Order* (Washington, DC, April 1, 1998).

24. Matthew Galbraith, "This Dog Don't Hunt," *South Bend (Indiana) Tribune*, May 29, 2000, p. A1.

25. Ibid.

26. Tom Harrison, "TVA Whistleblower Hospitalized; Watchdog Groups Assail NRC Response," *Inside NRC*, September 14, 1998, p. 1.

27. Department of Labor Administrative Review Board Case Nos. 98–111 and 98–128, *Final Decision and Order*, April 30, 2001.

28. "NRC Staff Proposes $88,000 Civil Penalty against TVA Based on Department of Labor Finding of Discrimination," News Release II-01-42, Nuclear Regulatory Commission, Washington, DC, October 16, 2001.

29. Letter from Lynne Bernabei, Esq., to Loren Plisco, NRC Region II Director, July 2, 2001 (available at NRC's Public Document Room).

30. David Lochbaum, "The Good, the Bad and The Ugly," Report, Union of Concerned Scientists, Washington, DC, 1998.

31. Letter (with attachments) from William R. Lagergren, Jr., to Nuclear Regulatory Commission, dated August 20, 2001, Nuclear Regulatory Commission Docket 50-290.

32. Westinghouse Electric Company, *Implementation and Utilization of Tritium Producing Burnable Absorber Rods (TPBARS) in Watts Bar Unit 1*, NDP-00-0344, Rev. 1, submitted to NRC in the TVA's license amendment request dated August 20, 2001 (available at NRC's Public Document Room, ADAMS accession number MLO23901060).

33. Edwin Lyman, "Plutonium Fuel and Ice Condenser Reactors: A Dangerous Combination," Report, Nuclear Control Institute, Washington, DC, October 19, 2000, available at <http://www.nci.org>.

34. Dave Airozo, "ACRS Urges Commission to Launch New Study on Shutdown," *Inside NRC*, April 28, 1997, p. 8.

35. Josh Meyer and Aaron Zitner, "Troops Uncovered Diagrams for Major U.S. Targets, Bush Says," *Los Angeles Times*, January 30, 2002, p. A1.

36. "NRC Orders Nuclear Power Plants to Enhance Security," NRC Press release No. 02–025, Nuclear Regulatory Commission, Washington, DC, February 26, 2002.

37. Nuclear Regulatory Commission, *An Approach for Using Probabilistic Risk Assessment in Risk-Informed Decisions on Plant-Specific Changes to the Licensing Basis*, Regulatory Guide 1.174 (Washington, DC, July 1998).

38. Nuclear Regulatory Commission, NRC *Regulatory Issue Summary 2001–2: Guidance on Risk-Informed Decisionmaking in License Amendment Reviews*, RIS 2001–02 (Washington, DC, 2001).

39. Jim Abrams, "Report: TVA Ought to Go Private," *Journal of Commerce*, November 21, 1997, p. 8A.

Chapter 7

1. Brenner, *Nuclear Power and Non-proliferation*, p. 11.

2. Ferguson and von Hippel, "U.S. Can Begin Cutting Its Tritium Needs and Arsenal without STARTing."

Appendix A

1. The 1990 estimate was $7.5 billion in 1990 dollars. A. M. Cunningham, "The Tritium Factor," *Technology Review*, Massachusetts Institute of Technology, vol. 93, no. 3 (April 1990):23. A life cycle cost of $90 billion was suggested by Congressman Lane Evans (*Washington Post*, July 31, 1990), p. A14.

2. Department of Energy, *Draft Environmental Impact Statement for the Siting, Construction, and Operation of New Production Reactor Capacity*, vol. 1, p. S-5.

3. The goal quantity in 1995 was three sixteenths of that in 1990, according to the "Record of Decision for Tritium Supply and Recycling," *Federal Register*, vol. 60, no. 238 (December 12, 1995), p. 63877.

4. Department of Energy, *Final Programmatic Impact Statement for Tritium Supply and Recycling*, vol. 1, p. S-5.

5. Letter from George K. Davis, ABB Combustion Engineering, reproduced in *Final Programmatic Environmental Impact Statement for Tritium Supply and Recycling*, vol. 3, p. TSR-NM-014.

Appendix C

1. U.S. Code, 42 USC 2014(aa).

2. NRCs responsibility in this regard appears in 10 CFR 70.4.

3. The text of the amendment is as follows:

Section 91 of the Atomic Energy Act of 1954 (42 U.S.C. 2121) is amended by adding at the end the following:
(d) The Secretary may—
    (A) demonstrate the feasibility of, and
    (B) (i) acquire facilities by lease or purchase, or
        (ii) enter into an agreement with an owner or operator of a facility, for the production of tritium for defense-related uses in a facility licensed under section 103 of this Act.

4. House of Representatives Report 105–340, p. 910.

5. Ibid.

6. Government Accounting Office, *Challenges Remain for Successful Implementation of DOE's Tritium Supply Decision*, GAO/RCED-00-24 (Washington, DC, January 2000).

7. Troy Wade II, Acting Assistant Secretary for Defense Programs at DOE, quoted in *The Tritium Factor: Tritium's Impact on Nuclear Arms Reductions* (Washington, DC: Nuclear Control Institute and the American Academy of Arts and Sciences, 1989), p. 62.

8. Edward Dowdy, ibid., p. 21.

Bibliography

Adato, Michelle, James MacKenzie, Robert Pollard, and Ellyn Weiss. *Safety Second: The NRC and America's Nuclear Power Plants.* Indianapolis: Indiana University Press, 1987.

Bailey, Kathleen C. *Doomsday Weapons in the Hands of Many: The Arms Control Challenge of the 90s.* Chicago: University of Illinois Press, 1991.

Bailey, Kathleen C. *Strengthening Nuclear Non-proliferation.* Boulder, CO: Westview Press, 1993.

Brenner, Michael J. *Nuclear Power and Non-proliferation: The Remaking of U.S. Policy.* New York: Cambridge University Press, 1981.

Carlisle, Rodney, with Joan M. Zenzen. *Supplying the Nuclear Arsenal.* Baltimore: John Hopkins University Press, 1996.

Carson, Rachel. *Silent Spring.* Boston: Houghton Mifflin, 1962.

Cochran, Thomas B., William M. Arkin, Robert S. Norris, and Milton M. Hoenig. *Nuclear Weapons Databook, Vol. II: U.S. Nuclear Weapons Warhead Production.* Washington, DC: Ballinger, 1987.

Ehrlich, Anne H., and John W. Birks, eds., *Hidden Dangers: Environmental Consequences of Preparing for War.* San Francisco: Sierra Club Books, 1990.

Ford, Daniel. *Meltdown.* New York: Touchstone, 1986.

Ford Foundation Nuclear Energy Policy Study Group and Mitre Corporation. *Nuclear Power Issues and Choices.* Report. Cambridge, MA: Ballinger, 1977.

Hargrove, Erwin C. *Prisoners of Myth.* Princeton, NJ: Princeton University Press, 1994.

Harvard Nuclear Study Group. *Living with Nuclear Weapons.* Cambridge: Harvard University Press, 1983.

Haynes, John Earl, and Harvey Klehr. *Venona: Decoding Soviet Espionage in America.* New Haven: Yale University Press, 1999.

Hewlett, Richard G., and Jack M. Holl. *Atoms for Peace and War, 1953–1961: Eisenhower and the Atomic Energy Commission.* Berkeley and Los Angeles: University of California Press.

Jones, Rodney W., and Mark G. McDonough. *Tracking Nuclear Proliferation.* Washington, DC: Carnegie Endowment for International Peace, 1998.

Kemeny, John, et al. *Report of the President's Commission on the Accident at Three Mile Island*. Washington, DC: U.S. Government Printing Office, 1979.

Kennedy, Paul. *The Rise and Fall of the Great Powers*. New York: Vintage Books, 1987.

Lavoy, Peter R., Scott D. Sagan, and James J. Wirtz. *Planning the Unthinkable*. Ithaca, NY: Cornell University Press, 2000.

Lilienthal, David E. *Change, Hope and the Bomb*. Princeton, NJ: Princeton University Press, 1963.

Masuzin, George T., and J. Samuel Walker. *Controlling the Atom*. Berkeley and Los Angeles: University of California Press, 1984.

McPhee, John. *The Curve of Binding Energy*. New York: Ballantine, 1973.

Moynihan, Daniel Patrick. *Secrecy: The American Experience*. New Haven: Yale University Press, 1998.

Müller, Harald, David Fischer, and Wolfgang Kötter. *Nuclear Non-proliferation and Global Order*. New York: Oxford University Press, 1994.

Nader, Ralph. *Unsafe at Any Speed*. New York: Grossman, 1965.

Nolan, Janne E. *An Elusive Consensus: Nuclear Weapons and American Security after the Cold War*. Washington, DC: Brookings Institution Press, 1999.

Nuclear Regulatory Commission. *Severe Accident Risks: An Assessment for Five U.S. Nuclear Power Plants* (NUREG-1150). Washington, DC: Nuclear Regulatory Commission, 1990.

Charles Perrow. *Normal Accidents*. Princeton, NJ: Princeton University Press, 1999.

Pool, Robert. *Beyond Engineering: How Society Shapes Technology*. New York: Oxford University Press, 1997.

Reiss, Mitchell, and Robert S. Litwak, eds., *Nuclear Proliferation after the Cold War*. Baltimore: Johns Hopkins University Press, 1994.

Rhodes, Richard. *The Making of the Atomic Bomb*. New York: Touchstone, 1986.

Rolph, Elizabeth S. *Nuclear Power and the Public Safety: A Study in Regulation*. Lexington, MA: Lexington Books, 1979.

Schell, Jonathan. *The Gift of Time*. New York: Metropolitan Books, 1998.

Schell, Jonathan. *The Fate of the Earth*. New York: Knopf, 1982.

Stever, Donald W. Jr. *Seabrook and the Nuclear Regulatory Commission*. Hanover, NH: University Press of New England, 1980.

Tomain, Joseph P. *Nuclear Power Transformation*. Indianapolis: Indiana University Press, 1987.

Weinberg, Alvin. *The First Nuclear Era: The Life and Times of a Technological Fixer*. New York: American Institute of Physics Press, 1994.

Index